Journal for the Academic Study of Magic

ISSN 1479-0750

ISBN 978-1869928-391

Published by Mandrake of Oxford, PO Box 250, Oxford, OX1 1AP, UK. http://www.mandrake.uk.net

In association with the Society for the Academic Study of Magic, c/o Dep't of Historical Studies, University of Bristol, 13 Woodland Road, Bristol, BS8 1TB, UK
http://www.sasm.co.uk/index.html

Bibliographic conventions: please cite as: Green, D (Ed.), *The Journal for the Academic Study of Magic*, 4, (Mandrake, Oxford, 2007)

Copyright of individual articles remains with the author(s), while editorial, style, layout etc of the Journal is © SASM, JSM and Mandrake of Oxford 2007.

All rights reserved. No part of this Journal may be reproduced or utilized in any form or by any means, electronic or mechanical including photocopying, recording or by any information storage and/or retrieval system, without express prior permission in writing from the Publishers.

Short extracts may be reproduced for review purposes. A copy of the review, and notification of where and when it appeared would be appreciated, sent to SASM please.

Contents

Editorial 5

Obituary 6

The Practitioner, The Priest, and The Professor: Perspectives on
Self-Initiation in the American Neopagan Community
Marty Laubach, Louis Martinie' and Roselinda Clemons 13

The Trinity of the Hebrew Goddess: A Guided Presentation Of Goddess
Narratives and Submerged Beliefs
Jayne Marie DeMente 35

The Topography of Magic in the Modern Western
and Ancient Egyptian Minds
Steven M. Stannish 64

The science of magic: A parapsychological model of psychic ability
in the context of magical will
David Luke 90

Is Magic Possible Within A Quantum Mechanical Framework?
Steve Ash 120

Angels with Nanotech Wings: Magic, Medicine and Technology
in *The Neuromancer* and *Brain Plague*
Catherine M. Lord 147

Rowling's Devil: Ancient Archetype or Modern Manifestation?
Lauren Berman 163

"Delivered From Enchantment": Cotton Mather, W. B. O. Peabody,
and the Struggle against Magic
Carl Sederholm 197

In a Mirror, Darkly : A comparison between the Lovecraftian Mythos
and African-Atlantic mystery religions
David Geall 214

The Journey of The Lion King and the Collective Unconscious
Melinda Marsh 252

"The Third Time's the Charm": Mythic Operative Magic
in the Merseburger Zaubersprüche
Michael Moynihan 268

The Old Irish Impotence Spell: The Dam Díli, Fergus, Fertility,
and the Mythic Backround of an Irish Incantation
Phillip A. Bernhardt-House 304

Reading the Turkish Coffee Cup and Beyond:
The Case of North Cyprus
Gulnara Karimova 326

Reviews 340

Editorial

Welcome (finally!) to the belated JSM 4. I want to keep this editorial as succinct as possible as the quality of the articles in this edition speak for themselves. They exemplify in their diversity, creativity and rigour the qualities for which this journal continues to stand:

In this issue we begin with three articles which, in their own way look at magic through the comparative examination of esoteric discourse: Laubach et al do this through different discourses on Neo-Pagan initiation, Jayne-Marie Peace via a phenomenology of Goddess Spirituality, and Steve Stannish through a comparative understanding of magical landscapes in Ancient Egypt and the contemporary West.

The next three articles observe, in various ways, relationships between magic, science and technology: David Luke looks to a parapsychological model of psychic ability, Steve Ash to the development of magical practices theorised and imagined through Quantum Mechanics, and Catherine M. Lord to the interplay between literature, technology and magic.

Indeed, Lord's article acts as a stepping stone to the next cluster of articles which examine the links between magic, literature and culture. Lauren Berman delivers a socio-historical analysis of J.K. Rowling's devilish Voldemort character from the Harry Potter books. Carl Sederholm, by contrast, takes us to the treatment of magic in the development of early American literature by looking to the lives of two distinctive men, Cotton Mather and W.B.O Peabody, who both attempted to deny magic in their work and throughout their lives. Following this, David Geall follows up his insightful article in JSM 3 with a comparative analysis of H.P. Lovecraft and African-Atlantic mystery religions. The final article in this section comes from Melinda Marsh who serves up a Jungian analysis of the Disney film *The Lion King*.

The last themed section of this edition looks at various aspects of European folk magics: Michael Moynihan examines the Old Germanic charms of The *Merseburger Zaubersprüche,* Philip Bernhardt-House considers the mythic narratives informing an Old Irish impotence spell and, finally Gulnara Karimova discusses tasseography - divination using coffee grounds - in Northern Cyprus.

On a personal note, this is my last edition (for now at least) as an editor and I would like to thank everyone who has made the last two editions, for which I have had editorial responsibility, possible. The Journal continues to make an interesting journey through the twin worlds of the academy and the occult. My stint as an editor has been enjoyable, if onerous at times. I wish the excellent and new editorial team of Susan Johnston Graf and Amy Hale the best for future editions. I am sure that the Journal will go from strength to strength.

Obituary

It is with great sadness that the death of Robert Anton Wilson was announced as the Journal was initially going to press. It only seems right and proper that we pay an all too brief homage to RAW here and hope that other contributors might wish to add more academic contributions and overviews in future editions.

RAW was one of those rare characters who managed not only to be a significant practitioner counter-cultural hero within the occult world but also, in a slightly different guise, a popular cultural hero who, often slyly, brought magic to the attention of the wider world. RAW is probably best known by the public for his Illuminatus Trilogy (co-authored with Robert Shea) published in 1975. The books were an outgrowth of their experiences at Playboy magazine in the 1960s where RAW and Shea observed that readers' letters were often marked by paranoia and conspiracy theories. The books are a heady and entertaining postmodern alchemy of the occult, Discordianism, Sci-Fi, conspiracy theory, psychedelia and shamanism and are as indebted to stylistic borrowings from writers such as Kurt Vonnegut, Thomas Pynchon and Philip K. Dick, as to the genius of the authors themselves. Central to these texts were one of RAW's main contributions to contemporary occultism – the importance of belief, and to an extent, disbelief. This was a development of RAW's commitment to a state of 'generalised agnosticism', a critique of the dogmas of rationality and the fixity of beliefs. This critique of dogmatism, conversely, was used as a tool not only interrogate the madness of contemporary culture, but also highlighted ways in which beliefs could be manipulated by individuals as ways of re-enchanting the self and that world. The latter, in particular, was taken up as a central tenet within Chaos Magic where ephemeral belief in particular philosophies and spiritualities is an important method of altering consciousness and exploring the nature of psychic self-defence mechanisms.

RAW was born in Brooklyn in 1932. He contracted polio as a child, which was to affect him for the remainder for his life, but solace came in his aptitude for engineering and mathematics. Rejecting the Catholicism of his early education, RAW had an eclectic career path which took in, amongst other things, ambulance driving, sales, advertising and engineering. After his marriage in 1958 to the writer Arlen Riley (who died in 1999), RAW turned to freelance journalism himself, eventually leading to his job as an associate editor at Playboy. His time at Playboy was spent honing his countercultural interests and literary style with a number of agnostic early works which discussed sex, magic, drugs – he was seen as an advocate of drugs, which assuaged the symptoms of his polio, and shamanic experience, a collaborator with Timothy Leary, and confirmed stoner - and the alteration of consciousness. These very much paved the way for the works for which he was to become best known.

His works post-Illuminatus form an important corpus for magicians, psychonauts and libertarians alike. In particular, RAW became fascinated with the nature and evolution of human consciousness. He paid special attention to the ways in which such consciousness could be constrained and restrained by the cultural effects of politics and the socialisation process and, conversely, the ways in which it could be liberated by the use of drugs and ritual. Central to these writings – such as *Neuropolitics* (1978), the *Schroedinger's Cat* trilogy (1980-1), *Prometheus Rising* (1983) and *Quantum Psychology* (1990) – is an almost Deleuzean regard for the process of *becoming*. RAW was an advocate of existential impermanence – another influence on Chaos Magic – and this attitude could be seen in his development of projects such as The Church of the Sub-Genius, the Association for Consciousness Exploration, and E-Prime. His commitment to overcoming the limitations of being human was exemplified by the fact that his daughter Luna's brain was cryogenically preserved after her death, ostensibly at the hands of robbers, when aged just 15.

After Arlen's death RAW himself began to suffer ill health exacerbated by the effects of polio. Just before his eventually death it became clear, especially through the efforts of the writer Douglas Rushkoff, that he was also in deep financial trouble. Fans and supporters came to his aid, raising enough money to see his remaining few months out in comfort. He was reportedly amazed at the response to the news of his financial plight and this highlights not only the modesty of the man but also the esteem in which he was held by many. Holding that death was absurd until the very end, RAW eventually died on January 11th 2007 survived by his remaining three children. He was cremated a week later with his ashes scattered on the waters of Monterey Bay – the same spot as those of his wife – on February 18th.

Robert Anton Wilson, writer, psychonaut and magician, born January 18th 1932; died January 11th 2007

Book Review Policy:

Following debate within the editorial panel about exactly what kind of books we should be reviewing (inspired by an unsolicited review copy of a very good practical magic book that we were sent by a publisher, and which is reviewed herein) we have reached the view that we would not be doing our job properly if we ignored what occultists are writing - this would be akin to producing a Journal about French culture yet reading nothing written in French or by a French person. This does not mean that we will be reviewing every last 'how to do spells' book, occult novel or collection of magical verse that is published, but we shall endeavour to cover some of the more significant books by practitioners in this and future issues, in a proportion of perhaps 1 practitioner titles to 4-5 academic titles. Would publishers and authors who wish to submit practical occultism books for review please contact us *first*, to discuss their potential review copies and whether we are able to review them. Thankyou.

Responses:

We welcome responses to articles, written in a reasoned, academic style and of less than 1000 words. If suitable these will be included in a future edition of the JSM, with a reply from the author of the original article. Responses of a longer nature will possibly warrant the respondent writing a full article for us.

A Technical Note for Prospective Authors:

As a multidisciplinary journal receiving articles from disparate scholars trained in multitudinous methods of citation we have decided that from JSM 3 onwards we will be moving to the somewhat more straightforward *Harvard* academic referencing system; since this seems to suit the majority of our submitting authors. Please see the website **sort this out (again):** **http://www.uwe.ac.uk/hlss/research/usrc/sasm/jsm_submission.shtml** for further details on the implementation of this process. Full details of how to submit an article to the JSM can also be found there.

Editorial Board

General Co-Editors: Dr Dave Green (University of the West of England, Bristol, UK) and Dr Susan Johnston Graf (Penn State University, Mont Alto, USA).

Peer Review Editorial Board:

Prof Ronald Hutton (University of Bristol, UK)

Prof Geoffrey Samuel (University of Wales, Cardiff, UK)

Prof Sabina Magliocco (California State University, Northridge, USA)

Dr Dave Evans (formerly University of Bristol, UK)

Dr Owen Davies (University of Hertfordshire, UK)

Dr Robert J Wallis (Richmond College, The American University in London, UK)

Dr Matt Lee (University of Sussex, Brighton, UK)

Dr Sarah Pike (California State University, Chico, USA)

Dr Jenny Blain (Sheffield Hallam University, UK)

Dr Justin Woodman (University of London, UK)

Dr William Redwood (University of London, UK)

Production Editor: Mogg Morgan (Mandrake of Oxford)

JSM 4 Contributors List, in alphabetical order

Steve Ash is a philosophy graduate and independent scholar and author concerning magical, scientific and Fortean phenomena.

Lauren Berman is currently currently pursuing a Ph.D. in English Literature at the University of Haifa. The topic of her dissertation is an exploration of evil in the Harry Potter series.

Phillip A. Bernhardt-House, formerly of University College Cork, Ireland, and now resident in the USA, is an independent scholar of Celtic myth and religion.

Roselinda Clemons is a longstanding Voodoo practitioner currently engaged in spiritual work with hospice residents in New Orleans.

Jayne Marie DeMente is Founder and Director of The Women's Heritage Project, California.

Dave Evans is a freelance researcher, occult author and a former General Editor of this journal.

David Geall teaches English language and linguistics at the University of Westminster, and researches English literature as an independent scholar.

Dave Green is a General Co-Editor of this journal.

Ronald Hutton is Professor of History at The University of Bristol, UK.

Neil L. Inglis is an independent scholar and author.

Gulnara Karimova is currently a PhD candidate and Teaching - Research Assistant in Communication and Media Studies at Eastern Mediterranean University, Turkish Republic of North Cyprus.

Marty Laubach has long engaged with American Neo-Paganism and currently teaches Sociology at Marshall University, Huntingdon West Virginia, USA.

Catherine M. Lord is an Assistant Professor in Film and Television studies at the Universiteit van Amsterdam.

David Luke is a Ph.D. student in the psychology of belief in magic and superstition at the University of Northampton, UK, and has research interests in altered states and entheogens in relation to magic and the paranormal.

Melinda Marsh is a recent graduate of the University of North Dakota with a Master of Science degree in Space Studies.

Louis Martinie' is an elder at the New Orleans Voodoo Spiritual Temple, USA.

Michael Moynihan is currently a postgraduate at the University of Massachusetts at Amherst specialising in philology and medieval Germanic texts.

Leslie Price founded the Theosophy History journal in 1985, was an important figure in the Society for Psychical Research, and is a longstanding independent historian of esoteric ideas.

Carl Sederholm is Assistant Professor of Humanities at Brigham Young University. He teaches courses on American Romanticism and American Gothic Literature.

Steven M. Stannish is an Assistant Professor of History at SUNY, Potsdam with a particular focus on the history of The Middle east.

Robert J. Wallis is a Peer Review Editor of this journal.

The Practitioner, The Priest, and The Professor: Perspectives on Self-Initiation in the American Neopagan Community

Marty Laubach, Louis Martinie' and Roselinda Clemons

Initiation is a religious practice that is generally understood as involving socialization and acceptance into a religious community, but American Neopaganism, with its emphasis on individualism and autonomy, has evolved a meaning that challenges that simple understanding. American Neopagan communities are marketplaces of ideas that are comprised of groups and solo practitioners, all in interaction in which they might conduct main holidays together, but not necessarily work together in what they would consider more "serious" practices in which they receive the spirit communications with which they develop the ideas. Among groups, these practices include initiations through which candidates are trained and authorized by their group to bring claims of spirit communication to the marketplace. However, one of peculiarities of American Neopagans is that solo practitioners also claim authority to bring communications from the spirit world to the marketplace based on claims that they received initiation from the spirits themselves. This practice of self-initiation effectively redefines a community into which the practitioner is initiated to directly incorporate the spirit world as the highest authority. While it offers community members tremendous flexibility and autonomy, it also confronts the broader community with the task of accepting or rejecting that claim. This study examines the phenomenon of self-initiation from the perspective of the solo practitioner and the community.

We propose an unusual methodology in this study. In response to the postmodern critique of an academic style in which a trained outsider presents the meaning world of a community using extracts of their words as data, this study offers a collaborative effort in which a practitioner, a trained leader in the religious community, and an academic engage in dialog over the issue at hand. We note that while we are directly engaging the social scientific debate over analytical perspective – insider vs. outsider, etic vs. emic, and most recently, postmodern vs. modernity – our real purpose is to explore spiritual phenomena that underlie religious meaning worlds from the unique perspectives of the authors. This format simply allows us to highlight the interplay between these perspectives in developing a fuller understanding of spiritually based religions.

We assert from the outset no precedence for any of these perspectives. We have discussed the issues in general and read each others' contribution but offered little more than requests for clarification and minor grammatical and stylistic comments. While we recognize that readers will likely feel drawn to one over the others, we hope that you will honor each for what it brings. Who better to offer the raw datum of experiences and consequences than the practitioner? Who better to contextualize these within a meaning world than the priest? Who better to contextualize all of these within a rational/empirical framework than the professor?

Furthermore, while each of us is well embedded in our respective networks, none of us claims to be representative of them. In fact, the collaborative relationship represented by this project offers us insights and opportunities to reflect on these issues in ways that are likely unavailable to other members of our networks. Hence our commitment to this project.

Our practitioner, Roselinda Clemons, has had psychic experiences since preschool age. She is currently employed at a nursing home where she works with hospice residents as a spiritual calling dictated by the Guedeh. This Loa is the "master of her head" within the New Orleans Voodoo path, and is just one of the spiritual guides she is in contact with. Ms. Clemons has taught spiritual movement on and off for twenty-five years, and reads tarot cards for various people in her community.

Our priest, Louis Martinie', has offered 15 years of service to the New Orleans Voodoo Spiritual Temple on Rampart Street as priest, lead drummer, and elder, but has offered personal service to the loa for many more. He co-authored the *New Orleans Voodoo Tarot*, founded the Black Moon Archives, and published books and journals on Voodoo and the Western ceremonial traditions through Black Moon Publications.

Our professor, Marty Laubach, teaches sociology at Marshall University. He has engaged with the American Neopagan community since 1979, and lived a career in information processing before returning to academe in 1994. He earned a Ph.D. in sociology from Indiana University for research into the ethnophenomenology, epistemology, and social effects of psychism.

The Practitioner

Visions have always been a part of my life. I sort of take them for granted. Not in an ungrateful way, but in a kind of way having any frequent experience for your entire life. You just know the visions are going to happen no matter what.

I remember as a child my mother giving me very strange looks when I would talk to her about my experiences. She had no understanding of my sensitivity. I had no support network. I had nonphysical guides, but my sensitivity levels were very acute and I needed guidance and support in both worlds. I just drifted along pulled wherever and incurring many bumps and bruises along the way. Some of which were quite dangerous.

As a parent of two daughters I realize how important it is to provide stability on the physical realm for sensitive children. I consider how lucky I am to have survived my childhood and into my adult years without being institutionalized. I still have a fear of not being able to cope and ending up in a mental hospital.

I believe I chose my ability to access other worlds and need to figure ways of using my sensitivity to help others and to evolve my spirit as well. There seems to always be sacrifices with the gifts we are given. Bouncing between worlds can be a difficult balancing act. Never feeling really connected in social settings or with people in general, spending lots of time alone, and spirit attacks from other realms are just some of the problems one might encounter.

If my parents or other knowledgeable adults had helped me understand what was happening, my early life would not have been so painful and confused. I really had to create my own survival techniques. I believe along with choosing my sensitivity I chose a resilient, strong willed nature to help me survive. I have a warrior's spirit. I've learned how to fight in other realms in the appropriate spiritual way.

Someone asked me "Why do you believe in the Loa?" My answer was and still is that I connect with whatever positive spirits come through to communicate with me. It has been said that you don't choose the Loa. They choose you." I've never chosen a particular path or spirit to connect with, except as a child I was always searching for places to ground my sensitivity and feel accepted. The Pentecostal church was a place where I could trance and be accepted, but the unhealthy emphasis on sin eventually seemed obsessive and I moved on. I now wait until whatever spirit shows up and then we establish a relationship and go from there. I must add that I always feel special and honored when these visions occur. I'm excited and humbled at the same time and continue to wonder why they're talking to me, why not someone more important. Hopefully I can help others gain more understanding of the spirits and the spirit realms.

The Guedeh are a Loa or spirit within the Voodoo path. They are the spirit of death itself. They are not to be confused with the morbid grim reaper image. The Guedeh are not out to scare anyone but to shake and wake you up to the realization that everyone will face death. The Guedeh are not an easy Loa to hang with. They are very dramatic by nature, and are high maintenance by way of how you choose to work them on the physical. Being initiated by the Guedeh certainly doesn't mean I'm always comfortable with them. My Roselinda ego has at times been embarrassed and generally discombobulated with their antics. They're usually demanding, coming and going as they please. By nature, they make one uncomfortable. That's what they do for specific spiritual reasons. Regardless, they're family and you deal with whatever because they're blood.

Just like any other relationship, it takes time to understand, build, and sustain that connection. I am honored and excited to work with my Guedeh family. They are my spiritual guides or what they call in the New Orleans Voodoo tradition, "Master of my Head."

My personal initiation by the Guedeh was totally on the spiritual realm. If a Priest or Priestess on the physical realm initiated me I would be honored and it would be meaningful, but until I hear directly from the source I have to question my initiation. This is my own personal feeling about my initiation process. I can't speak for others. Everyone has to assess their own initiation journey. No one else can do it for you. It doesn't matter anyway, the Loa have their ways of letting the community know who is or isn't connected. You can't fake the connection. One must have the passion, commitment, and faith to dive into the dark waters instead of paddling around on the surface with your head above water.

I do feel that if one is passionate and committed to whatever Loa they want to connect with then eventually they will get a confirmation in some way, shape or form. Have passion and commitment and then listen. Always listen. Be aware of signs from everywhere. I work very directly with the Loa by way of visions, but I'm always open to less dramatic signs of communication as well. Most spirits I connect with know that to get my attention they have to hit me in the head! I've even challenged certain spirits to bring me more proof of their existence. I'm a sensitive but a hard case to deal with as well. Maybe that's one of the reasons they chose me, because I feel it necessary and am willing and committed to sort through my personal issues that would cloud the connection.

When asked about what initiation means to me, I feel my entire lifetime so far has been a part of an initiation process. Many years of my life were spent in pain and confusion. Initiation is not a short journey that can be bought and paid for with the way mapped out and without any obstacles along the path. I feel the Guedeh spirits chose me because of what I have experienced so far on my life's journey as well as my sensitivity to other worlds. To be initiated by any Loa one has a very special and personal connection to that Spirit and must also follow a path on the physical that includes work specific to them. Initiation is a commitment to focus intently on spiritual growth. Initiation also means responsibility, whether you like it or not. One must be responsible for working the energy of the Loa and imparting information to the community.

It's fascinating and wonderful in retrospect how many Guedeh visions I've had and didn't understand during those periods of my life. I remember thinking "how strange, oh well, never mind." Years later, when I finally gained an understanding of the Loa, my odd visions made sense to me. It makes me wonder why the Guedeh would contact me when I had no knowledge of them. Among my first recollection of the Guedeh was the following sleep space vision:

> I was in a graveyard, it was night time, but similar to a full moon on a cloudless night with bright moon shadows everywhere. Skeletons surface from shallow graves, dancing happily. They invite me to join in. *(Roselinda Clemons, personal notes)*

I awoke feeling great until that voice from my childhood Christian background says "this isn't right." I had been taught that graveyards and skeletons were morbid and sad, and that dancing with skeletons was definitely devil-related. I have since learned to quiet that negative voice and continue to dance with the Guedeh in this realm and others. I even wrote a poem about this experience before I understood the word Guedeh or anything about Voodoo:

> *I dance with tall bony figures*
>   *carrying veils of darkness.*
> *Our movements are sharp and*
>   *lurking,*
>   *forever holding the mysteries*
>   *of the underworld.*
> *Come, we invite you into our dark*
>   *dance of mercilessly*
>   *passionate gestures.*
> *Embrace this enticing darkness.*

You will be filled with an exhilarating
   fear that will give way to
   illustrious power.

Take heed, use it wisely.

As we dance, we move out of the darkness into the light
   where my companions become
   clothed in beautiful radiant
   flesh

The warm heat of the light is equally
   as exhilarating as the dark.

We breathe in the light leaping and
   swirling around one another
   until the darkness calls once
   more,

and we return home where familiar
   shallow indentations in the
   earth await us for a rest,

before we again do our journey dance
   into the light.

I first heard the name Guedeh in a sleep space vision of a ritual officiated by Louis Martinie.' The participants formed a serpent line with Lu at the head and me next in line. Lu whispered the word "Guedeh" in my ear and I turned and whispered it to the next person who passed it down the line. I awoke thinking about the word, and knew it was special, but forgot it for a few months because I was rushed that morning and forgot to write it down.

I feel the following vision was an initiation into the Voodoo spiritual current. I was someplace tropical. I remember seeing old cars from the thirties or forties, black and white in color. I knew something was going to happen. I was led to a swampy pool of dark water. A black priest walked me into the pool and recited words I couldn't understand, but it didn't matter. I seemed to know what was going on. Other black people in African tribal costume and holding spears surrounded the pool. They poked their spears in our direction while chanting. Everything was intensely focused. The priest then went with me under the dark water. Instead of coming up out of the water, I was ejected very quickly out of an African totem pole like I was being birthed.

After becoming more familiar with the Guedeh spirits I had the following vision:

I was in a cemetery and there was a Guedeh on an elevated platform. He was standing over a coffin filled with another Guedeh. The Guedeh in the coffin was modeling a tuxedo coat with tails and the other Guedeh was very much like a used car salesman trying to sell me the coat that was being modeled. He would lift the Guedeh by the arm so I could get a better look at the coat and the model Guedeh would smile exceedingly big. When I didn't seem interested in the coat the salesman Guedeh would drop the model Guedeh back into the coffin. Other Guedehs would then bring another coffin filled with another model Guedeh for me to view and hopefully choose a coat. The whole scene was very much like a vaudeville comedy skit. The salesman Guedeh all at once stopped his humorous routine and became very serious, standing at attention. Approaching me from behind Baron LaCroix came around my left side and whispered in my ear, "We liked that you changed your name." Behind him a woman in a blue dress walked past me so close that she brushed my hair and face. She looked into my eyes with great intensity. She beckoned me to follow her down some steps that led underground under the cemetery. There were two beautiful stained glass windows on both sides of the stairway going down underground. I don't recall what happened while underground, but remember walking up the stairway still following the woman in the blue dress. As I was climbing the stairs the woman in the blue dress split into two identical women, twins. They turned their torsos inward, facing each other and then around to gaze at me. They turned back around and continued walking up the stairs. I came to the surface feeling connected, supported, like I had found a new family. *(Roselinda Clemons, personal notes)*

After this Guedeh vision I was in awe of the sacredness of the experience. I felt renewed, excited and most of all I had a spiritual knowing that I had been chosen or initiated somehow. How did I know? I just knew. Even if the Voodoo Pope refuted my experience, it wouldn't matter. If I don't experience that unwavering spiritual knowing then I usually discount the experience as an authentic vision. I'm very critical of my own process and am very careful of what I feel is or isn't a vision.

I integrate the Guedeh into my life through my job and the manner in which I work my spirituality. I work with spirit possession, letting the Guedeh spirits come through my body. They show me their specific dances and also give me personal warning visions that help me in my everyday life.

I also work the Guedeh into my daily life by working in hospice care within a nursing home setting. I have since had many rewarding experiences helping people pass on. It seems that after the Guedeh felt we were sufficiently acquainted that I needed to work in the trenches to fully understand their meaning. It's a difficult and necessary task, but also a beautiful and exciting transition. I still have a healthy fear of death, but at the same time I'm totally comfortable working so closely with the dying process. Sometimes I feel I reek of death, my flesh falling from my bones. I jokingly refer to my physical body as "My Bag of Bones." What would make most people uncomfortable; I'm quite at home with. I've literally witnessed people physically rot before they pass away and the Guedeh always remind me that we are all just of bag of bones. As I have heard it said in the Voodoo community, "Status makes no difference, no one of the flesh is immune."

The Priest

Blessings to you…Ah! The impudent humor of the Guedehs is apparent. They are such a pleasure. We are all in for surprises when they attend and they certainly do not disappoint in your vision. I can see the musty cloud of dust rise as the Guedeh model is rudely dropped back into the coffin.

When death laughs at us, the brave laugh back. Those who are both brave and wise laugh and willingly offer their hand. This day comes to us all and the humor of the Guedehs makes our common task a bit easier. If we can laugh with death, we can smile at most stuff the world throws at us. The Guedehs are certainly clowns but they are our holy clowns; sometimes they can teach in situations where the more serious Loa fail.

Your vision looks to be a calling or an invitation to serve the Guedehs and Barons. They offered you a tuxedo coat with tails, which is a fine Guedeh uniform. When someone is taken by the Loa at the Temple, they are offered clothing and other accouterments proper to the Loa that has nested in them. This is a common sign of honor and respect. If a beloved relative from far away were to pay you a visit, it would be a simple courtesy to offer him or her clothing, food, and shelter according to their taste. It's the same with the Loa.

You did not take the coat. This is very important. The Guedehs are tricky spirits. It would be an insult to accept their first offer. They love to haggle and respect those who can hold their own in affairs of the market (or cemetery, as the case may be). If you had bought the coat, the rank offered to you would have been diminished. You held your own and one of the big boys showed up. A Guedeh standing at attention is a rare sight. The Guedeh must have lost a bit of his composure when the Baron and his entourage entered your vision, if not I think he would have offered the Baron a mildly satirical salute.

Baron literally means "owner of the land." This is crucial to an understanding of the place occupied by the dead and the ancestors in our Voodoo. Soil is literally composed of the bodies of the dead. The mysterie here is not so much metaphysical as physical. We could not walk upon this earth; there would be no earth to walk upon without the animal and plant dead. We are supported every day by those who have gone before us. The Guedeh in your vision defers before an owner of the land.

The Barons are generally the named dead; the Guedehs are the dead whose names have been lost "in the seas of time," as we say. Here a big Baron shows up and compliments you on changing your name. This is an important moment in your confirmation into the realm of the Guedehs and Barons. You have been invited to change your name and an acceptance of this change has been voiced by the Baron even before you took a new name. My guess is that you hadn't even considered changing your name as of yet so there is a dry humor here. When they choose, The Barons can be a bit more sophisticated than the Guedehs. Perhaps the evils and the joys of our social positions even survive death.

At this point a woman appears. She wears blue; the color of the sky. A proper color for someone who would accompany the owner of the land. Her touch which brushed your hair and face appears to be both a purification and a blessing. In purification something is taken and in a blessing something is given. Her looking so intensely into your eyes is to confirm this exchange. Manman Bridgette is known to walk with the Barons. Bridgette is a great judge of the dead. It appears that she judged you and found you worthy of passage.

She is satisfied and takes you into a holy place beneath the cemetery. It is very impressive that you do not remember what happened in this holy, underground place. With initiation not only comes a new name but also new words. These new words are needed to describe the experiences of your new state not only to others but to yourself. Without these new words, it's harder to even recall the new experiences. You did not have the new words so what happened underground was hard to recall. Forgetting or lack of words to describe a spiritual experience is something that attests to the truth of the experience.

You describe two stained glass windows gracing the stairway. I believe that these windows foretell the woman splitting into twins. The twins are called Marassa and walk before even the Loa. Perhaps your underground experience was needed for you to see the double nature of the woman who led you. She may have always had this twin appearance up her sleeve and now you could see it.

You have indeed found a new family. That is a meaning of initiation. Confirmation is the act of acknowledging an initiation. It is much more common to confirm than to initiate in New Orleans Voodoo. The Loa and spirits do the initiating, a Priestess or Priest confirms the experience. As a Priest, I Louis Martinie' confirm your initiation.

That said, I think it is important that you understand the nature of this confirmation. New Orleans Voodoo is more similar to Protestantism than to Roman Catholicism in the matter of initiations / confirmations. Protestants emphasize a personal relationship their God and His spirits. You read the Bible and God speaks to you. He may tell you that you are saved, a Priest, or chosen in some other respect. People may agree with (confirm) what He told you, disagree, or have no opinion. What people say does not change the fact that God either did or did not speak to you. You know this in your heart in a deep way. Roman Catholics have beautiful rites to give people each of these chosen states. I believe that there is grace in the Catholic rites but it is no longer an individual matter between the practitioner and his or her God. New Orleans Voodoo believes in the primacy of an individual relationship with the Loa. As the old folks say, "Nobody needs to know (or do) your business."

A few years ago a Haitian Mombo came to New Orleans and wanted to meet with people from the various spiritual houses in the city. A shop in the Quarter sponsored this meeting. It's good to understand that there are all types of Voodoo in New Orleans. We have some houses that practice Haitian Voodoo, some that practice African Voodoo, and some, such as the House I am with, that practice New Orleans Voodoo. I went to the meeting so the New Orleans Voodoo Spiritual Temple could be present in welcoming the Mombo.

I sat with Creole Carol, another practitioner of New Orleans Voodoo. The Mombo was a nice person but she opened the meeting with exactly the wrong question. She said, "I want to get to know everyone. Let's start by saying who initiated you and their lineage." The practitioners of Haitian and African Voodoo were comfortable with the question and gave their well considered answers.

Ah! But there was such a silence from the practitioners of New Orleans Voodoo. I waited. I have the reputation as a bit of a trouble maker in our little community and didn't want to be the first to speak. Finally Queen Mother Margaret, her title is used to honor many years of service, said, "The spirits gave me my initiation." Perfect, she spoke with the humility a true queen offers an honored guest.

We believe that one is called by the Loa and is initiated directly by the Loa. Your vision is a good example of such an initiation and I am happy to confirm it as such but, and this is a big but, what I or others say is not all that important. You have heard the voice of the Loa. No human can give or take that voice from you. Your success or failure as a practitioner of New Orleans Voodoo is your most important proof to others. Papers can burn and the words of confirmation can be denied or revoked; your meeting with the Guedehs and Baron lives and confers grace from a place within you that is so strong it needs no protection.

The Professor

From a social scientific perspective, self-initiation is not supposed to happen. Religion is a social phenomenon involving communities, and a person cannot initiate him or herself into a community. However, Roselinda and Lu are discussing a religious community that skirts the edges of many social scientific theories – perhaps that is why they are so much fun to teach about in classes on the sociology of religion?

Scholars of religion who focus on New Age and American Neopagan religions note an emphasis on individualism and autonomy, which culminates in this peculiar acceptance of self-initiation (Bloch 1998; Berger et al 2003). My research (Laubach 2004) notes that the spiritual practices involving psychism, which are disproportionately practiced by Neopagans (Berger et al 2003), actually promotes autonomy and private practices. Bloch's (1998) work is especially interesting in that he demonstrates how inherently private magical practices actually serve as a basis for solidarity within spiritual communities that exist in tension with the dominant religions and rationalism of American society. My co-authors exemplify this with Roselinda's claim of private communication with spiritual entities and Lu's confirmation – i.e. that of a community leader.

Acceptance of self-initiation does not mean that American Neopagans do not crave long initiation lineages just like other religions – Lu's incident with the Haitian Mombo aptly demonstrates that fact – it is just that in a religion that is still under construction, with no Bible or founder to dictate canon, the ultimate authority reverts to a perceived direct experience of spirit.

This self-initiation phenomenon illustrates the importance of psychism as a tool for the construction of the American Neopagan religious community, and the problems and strategies of bringing such an individual experience into the sphere of community.

Self-initiation presumes the importance of psychism as a basis for belief construction the Neopagan community. The Theosophical Society defined psychism as "every kind of mental phenomena, such as mediumship and the higher sensitiveness, hypnotic receptivity, inspired prophecy, simple clairvoyance or seeing in the Astral Light, and truly divine seership; in short, the word conveys every phase and manifestation of the powers and potencies of the human and the divine Souls" (Judge 1943, p 246). From a social psychological point of view, I defined psychism as "perceptions of psychic intrusions into the stream of consciousness that are interpreted by the actor as not originating within the self's normal information channels" (Laubach 2004, p 242), and noted that its characteristics make the phenomenon uniquely "real" and allow it to serve as "evidence" (at least for initiates) of the reality of the spirit world.

My ethnographic research suggests that the importance of psychism is not limited to self-initiation. American Neopagans, who put such a premium on these kinds of experiences, increasingly see what religious scholars think of as "rituals" – repeatedly presenting religious symbols to reinforce community beliefs and practices – as empty acts. Neopagans are generally reluctant to invest in an initiation process that does not offer something that the student can interpret as direct experience of the spirit world. While they are not above taking shortcuts when possible, most recognize that attaining that experience of spirit is not easy, or cheap. They also know that the bill is paid not in cash - but in effort. They acknowledge a need to offer an exchange for the effort teachers give to them, but also understand that the kind of initiation experience they crave - the direct experience of spirit - is something that a student attains, not something that the teacher can give.

This is not to say that there is not a tremendous expectation pressure on initiation processes. Candidates are trained on symbol systems and on meditation, rhythms, dance, or other techniques that produce psychism. Initiation rituals then present symbols in a sequence, tempo, and drama designed to evoke additional psychic objects in the candidate's stream of consciousness that build on the ritual's symbols but are perceived as originating from the spirit realm. In this way, the experience ultimately recognized as initiation occurs as an encounter within the stream of consciousness of the candidate, not with the ritual actions of the priest. The best the officiator can do is to set up the initiation ritual properly, execute it skillfully, look for signs of success from its effect on the candidate, and attest to or confirm its success as Lu did with Roselinda's vision.

Self-initiation processes differ in the preliminaries that lead to the perceived encounter with the spirit realm. The most prevalent form has the candidate learning the system and conducting (maybe even designing) the ritual on her or his own. The rarer form, exemplified by Roselinda's account of her sleep-space experience, has the candidate encountering the psychic objects spontaneously. Note that Roselinda distinguishes these experiences from "dreams," a claim that is reflected in descriptions of visions by other esoteric communities (e.g., Tumminia 2002).

The community gets brought back into the picture through the confirmation process as described by Lu. Confirmation confers legitimacy on the initiate, validating the experience and authorizing the initiate to speak of it to the community, to make claims on the basis of the experience, sometimes to offer to help others reach their own initiation. Of course, this begs the question: how do community leaders confirm that the candidate has actually had the experience he or she has claimed?

While a full discussion is beyond the scope of this article, some elements can be seen even in my co-authors' writings. Some elements are pragmatic, others are esoteric. The first and most obvious pragmatic element is knowledge of the candidate. Lu and Roselinda have been friends for many years and have developed a sense of trust that comes from experience with each other. Accompanying this is a trust in the purpose to which the confirmation will be used. Lu's knowledge of Roselinda's history gives him confidence that she will not use his confirmation to make extravagant claims for money or power in the New Orleans Voodoo community.

On a more esoteric level, Lu notes that Roselinda is using the symbols correctly – even though she had not learned them at the time of the visions. She describes the correct form, contexts, and actions of the

Loa, and her actions and attitudes both in the visions and in her writing demonstrate that she has integrated the appropriate values expressed by the Loa. Furthermore, her writings indicate that these experiences are consistent with her prior history of encounters with the spirit realm, and are sequenced to culminate in an initiatory relationship. Along this line, Lu can note that she is demonstrating her dedication to a path consistent with the teachings or meanings of the Loa who initiated her by working with the hospice unit of the nursing home.

The final confirming element is consistent with what I encountered in my ethnographic research into spirit possession. While I emphasized that I was not interested in "judging" the validity of possession accounts I was recording, I was still asked how I knew whether someone was consciously lying to me. The consistent element I found in "believable" accounts, which can be seen in Roselinda's account, is a healthy respect or even fear of the experience. Experiences of psychism tend to challenge the essential foundations of what people come to believe is possible within their experience of reality, even if the type of experience is accepted within their cultural definitions of reality. Roselinda admits as much when she describes her continuing fear of ending up in a mental hospital.

The net effect of Lu's, or any community leader's, confirmation depends on the relative standing and interests of the people involved. It seems unlikely that the Haitian Mombo Lu describes would recognize Roselinda's initiation, but likely that Queen Mother Margaret would. Regardless, and this seems the strongest point made by Roselinda and Lu, neither response will change her understanding or responses of her experience.

Conclusion

The American Neopagan movement emerged from the 1960s countercultural mixture of spiritual seeking, feminism, eastern religions (see Melton 1993), indigenous American spiritual traditions, and British import spiritualities like Wicca, theosophy, and thelema. As is typical of American culture, these are blended with more regard for expediency than tradition, but always with an overriding concern for autonomy and individuality. These last factors have generated an emphasis on personal experience as a basis for beliefs, and psychism – spiritual experiences – has been a major tool in constructing the meaning worlds. With all of these influences, self-initiation claims, such as those described by Roselinda, can be seen as an obvious development from American Neopaganism.

References

Berger, Helen A., Evan A. Leach, and Leigh S. Shaffer, 2003, *Voices from the Pagan Census: A National Survey of Witches and Neo-Pagans in the U.S*, University of South Carolina Press, Columbia, SC.

Bloch, Jon P., 1998, 'Individualism and Community in Alternative Spiritual "Magic"' *Journal for the Scientific Study of Religion*, 37, 2, 286-302.

Judge, William Q., 1943, 'Cycles of Psychism', *Theosophy* 31, 6, 246-252.

Laubach, Marty, 2004. 'The Social Effects of Psychism: Spiritual Experience and the Construction of Privatized Religion', *Sociology of Religion*, 65, 3, 239-263.

Melton, J. Gordon, 1993, 'Another look at new religions', *Annals of the American Academy of Political & Social Science*, 527, 97-112.

Tumminia, Diana G., 2002, 'In the Dreamtime of the Saucer People: Sense-Making and Interpretive Boundaries in a Contactee Group', *Journal of Contemporary Ethnography*, 31, 6, 675-705.

The Trinity of the Hebrew Goddess: A Guided Presentation Of Goddess Narratives and Submerged Beliefs

Jayne Marie DeMente

Introduction

My expectations regarding human & historical heresies was *"surfacely"* to understand the historical context for primarily European heresy's or to understand more of history as it relates to the subject of Western Women's Thealogy.[1] What I am beginning to understand is different *ways of knowing* and how it affects women and my own stories. I consider myself a renaissance woman with considerable experience and knowledge. But I had a friend once who said to me that she had a lot of worldly experience but did not think that she really knew very much or how to apply that experience. I consider that the question or issue at hand. Do I have a broad enough understanding of "my" perspective to apply it to the information I am gaining in my field? Can I follow the information fast enough to apply it to the field? Will I be able to adjust to the ever-changing language, symbols & discoveries? It is an overwhelming path but none-the-less, it is the one I have chosen. Why, because it is ethical and right to tell the truth as we know it to be especially when discovering suppressed information.

I am informed by being a middle-aged American woman, wife and mother, of Scandinavian and French heritage in 2003 CE. One who has some professional knowledge of Greek mythology, Western psychology & ethics and cross-cultural transcendental ritual's of women internationally and throughout the human story. Like many in the United States, and of my generation, I was reared in protestant Christianity but left its practice to understand the aspects, rituals and traditions of other religions and their histories. My spiritual practice is a combination of the values I was reared with and those of others, whose story, truth, and practice made sense to me. Because of this knowledge and experience of many theologies, I find it interesting to muse upon their similarities and differences. My connection to the subject of the story of the "Hebrew Goddess" and the reason for pursuing the following endeavor, (regarding the sacred triangle and the Hebrew Goddesses) emerged from assignments during my Masters Program at the California Institute for Integral Studies.

I found that in doing the research, I began to theorize based upon three sources of knowledge. First, is my background in the study of philosophy, ethics and psychology gained during my undergraduate work at the University of Antioch in Los Angeles, California; second, is my background in storytelling and the study of archetypes during my past career as a film executive; and lastly is a combination from my upbringing as an evangelist's daughter, my study of religion and a guided spiritual experience. I have been fortunate in my quest to be *led* to certain spiritual understandings, based on concrete information as well as magical or spiritual insights. Some may call these *insights* psychic "breaks" or psychologically explainable. I have attempted to understand their meaning and in attempting to do so, I have come to understand that it all means the same. Experiences of *insight* are all metaphors for understanding the longing of the soul to have liberation and peace. I feel fortunate that in one of my encounters with Being,[2] or as I personified her as the *Mother*, led me on a path to know her and to bring me a clearer understanding of the Judeo/Christian tradition in which I was reared. And it has brought me peace.

In the world of Women's Thealogy, Cushe would be a good place to begin our story (better known as Ethiopia) in Africa.[3] We thealogians follow the many migrations of the people of Cushe into surrounding areas and then into other continents. It is time to place African origins and philosophies on equal standing with that of the Greeks, Europeans, Egyptians, and Aztecs, Indian and Asian philosophies. We attempt to understand what values and practices remained faithful to the early teachings of these peoples and the differences that led to the era of patriarchy and the diminishment cross culturally of women and their stories.[4] Intrinsic to theses stories and their mythologies and rituals is that until present, it has been held by those that follow the Yahweh cults, to be heretical to respect or question a female deity as an equal part of their respective mythologies.

Mara Keller, Program Director for Women's Spirituality at the California Institute of Integral Studies in San Francisco, California, points out that mythology constituted the religious beliefs of the ancients. As Merlin Stone and others have pointed out, the distinction between 'mythology' and 'religion' has been biased in favor of the latter, with religions often insisting on the truth of their own beliefs while holding the myths of others to be fictitious."[5] Personally, I hold to the idea that they all have the same origins and therefore, are invaluable in understanding the modern mind.

In this guided narrative story, I present three aspects of the Goddess in the Hebrew story and present why she continued to transform and change paradigm's that persist until today. I use the word *guided* because I felt compulsively drawn to the information and therefore, the books and people having knowledge of this topic - who appeared as if by magic and not by *coincidence*. According to one of these sources, Kathie Carlson, author of *Life's Daughter/Death's Bride*, a myth should be as pertinent to one today as it was in the past, even if the meaning has shifted. If we were able to ask mythologist Joseph Campbell, he would probably agree. He suggested before his death that the new emerging mythologies would be about partnership and planet sustainability. These are two of the main tenets of the Women's Thealogy movement and therefore, instrumental in the shaping of these emerging mythologies.

I acknowledge in this publication the academic and the empirical but I also wish to shed light on *other* ways of knowing. In the case of this narrative *knowledge* was given to me by a feminine spirit. I was placed in position over and over again to receive her information at a time when I and other women were open to receiving her information. It began with being moved to find information on Asherah, a widely worshiped Hebrew and Canaanite Goddess, (Canaanites are believed to be possibly the original people of Cushe[6]) and later to understand the stories of Lilith, her dark twin, who emerged out of Mesopotamia (also thought to be the peoples of Cushe) and then to theorize about the image of their *compassionate* cousin, Mary, of the Goddess and then Hebrew/Christian tradition.

Although written for academia, this reading was originally intended as a presentation piece or narrative because that was the way it was *given* to me. I hope you will find solace in its words. If you read my *discourse* you might recognize that it is meant to be a gentle way to present that early history indicates that humans are meant innately to live in peace. I do not find it heretical to muse on these Goddesses and their controversies within their traditions. In addition, through this journey, I have found a way to reconcile the story of women within the Judeo/Christian traditions. My wish is that this story will encourage others to find *her* within their own professions, religions, cultures and traditions. Hopefully, through the stories of women's deities, we may be able to create true gender and cultural *partnership* by having a partnership between spiritual *parents* and not just the male aspect of God. From out of a partnership of ancient values this mythology may lead us to save our planet and ourselves. **The Trinity of the Hebrew Goddess** is my contribution to this process – blessed reading!

The Trinity of the Hebrew Goddess

I have been fortunate in my quest to be *led* to certain spiritual understandings, based on concrete information as well as magical or spiritual insights. Some may call these *insights* psychic "breaks" or psychologically explainable. For many years, I have attempted to understand their meaning and in attempting to do so, I have come to understand that they both mean the same. Experiences of *insight* are all metaphors for understanding the longing of the soul to have liberation and peace. My insights led me to understand a part of the feminine human spiritual story that was left out of my education.

I do not find it heretical to muse about feminine deities and the controversies within their traditions. I have spent time with the following three Goddesses and they have guided me to the narratives that follow. Hopefully, through the stories of women's deities, we may be able to create true gender and cultural *partnership* by having a partnership between spiritual *parents* and not just the male aspect of God. From out of a partnership of ancient values a new mythology may lead us to save our planet and ourselves. *The Trinity of the Hebrew Goddess* is my contribution to this process in the following narratives about Asherah, Lilith and Mary.

Part I

ASHERAH

Goddess of the Cosmic Tree

The Lord by "Wisdom" (she) founded the Earth, by "understanding" (Being) established the Heavens.[7] And with thee is Wisdom, who is familiar with thy works and was present at the making of the world ... for she knows and understands all things.[8] She shall be the tree of life to all that lay hold on her.[9] Wisdom is/was as who kept guard over the first ... of the human race ...[10] She was called the "Queen of Heaven."[11] Wisdom is radiant and unfading and she is easily discerned by those who love her, and is found by those who seek her ... and she graciously appears to them in their paths and meets them in every thought.[12]

Who am I? I was called by Being to create the Universe. I was the word (Logos) before there was form and known as "Wisdom".[13] I spread my wings and caused the waters to form and my allurement became gravity and air.[14] I am Asherah, Queen of Heaven[15] known along the trade routes of Libya, Mesopotamia, Syria, Persia, Arabia and Crete.[16] I was called Ashtoreh, Astarte, Artemis, Innin, Inanna, Mama, Mit, Anat, Anahita, Ishtar, Isis, Au Set, Ishara, Attoret, Attar and Hathor – the many-named Ancestress.[17] Although I was there from the beginning, the following account is the "recollection" story of the time I spent with the Hebrews. I was recorded in their books of the Torah: I am recorded in the Wisdom books, Genesis, Exodus, Kings, Job, Jeremiah, Deuteronomy, Enoch and the book of Proverbs in their bible.

I was worshiped in the temple of Solomon for 236 years. I had 400 Priestesses and 400 Prophets knew my name.[18] I am known by the symbol of a tree - "the tree of life". After the Creation, I stayed among the people of Libya giving them all that they needed to know to thrive and be joyous. I then went back to "Being" to reflect upon creation.[19] Feeling their grief at my loss, I gave them a metaphor to reflect upon – the "cosmic tree".[20] It holds all wisdom. It is rooted in the Earth but stretches its branches to Heaven. Many replicas are made of my people stretching their arms like a tree to the sun.[21] I gave the metaphor of the tree because of its interconnectedness with air, soil and water. The analogy between wisdom and the tree was simple. I did not request or require worship therefore, any worship of me was simple and joyous and usually met with water, oil, bread or song.[22] Followers went to the grottoes or groves or to find bushes to pay homage to me. After the elders demoted me and changed my story in their book of Genesis,[23] what is left of that symbol is known as the nine branched *Menorah*. This symbol is now presided over by women in their homes.[24]

I was there in the beginning and I moved with the dark searchers during the great migrations. I was eventually connected to the trade harbors and many Goddesses attributed to this phase were considered my servants.[25] I am also known throughout the greater world as Hochma, Cardea, Hecate, Yemeya, The Tao, Tara, Bridget, Changing Woman, Kali, Mary and more, but we are all one. From as far as Iran and the Persian Gulf, to Arabia and the Red Sea, through Turkey and the Mediterranean Sea of Asia Minor, the advance of agriculture and trade moved along my seaways.[26] These waterways were crucial to the spread of Neolithic ideals.[27]

The qualities attributed to me were that I was free in love, fruitful in followers and a leader in peace and defense. The Israelites (Hebrews) in Egypt knew me as Isis and Hathor. The Israelites were composed of Egyptians, Canaanites and Semitic nomads (also known as the Cushites[28]) who joined together the ideals of the Goddess. The Goddess of these people exemplified "the infinite power and patterns of nature expressed through plant, animal and human life." … They described me as "Goddess as the lawgiver, who insured a high standard of moral conduct among her followers. She condemned lying, the breaking of promises and lack of proper respect for sacred things and for people."[29]

It was I who resided in the *Tent of Meetings* and nurtured the Hebrews in the desert. The oracles in their midst continued to call for me as Shekhinah.[30] After centuries of being enslaved in Egypt and forty years of wait in the desert, the Hebrews invaded Canaan. When the land was secured, the "sky god" is credited for the use of my ideals to set up a "Haven of Peace".[31] It was during this time that division was solidified between Hebrew men and women. Yahweh was given credit as the establishment of order and rule in the Universe! Previously, females held this status and were earthly as well as cosmic deities. Giving men this power gave the creative power of the Goddess to the state and it was then used to legitimize the king's rule.[32] The male religions then became the domain of the male cults. By the blood act of circumcision, creation was taken away from the blood rites of the Goddess and women were excluded from participation in the covenant.[33] The men changed my story by reversing the deities of the stories and attributing males my values and symbols.[34] The Hebrews attacked not Baal but Asherah as the target of their aggravations when they began to accept Yahweh as the one, true force of nature. Judea fell not because I brought bad luck but because the people neglected my rituals and Goddess worship had been forbidden.[35] The Emissary that came among the early humans suggested that our religion was a cult which co notated that we were less fine or civilized than his "religion". The followers of the Emissary, "the sons of Seth", began to look at the Priestess and her followers with different eyes. The garden story in Genesis became a watered down version of the story of where I first emerged in Libya. My attributes were divided into two trees, life and knowledge. Eve became the originator of sin. My lovely snake consort became the seducer of women and men and then the awareness of nakedness turned you away from the joy of sexual love and pleasures.[36] This is the joy that created you in the first place. This new story separated us, my "divine force is not distant or separate; the relationship is immediate and intimate".[37]

The Goddess religion was never monotheistic or dualistic - but pluralistic and represented by the trinity before it became part of the Hebrew male cult. It is the first trinity and known as the sacred triangle, or *yoni*.[38] This triangle represented various aspects of woman and the triangle of her vagina. The triangle is often referred to as maiden, mother and crone: innocent; then creator and nurturer; and then wise and magical and all are one and the same. Those of you seeking understanding of gender and cultural partnership, may find the answer to the question of partnership within the double triangle. These stars are the fully realized female and male narratives becoming parents to this planet. The symbol of partnership is the intertwining of two triangles into a six-pointed star – two triangles enmeshed together.

This male sky God, claimed what was not his to own. I was known not just as the eternal "Earth Mother" but also as the "Queen of Heaven". Therefore, I also held the distinction of the spirit of the sky. The worship of the Goddess was a geographically vast and major religion that affected multitudes of people over thousands of years until the fall of Crete.[39] It was totally integrated into the patterns of laws and society that translated into the later religions of the same regions and is held in your genetic memory awaiting cakes for the Queen of Heaven.[40] Remember me in your rituals and when lighting candles, especially when lighting Asherah's tree – my menorah tree.

PART II

LILITH

The Dark Twin

> *We share a god whom I do not share.*
>
> *We touch anyway. "Shekhinah" in our bones.*
>
> *You don't expect me to know the poems - Hebrew traces on the face of the sea.*
>
> *I have l earned these myths, I tore off my star of David,*
>
> *Whispered: Come to me Lilith,*
>
> *Waiting for a lover in exile, kiss of the demons,*
>
> *Surrendering the weight and breath of heaven.*
>
> *Israel; the far war, borders of ... Asherah, oranges, sand,*
>
> *So many hands surround me, Skin as dark as mine, more dust than night.*
>
> *Lo ira ra Ki at imadi*
>
> *(I shall fear no evil for you are with me);*
>
> *I mouthe these words in semblances of sound.*[41]

When Being called for creation our one self was divided. In the ascent our faces were torn from each other making us twins.[42] Forever we would have the quantum dialogue of sisters – twin sisters of opposing forces for the same cause. She was woman before the idea of woman.[43] In Libya[44] she was known as Yemeya – Mother of the Sea. Despite "religious fences" she has a multitude of names, Queen of Sheba, Proserpina, Lil, Lamassu, Partasshah, Rraphi, Anat, Ardad Lili, Avitu, Odam and Kali to mention just some of her names.[45] Her legacy is at the very nature of the secret of the universe. She is chaos. As I was the keeper of the blue print for creation,[46] her menstrual blood created all that you perceive.[47] She is a pulsating, throbbing, primal, wordless state of being.[48] She is found in the Sumerian's cosmological legends, Eleusinian sacred astrology, and Babylonian folktales. The Jewish Kabala, Zohar and the Talmud wrote the most of her story. Assyrian, Canaanite, Persian, Hebrew, and Arabic people and the Teutonic mythology of 3rd Century BCE also know her.[49]

Lilith became known under the heavens of the Gemini Twins. She is known as the Mistress of the Beasts, she rides a lion depicting her power over men and she is worshipped by the giving of food that has protective or healing qualities.[50] Her sculptured image is a part of many wedding dowries.[51] She knows the unspoken name of Being (God).[52] She is usually celebrated at the time of menses and the full moon.[53] She is dark skinned, she has long dark hair, and she is winged and full of persona. She is assigned the sea as am I, but the Hebrews changed the story to that of being created from dust because they wished to remove themselves even further from our origin stories.

Lilith is also assigned the heavens but cannot access Shekhinah, the life force. This is because Lil is chaos and is needed to keep the design of life in place. I hold the "grand concept" in contemplation with Shekhinah but I also, do not reside with her. We are all one but not.[54] Lilith is always the two sides of self and is your reflection. In Babylonia, the male son split "her" waters into two, just as Moses divided the Red Sea and Gilgamesh slashed the tree in the Sumerian folk story. These are not examples of the twin nature of myself, or my sister, but yet "other" examples of males taking power from the Goddess or the passing of

Goddess worship into patriarchy. Yet, for females these stories have merit in their psyche by representing the two sides of self coming together. Women, unlike men, do not shoulder a knapsack and sword in heroic challenge. Women, have no choice, they have felt cast out and "forced" into consciousness.[55] It is through knowing Lilith that ancient women became conscious of the inner self.[56] Without this reflection, the pathway to the female psyche, could be blocked and at its worse, one will go mad. It is my sister Lilith who leads women into the light and helps women find their voice – even if the voice is like a screech owl.[57]

Like myself, the Asherah, - Lilith is also known to Hebrew women as the Goddess. Abraham brought with him many stories from Mesopotamia when he settled in Canaan. He brought the myth of Innana (Nin-an-na) and her descent to the home of her sister Erishkigal, Ruler of the Underworld, who resides in the land of the dead. Innana ascends from there three days later.[58] Abraham thus brought a story that the Hebrews assigned to Lilith and eventually to Jesus. Again, in the Hebrew tradition, Lilith is also known to have rejected Adam's request for submission after she created the earth. It is important to note that Lilith is not the opposite of Eve. Eve is the story of the transition into patriarchy and is also a story borrowed from the changed stories of Gilgamesh or the Athena stories. Lilith is the remembrance of the Goddess and the resistance to patriarchy. She was insulted when the story about Eve's puberty became equated with Lil, as the serpent, seducing Eve into knowing her own body and sexual pleasures and the discovery of carnal knowledge. But because Lil left Adam we have the first divorce.[59] This establishes Lil as a woman operating both inside and outside the rules of her culture. As she becomes even more demonized in her stories, she will emerge as the wife of Samael (Satan) and therefore, instead of being the Queen of Heaven she became the Queen of the Realm of the Force of Evil. In an effort to denigrate the Mesopotamian sacred marriage rite, she is also assigned some responsibility for the denigration of sacred prostitution.[60] Paradoxically, in the Zohar my sister attains her most exalted position as "Mistress of God", God's divine counterpart, while Shekhinah travels with the Hebrews into "exile". Shekhinah was called into action to protect the wandering Hebrews, so then Lilith and I become moved about in our positions of power.

Probably the most important story of Lilith is when she came to King Solomon when he requested "Wisdom" from God. According to the Zohar, Book of Splendor:

> *God made two lights. The two lights "ascended" together with the same dignity. The moon, however, was not at ease with the sun, and in fact each felt mortified by the other ... God thereupon said to her, 'Go and diminish thyself. She felt humiliated and said "Why should I be as one that veileth herself? God then said 'Go the way forth in the footsteps of the flock' ... She was luminous, but as soon as she separated from the sun and was assigned the charge of her own hosts, she reduced her status and her light, and shells upon shells were created for covering the brain ... As this shell expanded it produced another, who was Lilith ... This became a quarrel of love ... it is the desire of Darkness to merge itself with Light, so it is the desire of night to merge itself in day ... 'Luminaries of light and fire' ... King Solomon, when he penetrated into the depths of the shell (of the nut-garden) drew an analogy from its layers to Lilith (and her spirits) ... The Holy one*

found it necessary to create all these things in the world to ensure its permanence ... The whole world is constructed on this principle, upper and lower, from the beginning ... so that one is a shell to another ... so that on this model man in this world combines brain and shell, spirit and body, all for the better ordering of the world.[61]

The Zohar offers detailed instructions (I 19b-20a) for deepening consciousness and individuation through knowing Lilith and her nature. Hers is also the story of the sacred hierarchy of a circle within a circle for within all opposites lies the same seeds of Lilith. This is the design of the mind, of heaven and of the sacred mysteries.[62]

Lastly, Lilith is also the keeper of secrets. She is the family member, which cannot be banished because she is needed. She regulates the margins of society and her role is distinct and necessary. Without her the family could not function and therefore, society would not function. Just as there are examples of men who return to obedient society,[63] Lilith leads females to know themselves by whichever path that takes them along.[64] Jewish families are instructed about preparing their house for the Sabbath. The house must be made to be lovely, as if receiving the bride "Shekhinah" and also for the "shadow" which is Lilith. "The two female forces are specifically contrasted because 'when one is fulfilled, the other is destroyed'".[65] Remember, the woman in the shadows knows God's secret name! Clearly, she is an integral part of the scene and not destroyed or banished. In the female psyche they are the obedient one and the disobedient one – finding their way to each other.

As her sister, I can say with pride that the important aspects of Lilith's story are those of her independence, strength, boldness, sexuality and courage. She is the flame of the revolving sword mentioned in the book of Genesis (3:24). That image of the flashing, revolving sword captures the essential quality of Lilith – now Goddess, now demon, now temptress, now murderess, now the bride of Satan, now the consort of God, ever flaming at the Gates of Paradise.[66] Understanding Lilith is only the beginning. Lilith will find peace when you know harmony for all people because then the twins will be one again. Lilith created all creatures and her seed is in all that lives. She is present for all life when Wisdom cannot be. She is the joy of sexual pleasure. She understands and leads each child through the veil into adulthood through the act of blood. She brings dark into light and light into darkness. She is allowed to marry with us in the unknowing of darkness. If she is the kidnapper, vampire, alien woman, owl, unclean, temptress, vanity, insanity, demon and child-killer, she is also the consort of God and Satan and the keeper of your story.

PART III

MARY

The Compassionate Cousin

Being remained one, the feminine became two
and then there was the child of action,
Mary our compassionate cousin.

This is the story of Mary, our cousin
She is Mary, the one they call Virgin
She is Mary the one they call Mother.
She is Mary the one they call Harlot. [67]

OUR MOTHER PRAYER

Our Mother, Thou who art in the darkness of the underworld
May the holiness of Thy name shine anew
In our remembering,
May the breath of Thy awakening kingdom
Warm the hearts of all who wander homeless,
May the resurrection of thy will renew eternal faith
Even unto the depths of physical substance.
Receive this day the living memory of Thee,
From human hearts,
Who implore Thee to forgive the sin of forgetting Thee,
And are ready to fight against temptation,
Which has led Thee to existence in darkness,
That through the Deed of the Son,
The immeasurable pain of the Father be stilled,
By the liberation of all beings
From the tragedy of Thy withdrawal.
For Thine is the homeland, and the boundless Wisdom, and the all-merciful grace,
For all and everything in the circle of All.[68]

Mary is what is left of the Lineage of the Hebrew Goddess and she is known by 100 names and is the feminine heritage for all people:[69] Covenant, Advocate, Blessed, Mother, Joy, Comforter, Immaculate, Reconciler, Grace, Mercy, Light, Annunciation and Assumption to name a few. She showed her spirit to those who asked and defined herself at Guadalupe taking on her predecessor's story of being the Mother of the

Sun and Moon. She appeared in Bosnia, Lourdes, Rue de Bec, Pompeii, Fatima, Korea, Cairo, China, India, Spain and in Los Angeles and will continue until we remember her fullness and grace. She took on the cloak of the color blue because she now represented heaven over the color of red for the ancient Goddess of Earth. I was the first and she is the last. She is the honored one and the scorned one. She is the whore and is the holy one. She began with me - Asherah, transformed into Shekhinah and is protected by Lilith. I begat our people through Eve and then passed into Mary as the last of our kind. She bore God from within … nursed him at her breast and taught him the secrets and chose him as her beloved. In my temple she made love to him to teach him the bountiful love that I am and prepared him. She wept at his feet, knowing he would be lost to me for a time and then she dried her tears with her hair. In our tradition, she anointed him with sacred oils in preparation for the sacrifice. And why do this you ask me? Because it was the time for men and they would not follow a daughter. Traditionally, the secrets pass to a daughter but I gave them a son, in order to carry on the values and secrets of the feminine, as the Goddess worshipers fade into memory. Mary dedicated her entire life to these ideals through her discipleship to her son.[70] She wept at the foot of the cross and watched … she accompanied him to the tomb. She administered the mystery of matter into light for his final sacrifice.

Mary, the mother Mirjim, and a Levi from the lineage of Levites, gave birth too many sons but Jesus, was destined to be clergy. Almost unnamed, she was remembered again by Christian scholars in the 17th Century after the death of her son. But longing for the feminine, some called her into their cults – giving her homage by recognizing the kinship with the Goddess of antiquity.[71] She was first recognized as dark and merged with the dark Goddesses of Europe. It was much later that she became depicted as light skinned. Her followers created over 500 dark skinned likenesses of her[72] and she presided over the European Goddesses, and then in the new world, as one by one they became saints. Her followers were of the Marion cult who blended aspects of Magdalene and the Mother. Unlike the competitive rule of the monotheists Gods, Mary gained remembrance as the Mother through the devotion of generations of Christian activists inspired by a "divine or holy longing" proving that "knowing the feminine" is a cultural force in its own right; that participates in the shaping of religious patterns. She always enters in peace and she is transformed by each generation that asks for her. She will bring in the "great convergence" and is the arbitrator between monotheism and the partnership of multifaceted religions.

Mary's son was trained in the carefully guarded secrets of two temples – mine was open for all and it flourished along side Christianity until the church decided to use murder to hold its followers in place. My temple held the mysteries of myth, science, symbols and ritual. Our stories of the mysteries of Isis, Mithraism and Cybele and the Gnostic, Hermetic and Apocalyptic movements influenced our son. Mary the Mother and Mary the whore priestess were trained in mystical practice and gave this knowledge to their son and lover. It was important to train him because in life and in the "shadow of death" initiations are crucial: because how one is instructed in the mysteries not only shapes life but also one's death. This is what Mary's son learned in his initiations. Otherwise one will wander around in life and death without purpose and abiding without trust of the blessing of the mystery. Your consciousness, or your subjective experience of self, is beyond the reach of today's neuroscience because it cannot explain how or why beings have self-aware minds. Minds that have the ability to project spirit in life and in death.

Mary in her compassion, choose to bear the son and used her temple ceremonial robes as swaddling, not because she had no clothes for him, but to honor him, as was her tradition. She reared him in the secrets that were available to not only women but also to men and children. The divine feminine will come to any who call her and she has appeared on all continents to all genders and to all cultures. She is one and she is many. Mary the Mother holds all the holy attributes of spirit. She gave witness to his life and deeds and she will appear again before the return of her son. She had several seasons but the next will be for always.

All Lords need consorts and muses, for without them the man fails at his task. Mary Magdalene, a sacred lover of the temple, joined to assist the cause of Jesus. She traveled to Rome to preach his true gospel and she kept ceremony with him. She later went to Marseilles, France to protect the mysteries. Her story became blended with her sister Sara's as seen represented in the Dark Madonna's of Europe. Magdalene and the son are the sacred partnership. She holds Christ in her allurement as he passes between worlds. Christ needs his mate and you need partnership to sustain yourselves. Given the choice to embrace the female, Christ for a time rebuked her and like Lilith is denied; she, like Eve must wait for the enjoining of partnership. It is my promise the Mother will present herself before the return of the Messiah and then the consort will be accepted. The sacred marriage will hold as it did at creation and you will know partnership and peace. Christ after the resurrection said of his beloved "it came to pass Mary, blessed one, who shalt inherit the whole Light Kingdom" and in saying this made her the Queen of Angels and Heaven. With this act he lifted humanity into partnership and into the realm of all possibility. [73] She is the most blessed of his disciples.

Unlike her cousins, Asherah and Lilith, the Mary's are mortal but take on the aspects and stories of the Goddess and in death merge with us. This is a difficult but compassionate feat. The Mother and daughter are linked into one and their compassion holds the feminine values and then they are able to blend us into one spirit. They are unparalleled and miraculous and the creation of the mind of God.[74] Christ's path was that of the will of the Father, but his life was promised to humankind by the Mother to alleviate suffering. When Jesus appeared after his death he was reconstituted (by the Mother and the daughter) thereby, reuniting God and Israel. This act is described in the *Song of Songs*, affirming the covenant.

Heaven and hell have their roots in the upper and lower Sophia[75] and God becomes incomprehensible but not greater than the Mother. The Mother is the first thought of God. Mary had independence from roles, was held above Joseph, she holds the feminine ethics and stature in her own right in the work of salvation. She was a virgin in that she was *virtuous* and became self realized through the Goddess initiation rites. She has the oldest thealogical[76] basis for all traditions. She is the consort, partner, lover and spirit of God and she will give you life, if you call she will answer. Find her and remember me.

Discourse: *A Goddess Meta Narrative*

I left you with a Goddess Meta-Narrative and it is found in the worship of the female and Mother earth. When the woman feels the first flutter of life in her womb – a universe is being born. This female paradigm suggests that the female immediately understands unconditional love, empathy, remorse and responsibility, in other words she understands the concept of self in "other". By studying the feminine, those who do not have children can also understand the concept of self in "other". It makes humans dependent on one another and interdependent. It socializes the community and leads one into the place of the unknown.

It is important to heed these words – a partnership is forming in your time – two trinities merging, father, son, holy ghost and mother, daughter, holy spirit. Together they form the six-pointed star – the star of love and peace. Now listen to the words of the "whore of Babylon", it is for every man to honor the Magdalene in every woman- as it is for every woman to honor the Christ in every man!" It is time to repair the damage to the web. Bring men back into the allurement and prosper again. Even in modernity, the Mother represents justice for all. We will then again nurture life, speak the truth, practice great generosity, approach the taking of life with great restraint and consider the consequences of action into many generations.[77] It is the promise of the covenant to have peace and you are asked to enforce this promise. The book of Hosea, chapter 79 speaks of ecology enjoining man who has failed his task to reunite with the fallen woman and become as it was before – returning to the first marriage an then there will no longer be devastation.

The greatest heresy is that these leaders of the one God movements scared humans into not knowing. They destroyed generations of followers of the Mother and later called them "witches". But that did not destroy us. I assure you, there will be a leader to come in the future. She is the many named and she will be reborn in your psyche and she comes in response to your seeking Wisdom.

> *Wisdom has built her house, she has set up her seven pillars,... she has set her table. She has sent out her maids to call... Come eat of my bread and drink of the nine I have mixed... walk in the ways of insight.*[78]

In closing, I wish to remind you, "Wisdom does not call upon any particular person or kind of person... not... only men or Israelites. She calls upon everybody – her grace, her abundance is universally available, to women, to men and to everybody who hears her."[79] In ancient times I was your gift of knowledge, now you must choose me. I am that moment in time and I am eternity. I am the Queen of Heaven and my body is given as a gift to you. I have born a dark daughter Sara, out of Egypt, out of Africa and the house of David lives on through the lineage of a beautiful and ancient dark woman.[80] Blessed Be.

Notes

1. A term created by feminist Naomi Goldenberg as the feminine of theology and coined by Feminine ethicist Coral Christ. It means the practices and rituals of women cross culturally throughout the human story.
2. Here loosely defined as the mind of God or of Universal Consciousness.
3. Ben-Jochanna 1988.

4   Birnbaum 2002.

5   Keller, Mara, *The Greater Mysteries of Demeter and Persephone*, unpublished, p xviii.

6   See Ben-Jochanna, Lucia Birnbaum, or Dunjee Houston for source.

7   Proverbs 3:19. Wisdom and Understanding are synonymous with Torah, known by the Hebrews as the feminine aspect of God

8   Wisdom of Solomon 9:9-11.

9   Proverbs 3:18.

10 Wisdom of Solomon 10:1-4. I Kings 11:5. II Kings 23:13. Solomon paid homage to her because of her instruction of "Wisdom" to him upon his request to (Being) God. In 10th Century BCE, he had a temple erected to her near Jerusalem). She is known here as Asthoreth.

11 Jeremiah 44: 15.

12 Wisdom of Solomon 6:12-16.

13 Darton & Todd 1995, Gen. 8:1 & 1:20.

14 Long, A.P. 1992, p 31.

15 Gadon, Elinor n.d., p126. (11th – 6th Century BCE)

16 Stone, Merlin, p 9.

17 Long, Asphodel P. 1996.

18 Long, Asphodel, P. 1998.

19 Long 1992 , p 33.

20 Derived from story in Karen Armstrong 1994.

21 Derived from a discussion with Mara Keller, director of WSE at CIIS.

22 Armstrong 1994.

23 Goldstein 1980.

24 Stone 1976.

25 A Cal Project n.d.

26 Gadon n.d..

27 Gimbutas n.d..

28 Houston 1926.
29 Gimbutas n.d., p 343.
30 Patai 1990.
31 tone 1976.
32 Gadon, p 183.
33 *Ibid.*
34 Armstrong 1994.
35 *Ibid.*, p 179.
36 Darton & Todd 1995.
37 Gadon, p 184.
38 *Ibid.*, p. 177.
39 See Gadon.
40 Stone 1976.
41 Dame et al, p 219.
42 Koltuv, p 7-10.
43 Dame et al, p 329
44 Birnbaum, p 127.
45 Davidson.
46 See Bridge, The.
47 Dame et al, p 27.
48 See Koltuv.
49 Probably drawn from earlier Cushite folklore.
50 Birnbaum.
51 Diamant.
52 Koltuv.
53 *Ibid.* p 24-30.
54 Paper, Jordan. *Through the Earth Darkly.* 1997. NY. Continuum Publishing.

55 Koltuv, Barbara Black. *The Book of Lilith*. 1986. NY. Samuel Weiser.
56 Ibid.
57 Personal theory.
58 See Paper.
59 Davidson.
60 Paper, p 36.
61 Koltuv, p 1-5.
62 Birnbaum, pp 127 & 4-7.
63 Luke 15:11-32.
64 Dame et al, p 311.
65 *Ibid.*, p 312.
66 *Ibid.*, p 17.
67 Taken from a handout in Charlene Spretnak's class at CIIS.
68 Prayer Given by Valentin Tomberg, *Gnostic Gospels*.
69 See Chiffolo.
70 *Ibid.*
71 Birnbaum.
72 Boyer (12th Century BCE).
73 Yogi, Maharishi, Mahesh.
74 Proverbs 76 tells of God and Wisdom consorting as earth forms.
75 See Pagels.
76 *Thealogical* is based upon the deity *Thea*, before *Theo*, and means the study of the divine.
77 Values defined by the ethicist Carol Christ.
78 Proverbs 9:1-6
79 Long 1992.
80 Personal theory.

References

A Cal Project, n.d., *Encyclopedia Judaica*, Keter Publishing House, Jerusalem.

Ann, Martha, 1993, *Goddesses in World Mythology*, ABC-CLIO, Santa Barbara, CA.

Armstrong, Karen, 1994, *A History of God*, Alfred A. Knoff, New York, NY.

Baring, Anne & Cashford, Jules, 1991, *The Myth of the Goddess*, Arkana, London.

Ben-Jochanna, AA., Yosef, Dr., 1988 [1971], *Africa. Mother of Western Civilization*, Black Classic Press, Baltimore, MD.

Birnbaum, Lucia, 2002, Dark Mother, Metaphor of the Third Millennium?, iUniverse, San Jose, CA.

Bridge, The, 1974, *The Ascended Masters Write the Book of Life*, Kings Park. Long Island.

Boyer, Marie-France, 2000, *The Cult of The Virgin*, Thames & Hudson, London.

Burkert, Walther, 1987, *Ancient Mystery Cults*, Harvard University Press, Cambridge, Mass.

Braud, William & Anderson, Rosemarie, 1998, *Transpersonal Research Methods for the Social Sciences*, SAGE Publications, Thousand Oaks, CA.

Carlson, Kathie, 1997, *Life's Daughter/Death's Bride*, Shambala, Boston & London.

Chiffolo, Anthony, 2001, *100 Names of Mary*, St Anthony Press, Cincinnati, Ohio.

Dame, Enid, Rivlin, Lilly, and Wenkar, Henry, 1998, *Which Lilith?*, Bookmart Press Inc, NJ.

Darton & Todd, 1995, *The New Jerusalem Bible*, Doubleday, New York, NY.

Davidson, Gustav, 1967, *A Dictionary of Angels*, Macmillan Pub, Canada.

Delaire, Jean., 1949, *The story of the Soul in East and West*, The Philosophical Publishing House, London.

Diamant, Anita, 1997, *The Red Tent*, Picador USA

Eliade, Mircea., 1958, *Rites and Symbols of Initiation*, Spring Publishing, USA.

Finch III, Charles, M.D., 1996, *Echoes of the Old Darkland. Themes from the African Eden*, Khenti, Inc., Decatur, GA.

Freke, Timothy & Gandy, Peter, 2001, Jesus & the Lost Goddess, Three Rivers Press, New York.

Gadon, Elinor, n.d., *The Once and Future Goddess*, Harper & Row, New York.

Gilligan, Carol, 1981, *In a Different Voice*, Harvard University Press,. Cambridge, Mass.

Gimbutas, Marija., n.d., in J. Marler, (ed.), *The Civilization of the Goddess*, HarperCollins.

Goldstein, David, 1980, *Jewish Legends*, Newnes Books, London.

Harding, M. Ester., 1971, *Women's Mysteries Ancient and Modern*, Putnam, New York.

Houston, Druisilla Dunjee, 1985 [1926], *Wonderful Ethiopians of the Ancient Cushite Empire*, Black Classic Press, Baltimore, MD.

Koltuv, Barbara Black, 1986, *The Book of Lilith*, Samuel Weiser, USA.

Long, Asphodel P., 1992, *In a Chariot Drawn by Lions*, Woman's Press, London.

Long, Asphodel P, 1996, *Asherah, the Tree of Life and the Menorah*, Sophia Papers.

Long, Asphodel, P., 1998, Asherah, Goddess of the Grove, the Menorah and the Tree of Life, *Goddessing Magazine*

Luker, Manfred, 1988, *Dictionary of Gods and Goddesses, Devils and Demons*, Routledge, London.

Macquarrie, John, 1990, *Mary for All Christians*, Eerdmans Publishing , Grand Rapids. MI.

Maier, Walter, 1986, *Asherah, Extrabiblical Evidence*, BL 1605 a7m358177.

Marler, Joan (Ed.), 1994, *From the Realm of the Ancestors: An Anthology in Honor of Marija Gimbutas*, Knowledge, Ideas & Trends, Manchester. CT.

Olson, Carl., n.d., *The Book of the Goddess Past and Present*, Crossroads, New York.

Pagels, Elaine, 1989, *The Gnostic Gospels*, Vintage Books, New York.

Paper, Jordan, 1997, *Through the Earth Darkly*, Continuum Pub., New York.

Patai, Raphael, 1990, *The Hebrew Goddess*. 3rd Edition, Wayne State Press, Detroit.

Russell, Letty M. (Ed.), 1985, *Feminist Interpretation of the Bible*, Westminster Press, Philadelphia.

Scholem, Gershom, 1954, *Major Trends in Jewish Mysticism*, Schockem Books, New York.

Stone, Merlin, 1976, *When God Was a Woman*, Dial Press, USA.

Swimme, Brian, 1984, *The Universe is a Green Dragon*, Bear & Co., Santa Fe. NM.

Tarnas, Richard, 1991, *The Passion of the Western Mind*, Ballantine Books, New York.

Walker, Barbara, 1998, *The Woman's Dictionary of Symbols and Sacred Objects*, Castle Books, Edison.

Yogi, Maharishi, Mahesh., 1963, *The Science of Being and the Art of Living*, MIU Press, Livingston. NY.

The Topography of Magic in the Modern Western and Ancient Egyptian Minds

Steven M. Stannish

Recently, in the pages of the *Journal for the Academic Study of Magic*, Aaron Cheak (2004) has shown that the Indo-European root **mag(h)*- and the Egyptian word *ḥk3*, usually translated "magic," both convey the idea of extraordinary "power." This conclusion agrees with Marvin W. Meyer and Richard Z. Smith's description of Coptic magical papyri as "texts of ritual power" (1999, pp. 1-6). Although Cheak's view has considerable merit, it is also important to acknowledge the fundamental differences between the European and Egyptian concepts of magic. This essay examines one such difference — that of topography. I maintain that, whereas modern Westerners have seen magic as a marginal activity associated with a mythical forest, the ancient Egyptians regarded *ḥk3(w)* as a gift from the gods and enshrined it in their society. In the simplest terms, one civilization cast magic beyond its boundaries; the other insulated it within them.

Before proceeding, two observations are in order. First, both of the cultures under investigation are complex and therefore marked by multiple opinions about magic. For the sake of economy, in each instance, I have decided to concentrate on the perspective of the literate male elite. In the case of the modern West, I have narrowed the focus even further, excluding the position of scientific skepticism. Second, I have elected to take a broad view of sorcery, including under its label practices as divergent as love magic and necromancy, weather magic and *defixio*, conjuring and midwifery. I hope that readers will forgive these choices.

Magic is one of the slipperiest terms in cultural anthropology. While most scholars today would reject James George Frazer's (1996) dichotomy between savage magic and civilized religion, many would be reluctant to go as far as Tom F. Driver (1991), who has maintained that all rituals employ magic in some way. Among other students of the subject, Bronislaw Malinowsky (1948) understood magic as an attempt to augment human ability in the face of formidable obstacles, Marcel Mauss (1972) and Emile Durkheim (1965) conceived of it as type of antisocial behavior, and David Aune (1980) classified it as deviant activity. For his part, E. E. Evans-Pritchard (1937) argued that any definition of magic should be based on the beliefs of the people under investigation, encouraging the appreciation of local peculiarities and nuances. Finally, Claude Levi-Strauss (1966), confronting the possibility that the concept of magic was of little or no value in cross-cultural analysis, suggested that it be "dissolved."

Given these diverse opinions, it would probably be futile to seek a universally valid definition of magic. I would submit, however, that any understanding of *Western* magic should begin with the word's etymology. English *magic*, French *magie*, German *Magie*, and Latin *magia* are all derived from the Greek *mageia*, a expression that denotes the activity of a Persian *maguš* or "specialist in religion" (Graf 1999, p 20). In the Greek imagination, the Persians were the ultimate barbarians. They spoke a different language, they had different political institutions, and they constantly menaced the Aegean world. Their rites emanated from beyond the boundaries of Hellenic society and were by nature threatening. So classical witches like Medea and Erictho hailed from remote regions, violated taboos, and blighted communities. Later, when Rome ruled the Mediterranean, magic was also disreputable (Graf 1999, pp 36ff.). One need only peruse Apuleius' *Metamorphoses* (1951) to find a whole company of low characters who dabble in the art.

The classical notion of *mageia*, then, constitutes the foundation for the Western concept of magic. But other factors certainly affected its evolution. The most significant of these, of course, is Christianity. In places, the New Testament attributes magic to holy men, but also associates it with foreign lands. Acts 7:22 suggestively remarks, for example, that Moses had been "instructed in all the wisdom (*sofia*) of the Egyptians" and was "powerful (*dunatos*) in words and deeds." Similarly, Matthew 2:1-14 records the celebrated visit of "wise men (*magoi*) from the East" to Judea. Elsewhere, however, the New Testament casts magic in a most unfavorable light. Acts 8:9-24 says that one Simon Magus "practiced magic" (*mageuôn*) in marginal Samaria, brazenly claimed to be "the Great Power of God," and tried to purchase the apostolic gift of imparting the Holy Spirit. Based on this tale of arrogance and ambition, Simon became the archetypal sorcerer as well as the first heretic of Christianity. Irenaeus of Lyons claims that "from [Simon] all heresies got their start" (1992, 23.2). Eusebius of Caesarea calls him "the prime author of every heresy" and likens his disciples to "a pestilential and scabby disease" (1989, 2.13, 2.1). In contrast to miracles, which won converts and benefitted humanity, magic was a contagion that festered on the edge of Christendom and that had to be kept at bay.

The binding of magic to heresy through the figure of Simon Magus profoundly influenced medieval thought on the subject. As enemies of Christ's Church, heretics were the servants of Satan and sought the ruin of humanity. If magic was itself heresy, then it was always malignant, whatever its professed goals were. Richard Kieckhefer writes: "The people who went out to gather apparently innocent herbs, or the midwife who seemed blameless and helpful might turn out to be in league with demons. … Indeed, for many writers in medieval Europe all magic was by definition demonic" (1989, pp 9-10). Related to this opinion was the conviction that wizards and witches made pacts with the Devil, sealing them with their own blood (McCall 1979, p 245). In exchange for money, revenge, and power, they promised to render homage, service, and their very souls unto the Prince of Darkness.

Besides the Church's notion of heresy and its crushing sense of the diabolic, two further developments served to fix the Western concept of magic (Russell 1986, pp 418-9). The first was the Scholastic corroboration of the mystical body of Satan, an enemy host that opposed the mystical body of Christ. This rival kingdom included sorcerers as well as Jews, pagans, and other unbelievers. The second development was the Inquisition, a movement that produced, in addition to a staggering measure of human suffering, an arsenal of manuals for the identification and prosecution of witches. The most infamous of these handbooks is *The Malleus Maleficarum* by Heinrich Kramer and James Sprenger. Permeated by farcical etymologies, tortured logic, and abominable style, the *Malleus* also exhibits a misogyny that is as rabid as it is vile. Kramer and Sprenger maintain that the great majority of witches are female, for "woman is a wheedling and secret enemy," at once "credulous" and afflicted by "insatiable carnal lust" (1971, 1.1, 1.6). No wonder, then, that she attempts to attain her ends through sorcery, the evils of which "exceed all other sin which God has ever permitted to be done" (Kramer & Sprenger 1971, 1.14).

Naturally, later movements like the Protestant Reformation, as well as local problems such as poverty, dislocation, and feuding also shaped ideas about magic. Nonetheless, I would argue that the concept had taken root by the time of the Italian Renaissance. In Malcolm Gaskill's recent study (2005) of witch-hunting during the English Civil War, for instance, we find ecclesiastical officials who regard even cunning folk as diabolists, fanciful stories of magical rites that kill people and damage property, and a general fear of women subverting patriarchal society. With considerable aptitude, Gaskill describes an imagined alliance of royalists, papists, midwives, and witches on the outskirts of Cromwell's utopia, a fantasy that inspired a persecution of individuals who were both guiltless and harmless.

Based on these initial remarks, we may begin to situate magic in the mythical landscape of Western civilization. As heresy, the practice originates on the margins of Christendom, threatening to infect and destroy the realm. So Pope Innocent VIII's Bull *Summis desiderantes affectibus*, a document addressing witchcraft in Germany, proclaims that "all heretical depravity should be driven far from the frontiers and bournes of the Faithful" (Summers 1978, p 553). But what exactly is magic's liminal zone? I submit that it is the forbidding waste, the eerie heath, or, most commonly, the dark forest. The forest is, of course, the traditional site of the hero's adventure, the domain through which the Arthurian Knights cut their individual paths on the Grail Quest (Campbell 1968a, pp 36-37). More generally, it is the place where the society's rules are suspended and things do not conform to expectation (Campbell 1968b, pp 79-83). Hence, the woods are the ideal place for the black arts. I do not mean, of course, that, like the crone in *Hänsel und Gretel* (Grimm 1969, pp 120-132), practitioners always *live* there. Indeed, according to Sir Thomas Malory's *Le Morte Darthur*, the arch-sorceress Morgan le Fay was "put to school in a nunnery, and there learned … necromancy" (1961, p 4). I simply maintain that the forest, as the locus of the weird, is also the site of spectacular witchery.

To test whether this is indeed the case in the modern Western imagination, I have selected two books, Jules Michelet's *La Sorcière* (1964) and Montague Summers' *The History Witchcraft and Demonology* (1993), as well as two films, *The Blair Witch Project* (1999) and M. Night Shyamalan's *The Village* (2005). I have chosen these sources not necessarily for their quality, but for their popularity. The volumes remain in print, despite their obsolescence, and the films grossed over $248 million and $256 million, according to The Numbers web site. *The Blair Witch Project*, produced on a minuscule budget of $35,000, profited from the belief that it was a "true story," reconstructed from surviving footage. This misunderstanding was intentionally fostered by Internet advertising and by a television special titled *Curse of the Blair Witch* (Harris 2001).

The Village, despite being somewhat bland and predictable, managed to capitalize on the success of Shyamalan's previous ventures, *The Sixth Sense* (2000) and *Signs* (2003).

There can be no doubt that Jules Michelet imbued *La Sorcière* with his own anti-authoritarian and anti-ecclesiastical biases. Yet, he also drew on numerous historical documents. As a result, his portrait of the witch is at once revolutionary and medieval. So, while Michelet seeks to reverse magic's negative polarity, he still associates it with the Orient, with infidelity, and with women. "Reines mages de la Perse," he writes, "ravissante Circé, sublime Sibylle, hélas! qu'être-vous devenues? et quelle barbare transformation!" (1964, p 22). Indeed, in first sentence of *La Sorcière*, he quotes the *Malleus* on "*l'heresie des sorcières*, et non des sorciers" (1964, p 21, Michelet's italics).

For Michelet, magic belonged to the common folk and was rooted in a natural world that terrified and disgusted the Church. Satan, besides being "le roi des morts," was "le prince de la nature" and "toute la nature" was "démoniaque" (1964, chs. 7-8, p 41). As such, Michelet situates sorcery on the edge of the community, in the teeming woods. "Si le diable est dans une fleur," he remarks, "combien plus dans la forêt sombre!" (1964, p 41). Michelet even invents a story in which a widow, longing for her dead husband, considers obtaining the help of a witch who dwells in the woods. For the time being, the widow decides not to go, since "Maintes fois on a vu sur la lande des choses qui n'étaient pas à voir" (1964, p 95). One night, she adds, her neighbor wandered into the forest in search of a lost sheep and came out mad (1964, pp 95-96). As expected, magic's place is that marginal area where society's rules break down and insanity reigns.

In many respects, Montague Summers was the antithesis of Michelet. A Catholic priest and a believer in the Church's saving mission, Summers accepted the existence and efficacy of witches, and endorsed and their execution. He was, essentially, a medieval man caught in the twentieth century. In the first pages of his *History*, Summers characterizes the witch as a heretic and an anarchist (1993, ch. 1). By polluting the Church, she both imperils souls and sews discord. Like his predecessors, Summers also traces sorcery back to Simon Magus, "so early do heresy and magic go hand in hand" (1993, p 193). Finally, he suspects that all magic is malevolent and even quotes the *Malleus* on the harmfulness of midwives (1993, p 160).

Given these opinions, it is not surprising that Summers locates magic on the boundary of Christendom: "sceptics do not, will not, realize the monstrous things that lie only just beneath the surface of our cracking civilization" (1993, p 95). Discussing the Witch's Sabbat, Summers notes that the ritual can take place indoors or outdoors, but that "it was advisable that the selected locality be remote and deserted to obviate any chance of espionage or interruption" (1993, pp 113-114). He cites Christian Stridtheckh's remark that "meetings are generally held in wooded spots, or on mountains, or in caves" (1993, pp 114-115). Such areas mediate between the world of men and the kingdom of hell, so that Satan — sometimes a costumed degenerate, other times an actual shade — might join the celebrants (1993 pp 8-9). Summers even records an English witch's description of the Fiend's aspect: "The deuell wes cled in ane blak goun with ane blak hat vpon his head. ... His faice was terrible, his noise lyk the bek of ane egle, greet bournyng eyn; his handis and leggis wer herry, with clawes vpon his handis, and feit lyk the griffon" (1993, p 9).

One might argue that Michelet and Summers were extraordinary men, the former being a Romantic scholar, the latter an atavistic priest, and conclude that they held unusual views. Nonetheless, many of their ideas reappear in the films under consideration. *The Blair Witch Project* concerns three college students — Heather Donahue, Josh Leonard, and Mike Williams — who are making a documentary about Elly Kedward, a witch from Blaire, now Burkittsville, Maryland. According to the aforementioned television special, Elly was an outsider who possessed unacceptable religious sensibilities. An Irish Catholic immigrant to a Protestant town, she was convicted of using pagan magic and banished to the Black Hills Forest in the winter of 1785. Over the next two centuries, several mysterious murders took place in the vicinity of the woods, suggesting Elly's continued presence. Supposedly, the students interviewed local people and traveled to relevant sites.

The Blair Witch Project sharply distinguishes between the normality of Burkittsville and the uncanniness of the Black Hills Forest. Many of the town's citizens cultivate a healthy respect for the legend of Elly Kedward, but only one, Mary Brown, is certain of its veracity. Described as "crazy," Mary lives in a trailer park, seemingly on the edge of community. She claims to have encountered the witch one day in the woods and says she was "like a woman" but "hairy from head to toe."[1] Mary's story is unsettling both because of her labored speech and because she looks a lot like a witch herself. She carries a Bible and wears what appears to be a rosary around her neck, but she also has a hooked nose, a protruding chin, and wild eyes.[2] Whether or not she is really the

Catholic/pagan Blair Witch, Mary serves as a warning against violating Elly's abode. Of course, after the students enter the forest, the signals become more intense. Three piles of rocks appear around their tent, strange noises emerge from the dark, and figures made of bound sticks dangle from the trees.[3] As their supplies dwindle, the students become disoriented and agitated. In his anger, Mike even throws the map showing the way out of the woods into the river. The film concludes with Josh's disappearance, a bundle of sticks being left in his stead, and Heather and Mike's apparent murder in an abandoned cabin. Once again, the forest is the place of adventure, the location of the weird, and the realm of witchery.

Unlike *The Blair Witch Project*, *The Village* does not claim to be anything more than fiction. It may seem to be an odd source for an essay on magic, since it mentions the concept only once, in connection with a handful of protective rocks, but it does shed considerable light on the mythic landscape of Western civilization. The film is set in a rural community in what seems to be late nineteenth century Pennsylvania. Surrounding the settlement is Covington Woods, a "forbidden forest" inhabited by "those we don't speak of." The boundary between the two areas — "their woods, our valley" — is marked by lanterns and monitored by a tower. Beyond the forest sit "the towns" to which the community's founders vowed never to return.

There are some correspondences between *The Blair Witch Project*'s Black Hills Forest and *The Village*'s Covington Woods. A sorceress is not associated with the latter region, but strange and dangerous creatures are. To an extent, "those we don't speak of" combine the features of Elly Kedward as described by Mary Brown and those of Satan in

Summers' *History*. They have hairy bodies and long claws on their hands and feet, as well as boar's snouts and spinal quills. "Those we don't speak of" are generally content to remain in the forest and make menacing sounds, unless a member of the community breaches the boundary, and then they become aggressive. One last detail: the creatures wear red cloaks. In fact, the community calls red "the bad color" because it attracts them. At the risk of forcing a comparison, I would point out that red is also associated with witchcraft (Summers 1993, pp 102, 196). It is the color of blood — "the life of all flesh" (Leviticus 17:14), the seal of the Devil's bargain, and the nourishment of a sorceress' familiar.

The plot of *The Village* centers on the romance of Ivy Walker and Lucius Hunt, children of two of community's Elders. Their relationship is jeopardized when Lucius is stabbed by a jealous and deranged boy named Noah Percy. Despite the fact that Ivy is blind and intensely afraid of "those we don't speak of," she resolves to journey through forest to the "wicked" towns that possess the means of healing her love. At this point, *The Village* begins to reveal its deceptions. Ivy's father tells her not to fear "those we don't speak of," because they are only "a farce" designed to insulate and unify the community. Then, Noah, disguised as one of the creatures, attacks Ivy in the woods, but falls into a pit and dies. Evidently, he had discovered the truth about "those we don't speak of" and had been using the knowledge to carry out brutal attacks on animals. Thoroughly unnerved by the forest, Ivy finally reaches its outer limit and encounters a park ranger driving a Land Rover Defender 90 with the words "Walker Wildlife Preserve" emblazoned on its door. The audience learns that each of the Elders lost a loved one during 1970s and went to the same grief counseling center. Forsaking the savagery of twentieth century, they used Ivy's father's inheritance to buy an isolated refuge. The real year, printed in a newspaper at the park's headquarters, is 2004.

The Village clearly divides the world into three concentric circles: the community of the elect, the threatening forest, and the kingdom of the damned. The second circle menaces the first, overturns its rules, and disorients its inhabitants. It is the realm of the barbaric, the threshold of the adventure, and the site of the unusual. As in Dante's *Inferno* (1994, 1.1-3), the forest is also closer to hell, whence magic draws its inspiration. Interestingly, Ivy, the heroine who enters the woods on "a quest" for medicine, has red hair. While she is a member of the community, she is also physically linked to the margins. *The Village* thus makes a series of clever but also very traditional connections: forest-outside-individual quest-red-power-life. Of course, the film also deviates from custom in certain respects. It does not, for instance, feminize the strange and subversive. I do not consider such departures to be problematic, however. Instead, I see them as signs of specific psychological changes, in this case the erosion of medieval hostility towards women, at least in Shyamalan's mind.[4]

At this point, we turn to ancient Egyptian thought. As previously noted, scholars usually translate the word *ḥk3(w)* as "magic." Lending support to this modern convention, late antique scribes equated the Coptic derivative *hik* with the Greek *mageia*, claiming, for example, that Simon Magus "did *hik*" in Samaria (Crum 1939, p 661a). Although this equation suggests an affinity between the two concepts, we should not therefore neglect their differences. Herman te Velde has convincingly argued that *ḥk3(w)* comes from the expression *ḥwi k3*, the "consecration of the *ka*" or "vital essence" (1970, pp 179-180). The Egyptians seem to have believed that magic penetrated a being's very life force, either for good or for ill (Ritner 1993, p 25). Linked to *ḥk3(w)* are *3ḥw*, sometimes called "spells." Strictly speaking, the word means "effective things," implying that magicians possess the ability to accomplish remarkable tasks (Cheak 2004, p 272).

ḥk3(w) is closely associated with and, indeed, often inseparable from the god Heka (Ritner 1993, p 16). Spell 261 of *The Coffin Texts* describes this deity as the son and heir of the solar demiurge, Re-Atum, and as the "protection" (*sa*) of the cosmos (de Buck 1947, pp 382-389). The charm also reveals that Heka gave life to the Heliopolitan Ennead and calls him the "lord of *kas*." The god's role as caretaker of the universe is underscored by a later funerary vignette, which positions him alongside Maat (*m3't*), the apotheosis of order and justice (Pinch 1994, fig. 2). This scene also depicts Heka's principal symbol: the snake. The god holds two snake wands across his chest and is preceded by "Great of Magic" (*wrt ḥk3(w)*), a divinity with a serpentine head. It is important to note that, for the Egyptians, the snake represented both protective and destructive power (Clark 1978, pp 239-245). The king wore the uraeus-serpent on his brow as an apotropaic device even while his priests intoned hymns to help the solar bark overcome Apophis, the dragon of inertia.

In addition to being linked to Heka and to snakes, *ḥk3(w)* figures prominently in the mythology of Isis, who was herself called "great of magic." According to a New Kingdom (ca. 1539-1075 BCE) tale, Isis once fashioned a viper out of spittle and dust, and sent it to bite Re, the elderly king of the gods (Pritchard 1955, pp 12-14). Then, she offered her victim a magical cure in return for the disclosure of his "secret name." Unable to work a deception, Re transmitted his name to Isis, but forbade her to communicate it to anyone except her son. The story highlights the resourcefulness and power of Isis and explains the political authority of Horus, whose incarnation was the living king. In addition, it was to be recited over a divine image or copied onto a papyrus and dissolved in beer as a remedy against scorpion stings.

These observations suggest that $ḥk3(w)$ did not originate among savages or reside on society's margins. Its patron was an early and integral part of the cosmos, and its practice was sanctioned by myth. To quote John Baines, "Egyptian magic was a realm of legitimate action … which … involved all of creation from the highest to the lowest. It was a force that had existed from the beginning of time and had been essential to the creation of the world" (1991, p 165). As a protection, $ḥk3(w)$ even helped keep chaos at bay. *The Teaching for Merikare*, a wisdom composition that may date to the First Intermediate Period (ca. 2198-2160 BCE), describes it as "a weapon ($ʿḥ3w$) to ward off what may happen" (Helck 1977, p 47), and execration texts from the Middle Kingdom (ca. 1938-1759 BCE) use it to cripple both foreign and domestic enemies (Sethe 1926).

We should take care not to overdraw the picture of $ḥk3(w)$'s respectability, however. Just as the snake had an ambivalent nature, so too did magic. While the Egyptians believed that $ḥk3(w)$ was a boon, the story of Isis and Re hints that it might be employed for sinister ends. This is not to say, of course, that the Egyptians saw Isis' actions as ignoble. She replaced an old and faltering ruler with a young and vigorous one, thereby preserving the order of the world. Some must have wondered, though, whether a villain might employ similar tactics to spread anarchy. Magic pervaded a world populated by rebels, foreigners, and malevolent shades as well as legitimate kings, loyal subjects, and irreproachable deities (Ritner 1993, p 23). To investigate the situation further, I will use three sources: the Middle Kingdom text *Khufu and the Magicians*, the New Kingdom *Book of the Celestial Cow*, and the body of records from the harem conspiracy under Ramesses III (ca. 1186-1155 BCE).

Khufu and the Magicians consists of four tales ostensibly from the court of the builder of the Great Pyramid. Unfortunately, the beginning of the manuscript is lost and most of the first story is missing. Set in the time of Djoser, it concerned the magic of an unknown lector priest, perhaps the fabled Imhotep (Simpson 2003, p 14, n. 1). The second tale narrates a "marvel" (*bi3yt*) performed by the lector priest Webaoner during the reign of Nebkare (Blackman 1988, 1.17-4.17). Webaoner learns that his wife is having an affair and transforms a wax crocodile into a living one in order to terrorize her paramour. At the end of the story, the wife is burned and cast into the Nile. The third tale describes a wonder performed by the lector priest Djadjaemonkh during one of King Snefru's boating picnics (Blackman 1988, 4.17-6.22). In the course of the outing, a harem woman accidentally drops her fish-shaped charm in the palace lake, and the king orders Djadjaemonkh to rescue it. Using *ḥk3(w)*, he folds one side of the lake onto the other and retrieves the object from dry land. In the fourth tale (Blackman 1988, 6.22-9.21), Khufu's son Hardedef points out that the previous stories are all unverifiable. He, however, knows a man in the village of Ded-Snefru named Dedi, who is 110 years old and can himself perform magic. Khufu summons Dedi to the palace and asks him to reattach a head that has been severed from its body, a power he is said to possesses. The king even offers to decapitate a prisoner to facilitate the spectacle. Although Dedi refuses to use a human subject, he does work his magic on a goose, a waterfowl, and an ox. In addition, he predicts the end of Khufu's dynasty in three generations. This forecast segues to a climactic account of the next regime's origins (Blackman 1988, 9.21-12.26). With the help of five deities — Isis, Nephthys, Meskhenet, Heqet, and Khnum — a woman named Reddedet gives birth to three future kings. Besides hastening the triplets' delivery, the divinities also fashion their crowns and summon a storm as an excuse to depart (Simpson 2003, p 23, n. 21).

It is significant that all of the tales in *Khufu and the Magicians* associate *k3w* with civilization. In the first three, the sorcerers are lector priests (*ḫryw-ḥbt*), literally "those who carry the book." These men should not be understood as Catholic clergy, but rather as learned scribes (Sauneron 2000, p 61). Their activities were connected, in particular, with the "House of Life" (*pr ꜥnḫ*), a scriptorium that compiled works on religion, medicine, and magic, among other topics (Gardiner 1938, pp 175ff.). Archaeologists have discovered an example of this institution at Amarna, where it abuts on "the Place of the Correspondence of Pharaoh" (*t3 st t3 šꜥ pr-ꜥ3*) (Gardiner 1938, pp 160-161). Evidently, it was closely tied to the affairs of state. In the fourth tale, the magician is of uncertain rank, but he is a full member of society, on good terms with the prince, and a welcome guest at the palace. Finally, the prediction of the birth of the kings links *ḥk3(w)* with prophesy, midwifery, kingship, and weather. *Khufu and the Magicians* thus presents a world where magic is an acceptable feature of life. The art rests with the gods and with erudite men, who use it for the benefit, or at least the entertainment of society. And while it might be naive to presume that a local court (*nbt*) would have approved of Webaoner's actions (cf. Meskell 2002, pp 99-100), many doubtless would have seen them as supremely just. It was not the wizard who undermined order and suffered public immolation, but his promiscuous wife.

The funerary text called *The Book of the Heavenly Cow* is best known for its account of the destruction of mankind by Re. Yet, there is more to this work than just righteous slaughter. The fourth section includes a dialogue in which Re warns the earth god Geb, "Beware your snakes that are in you ... you know their magical potencies (*3ḫw*)" (Hornung 1982a, 207-208). Re instructs Geb to tell Nun, the watery abyss, to "keep watch over the snakes in the earth and in the water" (Hornung 1982a, 211). Geb himself should "Beware also of these spells (*ḥk3(w)*) that [magicians'] mouths know. Behold, Heka himself is therein" (Hornung 1982a, 218-219). The fifth and final part of the book contains instructions for three protective incantations. It says that the wizard should identify himself with Re, that "the *ba* of every god and goddess is in the snakes," and that "the *ba* of Re is in *ḥk3(w)* throughout the world" (Hornung 1982a, 284, 286).[5]

The outline of *The Book of the Heavenly Cow* is certainly old, appearing already in *The Teaching for Merikare* (Helck 1977, 46-47). Its *Vorlage*, on the other hand, was probably composed much later, during the reign of Amunhotep III (ca. 1390-1353 BCE) (Spalinger 2000, pp 281-282). The text's warnings about snakes and magicians are interesting given the implication of *ḥk3(w)*'s dangerous character elsewhere. Those who possess it must be watched, presumably because they are capable of undermining the order of the universe. More enigmatic are the book's remarks about divine *ba*s (*b3w*). *Ba* is sometimes translated as "soul," and misleading so, for the Egyptians did not conceive of the self as a unity (ðabkar 1968, p 162). Rather, it was a composite of the body, the shadow, the name, the *ka*, and the *ba*. In funerary contexts, *ba* is best understood as a quality or facility that enables the deceased to travel between this world and the next (Traunecker 2001, pp 22-23). For this reason, it is depicted as a bird with a human head. At its root, however, *ba* denotes power, especially in the context of divine wrath and punishment (Sauneron 1963, pp 49-51). Thus, according to *The Book of the Heavenly Cow*, divine power dwells in the embodiments of magic, and the energy of the venerable king of the gods resides the *ḥk3(w)* that pervades the cosmos. Once again, magic does not emanate from beyond the pale of civilization or necessarily threaten it. It is a vital part of created world.

Our final source is the body of records from the harem conspiracy under Ramesses III: the Turin Juridical Papyrus, Papyrus Rollin, Papyrus Varzy, Papyrus Lee, and Papyrus Rifaud (A, B, C, and E) (Devéria 1858; Redford 2002, pp 11-22). These records were originally sections of a single scroll and not separate documents. To summarize their contents, the plot began with the royal wife Teye's wish to eliminate the elderly Ramesses III and elevate her son, Pentaweret, to the throne. Eventually, she gained the support not only of the women and eunuchs of the harem, but also of soldiers and officials. Her confederates included two scribes of the House of Life, the court magician (*ḥryw-ḥbt*) Prekamenef, and the royal physician Iyry (Juridical Papyrus 5.5). Susan Redford explains the function of these men: "Besides the rather mundane task of immobilizing the sentry, [the conspirators] had to remove a king from his throne — a man who by his position was in the full protective custody of the gods. Such an undertaking would require the help of some very powerful sorcerers" (2002, p 8). Pascal Vernus agrees: "Recourse to magic, far from being an original initiative on their part, was simply imposed by the very apparatus that surrounded Pharaoh's person" (2003, p 116). Apparently, Teye and her accomplices did manage to mortally injure Ramesses III, for Papyrus Rifaud says that "the royal bark … was overturned" (A.3).[6] Still, the conspirators failed to secure the succession of Pentaweret. Surprisingly, during the ensuing treason trial, some of the judges were found to be in the harem women's thrall and punished by mutilation (Juridical Papyrus 6.1).

One of the more interesting details of the plot is that the conspirators obtained their *ḥk3(w)* from disaffected royal servants. Papyrus Lee explicitly states that they used copies of magical scrolls housed in the king's library itself (1.3). In other words, their sorcery was evil only by intention, and not by nature. At the same time, they enacted the very abuse of magic that the story of Isis and Re portends and *The Book of the Heavenly Cow* fears. Redford has even argued that Teye, like Isis, employed snake venom to harm her lord (2002, pp 109-114). If she is correct, the intrigue must have seemed very perverse indeed.

Happily, the Egyptians possessed a healthy measure of the human capacity for transforming appalling disasters into splendid triumphs. Their distinctive genius in this operation was part and parcel of their understanding of time as a cyclic yet static phenomenon. In the filter of the Egyptian imagination, events inevitably followed an A-B-A pattern, whereby the order of the world (A) repeatedly confronted and overcame crises (Bs) (Assmann 1975, pp 41ff.). With regard to the harem conspiracy, the records thus say that, ultimately, nothing happened. Hints of the Ramesses III's death aside, the papyri indicate not only that the plot failed, but also that its architects never truly occupied their lofty positions in the first place (e.g., Papyrus Rollin 1; Papyrus Rifaud A.5, 9; B.1; C.6-7; E.1). Naturally, these claims reflect a *damnatio memoriae* visited on the traitors, a policy also suggested by the replacement of their real names with similar pejoratives (Posener 1946). We should not, however, lose sight of the idea behind these artifices. Corruption might assail the state, but it could never overwhelm it. As *The Maxims of Ptahhotep* proclaim, "Order (*m3't*) is great and its effectiveness (*spdt*) endures; it has not been confounded since the time of Osiris" (Dévaud 1916, 5).

The Egyptians' belief that "evil" (*bin*) and "disorder" (*isft*) were in the end impotent shaped their concept of magic. Their difficulty envisioning a single victory of chaos, let alone an apocalypse of Biblical proportions, situated *ḥk3(w)*, which was an effective activity, very close to home.[7] According to John A. Wilson, the Egyptians divided the universe into five ideal regions: the ordered Nile Valley (*kmt*), the savage desert (*dšrt*), the enveloping abyss (*nnw*), the underworld (*dw3t*), and the upper and lower skies (*pty*) (1977, pp 44-48). Although *ḥk3(w)* was a basic part of the entire world, it was ensconced in the first, civilized realm, particularly in the palace and its adjuncts. As such, it was insulated from the marginal waste. Far from being an individualistic activity opposed to the establishment, magic was the establishment activity *par excellence*. In more poetic terms, the sorcerers who challenged Moses and Aaron in Exodus 7:8-13, transforming their staves into serpents, may be heathen outsiders in the Torah, but they are the guardians of social stability in Egyptian lore.[8]

In conclusion, I would like to emphasize that my purpose is not to discount the similarities between Western and Egyptian magic, but merely to underscore their difference in terms of topography. Certainly, several congruities exist apart from the shared meaning of **mag(h)-* and *ḥk3(w)*. For example, even though the Egyptians enshrined magic in their community, this did not stop them from, like Westerners, imbuing it with exotic qualities. Indeed, texts sometimes refer to Isis as "the Nubian" and express apprehension about sorcerers living to the south of the kingdom (Koenig 1987). Also like Westerners, the Egyptians associated magic with the color red, despite the fact that this hue also stained the desert waste (Wilkinson 1994, pp 106-107). It is, of course, only through an appreciation of differences as well as similarities that good cultural comparisons can be made.

Notes

1 "Hairy from head to toe" is how Heather paraphrases Mary's description of the witch.
2 Cf. the representations in Gaskill (2005, pp. 148-149).
3 The latter are especially interesting, for Mary's "gate" is also made of bound sticks.
4 Shyamalan is Indian-American, and it would be interesting to see how many aspects of *The Village* resonate with Hindu beliefs.
5 Not simply "der Ba des Re [ist] durch die ganze Welt," as in Hornung (1982a, p. 47).
6 Redford (2002, esp. ch. 6) presents a strong case for this result based also on a daybook record of a rebellion two and a half weeks before the king's death.

7   There is an ongoing debate over whether the Egyptians foresaw an end to the cosmos. Based on phrases like "the limits of eternity (*n*) and everlastingness (*t*)," Erik Hornung has answered the question in the affirmative (1982b, p. 183). Jan Assmann, on the contrary, has argued that such expressions are either rhetorical or aberrant (1975, pp. 18-36).

8   This difference was already noted by Sigmund Freud in his work on Moses and monotheism: "the one religion severely condemns any kind of magic or sorcery, which flourishes so abundantly in the other" (1967, p. 20).

References

Alighieri, D., 1994 [ca. 1306-1314], *The Inferno of Dante*, trans. R. Pinksy, Farrar, Srauss and Giroux, New York

Apuleius, 1951 [ca. 180], *The Transformations of Lucius, Otherwise Known as the Golden Ass*, trans. R. Graves, Farrar, Srauss and Giroux, New York

Assmann, J., 1975, *Zeit und Ewigkeit im alten Ägypten*, C. Winter, Heidelberg

Aune, D. E., 1980, 'Magic in Early Christianity', *Aufstieg und Niedergang der römischen Welt*, part 2, vol. 23, no. 2, pp. 1507-1557

Baines, J., 1991, 'Society, Morality, and Religious Practice,' in *Religion in Ancient Egypt: Gods, Myths, and Personal Practice*, ed. B. Shafer, Cornell University Press, Ithaca, pp 123-200

Blackman, A. M, 1988, *The Story of King Kheops and the Magicians, Transcribed from Papyrus Westcar (Berlin Papyrus 3033)*, ed. W. V. Davies, J. V. Books, Reading

The Blair Witch Project, [DVD] 1999, dir. D. Myrick and E. Sanchez, Artisan Entertainment, Santa Monica

de Buck, A., 1947, *The Egyptian Coffin Texts, Vol. 3, Texts of Spells 164-267*, Oriental Institute publications, University of Chicago Press, Chicago

Campbell, J., 1968a [1949], *The Hero with a Thousand Faces*, Princeton University Press, Princeton

   1968b, *The Masks of God: Creative Mythology*, The Viking Press, New York

Cheak, A., 2004, 'Magic through the Linguistic Lenses of Greek *mágos*, Indo-European **mag(h)-*, Sanskrit *māyā*, and Pharaonic Egyptian *ḥekˁ*, *Journal for the Academic Study of Magic*, vol. 2, pp. 260-286

Clark, R. T. R., 1959, *Myth and Symbol in Ancient Egypt*, Thames and Hudson, London

Crum, W. E., 1972 [1939], *A Coptic Dictionary*, The Clarendon Press, Oxford

Dévaud, E., 1916, *Les Maximes de Ptahhotep, d'après le Papyrus Prisse, les Papyrus 10371/10435 et 10509 du British Museum, et la Tablette Carnarvon*, Freiburg

Devéria, T., 1858, *Le Papyrus Judiciare de Turin et Les Papyrus Lee et Rollin*, Imprimerie Impériale, Paris

Driver, T. F., 1991, *The Magic of Ritual: Our Need for Liberating Rites That Transform Our Lives and Our Communities*, HarperSanFrancisco, San Francisco

Durkheim, E., 1957 [1915], *The Elementary Forms of the Religious Life*, trans. J. W. Swain, G.Allen & Unwin, London

Eusebius of Caesarea, 1989 [ca. 325], *The History of the Church*, trans. G. A. Williamson, Penguin Books, New York

Evans-Pritchard, E. E., 1937, *Witchcraft, Oracles, and Magic among the Zande*, Clarendon Press, Oxford

Frazer, J. G., 1996 [1922], *The Golden Bough: A Study in Magic and Religion, Abridged Edition*, Simon & Schuster, New York

Freud, S., 1967 [1939], *Moses and Monotheism*, trans. K. Jones, Vintage Books, New York

Gardiner, A. H., 1938, 'The House of Life', *Journal of Egyptian Archaeology*, vol. 24, pp 157-179

Gaskill, M., 2005, *Witchfinders: A Seventeenth-Century English Tragedy*, Harvard University Press, Cambridge, MA.

Graf, F., 1999, *Magic in the Ancient World*, trans. F. Philip, Harvard University Press, Cambridge

Grimm, J. & W., 1969 [1812-1815], *Kinder- und Haus-Märchen*, 2 vols., Manesee Verlag, Zurich

Harris, M., 2001, 'The "Witchcraft" of Media Manipulation: *Pamela* and *The Blair Witch Project*', *Journal of Popular Culture*, vol. 34, no. 4, pp. 75-108

Helck, W., 1977, *Die Lehre für König Merikare*, O. Harrassowitz, Wiesbaden

The Holy Bible, Containing the Old and New Testament, New Revised Standard Version, 1989, Thomas Nelson Publishers, Nashville

Hornung, E., 1982a, *Der ägyptische Mythos von der Himmelskuh: Eine Ätiologie des Unvollkommenen*, Universitätsverlag, Freiburg/Vandenhoeck & Ruprecht, Göttingen

— 1982b [1971], *Conceptions of God in Ancient Egypt: The One and the Many*, trans. J. Baines, Cornell University Press, Ithaca

Irenaeus of Lyons, 1992 [ca. 175], *Against the Heresies, Volume 1, Book 1*, trans. D. J. Unger, The Newman Press, New York

Kieckhefer, R., 1989, *Magic in the Middle Ages*, Cambridge University Press, Cambridge

Koenig, Y., 1987, 'La Nubie dans les textes magiques: «L'inquiétante étrangeté»', *Revue d'Égyptologie*, vol. 38, pp. 105-110.

Kramer, H. & Sprenger J., 1971 [1484], *The Malleus Maleficarum*, trans. M. Summers, Dover Publications, Inc., New York

Levi-Strauss, C., 1966, *The Savage Mind*, University of Chicago Press, Chicago

Malinowski, B., 1948, *Magic, Science and Religion and Other Essays*, The Free Press, Glencoe

Malory, T., 1961 [ca. 1470], *Le Morte Darthur: The Book of King Arthur and his Knights of the Round Table*, ed. A. W. Pollard, University Books, Inc., New York

Mauss, M., 1972 [1901-1902], *A General Theory of Magic*, trans. R. Brain, Routledge and Kegan Paul, London

McCall, A., 1979, *The Medieval Underworld*, H. Hamilton, London

Meskell, L., 2002, *Private Life in New Kingdom Egypt*, Princeton University Press, Princeton, NJ.

Meyer, M. W. & Smith, R. Z., 1999 [1994], *Ancient Christian Magic: Coptic Texts of Ritual Power*, Princeton University Press, Princeton

Michelet, J., 1964 [1862], *La Sorcière*, Éditions Julliard, Paris

Nestle-Aland Novum Testamentum Graece, 1979, Deutsche Bibelgesellschaft, Stuttgart

The Numbers, accessed 7-29-2006, [on-line], http://www.the-numbers.com

Pinch, G., 1994, *Magic in Ancient Egypt*, University of Texas Press, Austin

Pritchard, J. B., 1955, *Ancient Near Eastern Texts Relating to the Old Testament*, Princeton University Press, Princeton

Posener, G., 1946, *Revue d'Égyptologie*, vol. 5, pp. 51-56

Redford, S., 2002, *The Harem Conspiracy: The Murder of Ramesses III*, Northern Illinois University Press, Dekalb

Ritner, R. K., 1993, *The Mechanics of Ancient Egyptian Magical Practice*, Studies in Ancient Oriental Civilization, no. 54, University of Chicago Press, Chicago

Russell, J. B., 1986, 'Witchcraft' in *The Encyclopedia of Religion*, vol. 15, ed. M. Eliade, MacMillan Publishing Company, New York, pp. 415-423

Sauneron, S., 1963, 'Remarques de philologie et d'etymologie', *Revue d'Égyptologie*, vol. 15, pp 49-62

2000 [1957], *The Priests of Ancient Egypt*, trans. D. Lorton, Cornell University Press, Ithaca, NY.

Sethe, K., 1926, *Die Ächtung freindlicher Fürsten, Völker und Dinge auf altägyptischen Tongefassscherben des Mittleren Reiches*, Akademie der Wissenschaften, Berlin

Signs, [DVD] 2003 [2002], Touchstone Pictures, Burbank, dir. M. N. Shyamalan

Simpson, W. K., 2003, *The Literature of Ancient Egypt: An Anthology of Stories, Instructions and Poetry*, Yale University Press, New Haven

The Sixth Sense, [DVD] 2000 [1999], Buena Vista, Burbank, dir. M. N. Shyamalan

Spalinger, A., 2000, 'The Destruction of Mankind: A Transitional Literary Text', *Studien zur altägyptischen Kultur*, vol. 28, pp 257-282

Summers, M., 1978 [1927], *The Geography of Witchcraft*, Routledge and Kegan Paul, London

1993 [2nd ed. 1956], *The History of Witchcraft and Demonology*, Carol Publishing Group, New York

Traunecker, C., 2001 [1992], *The Gods of Egypt*, trans. D. Lorton, Cornell University Press, Ithaca, NY.

te Velde, H., 1970, 'The God Heka in Egyptian Theology', *Jaarbericht van het Vooraziatisch-Egyptisch Genootschap*, no. 21, pp 175-186

Vernus, P., 2003 [1993], *Affairs and Scandals in Ancient Egypt*, trans. D. Lorton, Cornell University Press, Ithaca

The Village, [DVD] 2005 [2004], Touchstone Pictures, Burbank, dir. M. N. Shyamalan

Wilkinson, R. H., 1994, *Symbol & Magic in Egyptian Art*, Thames and Hudson, London

Wilson, J. A., 1977, 'Egypt', in *The Intellectual Adventure of Ancient Man*, University of Chicago Press, Chicago, pp. 31-124

ðabkar, L. V., 1968, *A Study in the Ba Concept in Ancient Egypt*, University of Chicago Press, Chicago

The science of magic: A parapsychological model of psychic ability in the context of magical will

David Luke

Crowley defined magic as the art and science of causing change in conformity with will. There has been much written about the art of magic, but very little of the abstract science of that art has taken on truly empirical edicts. The following paper describes a parapsychological model of psychic ability in terms of its intrinsically magical undercurrent, thereby providing a bridge between science and magic that has seldom been remarked upon, save for occasional discussion (e.g. Roney-Dougal 1991). The model, termed 'psi-mediated instrumental response' (PMIR), seeks to explain the unconscious everyday use of 'psi' (precognition, telepathy, clairvoyance, or psychokinesis) as a means of serving the needs and desires of the organism. While the model is based on the principles and research of cognitive, behavioural, and para- psychology, it is intended that by extending the inferences of this model and by subtly re-orientating it to a magical perspective it can serve as a useful psychology of magical operation, or an aspect of it at least, in a truly scientific sense.

Solve...

Coming from a purely psycho-biological perspective Rex Stanford initially put forward his PMIR model of psychic functioning in 1974, and then gently tweaked it and supported it over a period of successive publications spanning sixteen years, but fundamentally altered it little (Stanford 1974a, 1974b, 1977, 1982, 1990). Synchronously, with the publication of SSOTBME by Ramsey Dukes 1974 also heralded the formation of the bare principles of chaos magic (Dukes 2000; Illuminates of Thanteros 2002), to which Stanford's propositions have an uncanny resemblance, as will be demonstrated, although, PMIR corresponds most closely with the works of Austin Osman Spare, which preceded them both. Nevertheless, from the lack of corresponding literature it is apparent that Stanford was not even covertly familiar with such work (a matter confirmed by personal communication – Stanford 2005), nor occultists with his, despite the similarities. His model, while even now remaining somewhat obscure, straddled the theoretical any-man's land of the period by relying largely on the then newly flourishing foundations of cognitive science while simultaneously representing vestiges of the aged and declining school of behaviourism. The behaviourist aspect is apparent from the model's name, which offers the concept of there being an 'instrumental response' to a given stimulus, albeit in this case the stimulus, desire, is internal. Furthermore, the corresponding behavioural response to the stimulus need not be physical either but, according to Stanford's model, can be psychic too, as in psychokinesis – the ability to affect matter directly with the mind.

The model also assumes a particularly evolutionary flavour by considering psychic ability as an adaptive function, which is made available to serve the needs of the individual. Taking this needs-serving function of psi as a basic assumption allows the model to offer a useful account of *why* psi works, and this acts as a forerunner to explaining *how* it works. By making the theoretical assumption that psi is need-serving Stanford was able to break down the concept of need into some testable psychological mechanics. For example, according to PMIR, the primary motivating factor for psi to occur depends on both 'need strength' and 'need relevance'. Such that the greater need there is for psi to serve the organism then the more likely it is to occur. So, for instance, though somewhat banally, your need to stay alive is probably strong enough to warrant your using psi to find a restaurant when you get hungry, but the relevance of the food incentive may prevent you from detecting a greasy fast-food outlet when a tastier option also lies within equal reach.

For Stanford (1974a), the needs-driven supposition also incorporated desires under the rubric of needs, although he later altered the terminology of this proposition to additionally include mere 'dispositions' (Stanford 1977), thereby covering a far looser range of motivating factors, semantically at least. Yet, for all its inclusivity of expression, by 1977 Stanford had constricted his earlier generosity and redefined his 'dispositions' so that they only actually amounted to biological tissue needs, learned needs, and conditioned responses, thereby distilling human desires down to a rather reactive robotic brew of behavioural drives. However, this quite Skinnerian view rather chokes the spirit out of being, and it need not be fundamental to the PMIR model. If we instead focus on Stanford's original central concept of desire, rather than the purely behaviourist images of need that came later, the model can be seen as a useful psychological framework for the magical function of the will. By considering PMIR's needs and desires in equivalence to the will of the magician, Stanford's following psychological portrait of the psychic organism takes on a wholly thelemic hue. Thelemic, that is, primarily in the sense that it relates to magical will, and less in the sense of the Crowley-ian magical current, because here I have chosen to parallel the model mostly to the magical doctrines of Austin Osman Spare.

> "What is desired of the Self is given – eventually. The desire is sufficient." (Spare 1921, p 3)

In essence, what Stanford's model suggests is that desire is the sole requisite for ensuring that the organism tacitly and psychically attracts its desire towards itself, and itself towards its desire. Be it through the psychic reception of information relevant to the desire, or through the psychic exertion of one's will upon the environment. By this means we see that 'need strength' and 'need relevance' are psychological correlates of psychic attraction. Somewhat like magnetic metrics for magical manifestation of the will, if you will. The greater the desire, and the more relevant the object or event is to that desire, then the more likely it is that there will be a psychic response to ensure the two unite. In an evolutionary sense this is born out of the needs basic to the survival of the organism, such as sensing immanent danger, or preventing an impending accident from occurring. On a fundamental level though, this equates to the satisfaction of the needs and desires of the individual, and here we see that this 'goal-orientated' concept of psi is literally 'thelemic' in nature because it defines a psychic reality contingent upon the will alone.

> "…That which is indeliberate is the more vital and is will."
>
> (Spare 1921, p 7)

The twin functions of the magician's perception and will, which Carroll (1987) used to define Spare's *Kia*, could here equate to psi. Yet, the real harmony in equating PMIR to magical divination and manifestation comes through the model's following assumptions. The first of which stipulates that no conscious awareness of the psychic act, or awareness even of the desire, is required for the PMIR to occur. Stanford also proposed that psi works through the most economical means available, because it serves a purpose by attending to the needs of the individual. That is, the psychic agent may well be an unwitting wizard, but furthermore, the PMIR actually works better where the individual is unwise to its action. To this end, Stanford offered that humans tend to react more successfully to their unconscious primary drives rather than their conscious cognitions, an idea which is supported by the notion established in cognitive psychology of 'implicit knowledge' commonly driving behaviour. For Stanford, the individual reacts to psi information in the same way as they would react to subliminal or other 'implicit' information. So conscious awareness of psi-accessed information, for example, is redundant if the function of that information can be better utilised unconsciously, and therefore directly, through a 'psi-mediated instrumental response'. Or quite simply put, you don't have to know psi is working for it to work, and it actually works better if you don't, because there's less interference that way. The same might be said of magic.

Receptive magic – perceiving the web outside of time and space

Focusing here on the case of 'receptive psi' serving the organism (telepathy, clairvoyance, or precognition, terms that have, perhaps misleadingly, been called extra sensory perception, ESP), psi is proposed to function better unconsciously because the conscious cognition of the psi information may easily get confabulated and distorted by ongoing cognitions, and this is obviously counterproductive. Expressing this in data language, the information is more likely to become degraded by data noise if it becomes conscious and, according to Stanford, it would most often be better responded to instead by unconscious alterations to behaviour, memory, thinking, emotions, or even desires. This sits comfortably with the techniques used by the practitioners of the divinatory arts, who may endeavour to clear their mind of conscious thoughts before they scry, or at least settle them, yet most will also use tools flexible enough to channel through the subtleties of the signal before they even attempt to cognise it. Elsewhere, in parapsychological research, free association of one's stream of consciousness in an altered state seems to be the favoured method of eliciting divine information (as in the Ganzfeld method), although this also gives a lot of superfluous verbal flotsam. Yet, bypassing the conscious mind completely by tapping directly into the unconscious psi information has been superbly demonstrated by research recently demonstrating the apparent psychic anticipation of arousing images. This psychic anticipation was indicated solely by psychophysiological markers, such as galvanic skin conductance, a general measure of physiological arousal (e.g. Beirman 2000; Radin 1997). This research has shown a small but quite distinct *bodily* presentiment to arousing stimuli several seconds before their delivery, strongly supporting Stanford's unconscious psi hypothesis.

Going a little beyond Stanford's vision, others have noted that the conscious awareness of psi information has the added hazard of having to contend with that most ingrained rationalist abhorrence common to modern wo/man, the fear of psi (e.g. Braude 1993; Tart 1984). Given all the terrifying psychotic implications of psychic transparency that are loaded within the idea of our being latently omniscient, and then mixed with the quite blasphemous possibility that we may also be latently omnipotent too, the fear of psi would seem a well buried yet determined phobia of our own psychic abilities, no doubt common to many, even magicians. Given this fear of psi, any conscious psi cognitions, assuming they can be recognised as such, would cause a 'cognitive dissonance' between subconscious belief and experience in all but the most mentally liberated individuals, rendering the information useless. The logic in this cognitive dissonance concept combined with Stanford's cognitive distortion of conscious psychic information seem jointly more than capable in accounting for why only the most extreme incidences of psi-information make themselves known spontaneously to the individual, such as in crisis apparitions (e.g. visions of absent relatives as they die).

"Magic, like Science is reluctant to shatter our basic beliefs."
(Dukes, 2000 p 24)

However, in the usual case, Stanford proposed that everyday psi-information attempts to satisfy its desire-driven goal by expressing itself through unconscious behaviour, thought, desires, memories, emotions, and even psychokinesis, in such a way as to be maximally economical.

To do so, the PMIR manifests itself through 'ready responses', i.e. processes which are very likely to happen, so that no major deviations in conscious action are necessary, merely the subtle alteration of a normal impending action. This occurs through various mechanisms such as unconscious timing changes, so, for example, that you may unconsciously speed yourself up to 'serendipitously' bump into someone you hoped to see. Alternatively, the response may be expressed through one's memory, by forgetting to do something, or remembering something else, or it may happen through an unconsciously psi-mediated mistake. Additionally, the PMIR may exert itself through association, either made emotionally or through a train of thought. Psi-information may even be best expressed through unconscious psychokinesis. But only in the extreme case, as explained already, does psi-information naturally manifest itself to the conscious mind. Through these means 'magic' occurs very much more frequently than is ever actually noticed by the casual observer, and this resembles Dukes' (2000, p 78) point that, "we might not see magic only because we are taught not to believe in it". Here perhaps, knowledge of PMIR would help the aspiring mage to spot when such subtle magic is happening.

> "Instead of defying causality, modern Magic tends to stretch it slowly, within the operator's subjectively conceived world" (Dukes 2000, p 23)

For Stanford, what mattered most was that the PMIR occurs economically, and for that, it is best expressed unconsciously and in accordance with the individual's current action. This concept may have more accord with the tacit practicalities of reality than with established occult doctrine concerning the economics of magic, but it has pragmatic appeal for the demands of both the will, and the imagination, if magic expresses itself often through mundane and invisible means, save for the end results. This is akin to the Robert Anton Wilson adage that 'reality is what you can get away with', and lets face it, it should be a damn sight easier to get away with profound, but little, tweaks in the normal construction of reality than straining to summon an enormous visible Cthulhu-type entity to eat your foe in the living room. Not that I'm being pessimistic about the bounds of possibility I just recognise that magical manifestation in general, and any ordinary unwitting magic particularly, is seemingly limited by a Reality Violation Principle. This, I propose, is nothing more than the sense that whatever one wills or desires to happen can only occur within the limitations of one's will and imagination. Given that these are suitably focused and capable of completely convincing the mind of the magician, gaining their absolute belief, and possibly those of others involved, then theoretically anything is possible. But it's a far tougher job cutting across the grain of perceived consensus reality than it is working with it. This idea is self-evident in the peculiar and often unexpected way that desire tends to manifest itself magically. As noted by Dukes (2000, p 23) "Nowadays the Magician…is unlikely to find his spells will defy causality – e.g. instead of materialising gold coins, he might have 'luck' on a state lottery". It is probably easier to change consensus reality enough for the magic to occur than it is to transgress its integrity, and this is the basis of creating temporary yet complete magical belief during group ritual.

Expressive magic – the manifestation of desire

"The desire determines, and no later belief will alter it one whit." (Spare 1921, p 6)

Applying his model to so called 'active psi', Stanford (1974b) looked to research of spontaneous cases of psychokinesis (PK) primarily, and found these reflected the same unwitting expression of desire specified by his model for receptive psi. In one-off cases, such as the stopping of a clock at the time of someone's death, the PK appears to be unconsciously concocted, yet always expressive of something relevant or important to the person involved. In cases of recurrent spontaneous psychokinesis (known as RSPK), such as so called poltergeist activity, there is always a central person around which the activity occurs, and also ceases in their absence. In such instances, the poltergeist activity is seen as the expression of suppressed hostility towards others, which, because it rarely hurts anyone physically, is a safe form of harassment. This is because the agent has no conscious control, and therefore no ownership or responsibility for the events. A prime example of such a case involved torrents of water gushing inexplicably from the ceiling, whilst all the vessels in the house containing liquids spilled themselves on the floor (Auerbach 1996). These events occurred to a family whose son was forced by his father to stay in the swimming team against his will, thereby demonstrating RSPK as a poetic manifestation of anger. Despite the scarcity of spontaneous PK cases, laboratory PK has proven even more rare and difficult to manifest on a visible (macro) scale, although there is very good laboratory evidence to suggest the influence of PK on randomly controlled micro systems, such as the outcome of dice rolls or other random event generators (e.g. Radin & Nelson 1989). In such research, the results seem to suggest that the greatest effects, usually measured statistically, occur in the moment when the agent stops trying to cause the PK to happen, and this is called the 'release of effort' effect.

> "Conscious desire is the negation of possession: the procrastination of reality. Make thy desire subconscious; the organic is creative impulse to will." (Spare 1921, p 3)

That visible psychokinesis occurs so rarely and is never owned by the individual is, for Stanford, a fundamental feature of the necessity for unconscious active psi. The fact that efforts to manifest PK in the laboratory are much less dramatic than those occurring spontaneously reflects the hindrance of consciously aware and owned attempts at PK. This quirk has been aptly demonstrated by the likes of Batcheldor (1966), who was able to demonstrate remarkable table tipping phenomena during experimental pseudo-séances. Batcheldor accounted for these pronounced PK effects with the explanation that ownership inhibited PK, but could be bypassed by abdicating responsibility to the group. Furthermore, by invoking the mercurial trickster and utilising a 'deliberate deception technique' to get things started, Batcheldor was able to overcome what he called 'witness inhibition' to PK by deceiving his group into thinking that the table tipping was caused by unseen, normal forces, which it was - initially at least. Once witness inhibition had been overcome, amid much humour, by the spectacle of observing oneself performing pseudo-PK in a group, the deliberate deception was unknowingly (i.e. deceptively) ceased and real PK began; unwittingly. Thereby demonstrating that you may need to 'fake it till you make it' to surmount the barriers of belief.

That such barriers of belief exist makes unconscious, un-owned, unknowing, and released desire near essential to the spontaneous manifestation of will as psi, or perhaps even magic? This has been expressed nowhere more succinctly than by Spare (1913/1975, p 2) when he wrote that "Unless desire is subconscious, it is not fulfilled, no not in this life. Then verily sleep is better than prayer." Indeed, to support this notion of unconscious nonattachment Stanford cited research by McConnell (1955) that demonstrated a successful attempt to affect dice rolls during sleep. Furthermore, despite his clearly non-occult academic-psychology stance, Stanford (1974b) also drew upon parallels from prayer, spiritual healing, and religious or magical rites to further inform his model. Stripping down these rituals into constituent parts Stanford begins to seem like an early chaos magician searching for the bare principle components of spell casting when he identified that, for the desire to manifest, an appeal must be made to a supernatural agency through the use of ritual. However, more importantly he informed us that the ritual is necessary but not sufficient to produce the effect, but through this action the responsibility becomes mediated to a supernatural agency. For the magician, this supernatural agency can be the angel, demon, god, spirit, element, or even just 'sympathy' that is evoked or invoked.

Dukes (2000, p 53) has noted that magicians have long since identified demons and angels as being part of their own mind but regrets "the implicit Scientific deduction that being part of our own minds means that they 'don't exist'". Yet for Stanford, whether the supernatural agency exists or not was largely irrelevant, perhaps because it went beyond the realms of his field. What was important is that the agency serves to displace any inhibitory ownership, a matter which is convenient in preventing the magical or religious belief system from collapsing should the ritual fail. Yet astute as this observation is, here Stanford failed to also recognise that the displacement of ownership insures against the surfacing of those submerged fears of omnipotence that provoke the inhibitive fear of success, and furthermore, should the ritual actually be successful, it also prevents against inducing megalomania.

> "The soul, proud and blighted… is a civil war of desire"
>
> (Spare, 1921, p 8)

It was further offered by Stanford that intentional psychokinetic research anecdotes teach us that a seemingly paradoxical sense of hope, yet complete abandonment, creates a psi-conducive balance of beliefs. Recent research has shown that the most psi-conducive volitional strategy in tests of intentional psychokinesis is best described as an 'effortless effort' (Houtkooper, 2004). Stanford offered that such a contradictory condition is necessary because otherwise ego-involvement leads to a fear of failure, which only induces desperation and scattered efforts. This is a point aptly delivered by Spare (1913/1975, p 51) with his art of sigilisation. "The sigil, being a vehicle, serves the function of protecting consciousness from the direct manifestation of the (consciously unacknowledged) obsession, conflict is avoided with any incompatible ideas and neither gains separate personality". Here conflict applies to the contrary urges reflective of the original desire competing against its corresponding distortions that may emanate as the fear of success, the fear of failure, or any other such competing desires.

> "Complex desire is the further creation of different desire, not the realization of (particular) desire." (Spare 1921, p 3)

In generalising about the function of ritual in manifesting desire, Stanford offered that the act of manifestation should be 'ego-alien', because this prevents the ego misdirecting the will, abnegates personal responsibility, and provides a sense that the outcome will be meaningful and comprehensible. Despite offering no further explanation on this latter point it is presumed that the miraculous outcome is meaningful because it occurs within the context of the magical or religious belief system, although even a parapsychological belief system such as the one implied by this model should do. Here Stanford also pointed out that the dominant belief system conditions the specific nature of the phenomena produced, and gave the example of the cold war Russian psychokinetic star, Nina Kulagina, who couched the cause of her rare skill in terms of 'bioplasma' (Pratt & Keil 1973).

> "To will well, to will long, to will always, but never to lust after anything, such is the secret of power"
>
> (Levi 1856/1968, p 245)

Before influencing the external object, Kulagina would build up great physical stress, and Stanford used this as an example of how intense ritual focus also serves to absorb the attention of the agent so that the ego becomes detached from the operation. However, Stanford speculated that in most other situations focused attention on PK targets inhibits its manifestation, which he called 'attention wishing inhibition', and hence the release of effort effect. This release of effort is the psychological equivalent to Spare's quiescence, the art of letting go of the desire and releasing the will. It is also the act of banishing, which seeks to detach the mind of the magician from the act.

> "Why is belief always incarnating? Though oft times not even a sincere wish?" (Spare 1921, p 10)

Conversely to the 'attention wishing inhibition', Stanford also proposed that even focused attention on desired events that are about to unfold naturally can cause a counterproductive PK inhibition or retardation of the event. As an anecdotal example you need only think about urging-on a sluggish piece of technology whilst desperately requiring its slick performance in a moment of need, such as the observed malfunction of one's printer while dancing on the edge of a deadline. Essentially, direct attention on one's desire, although initially necessary, is inhibitive of its manifestation, so truly a watched pot never boils.

> "The will, the desire, the belief, lived as inseparable, become realization." (Spare 1921 p 3)

In essence of PMIR, for the desire to manifest itself outside of the body, the desire, or need, should be suitably strong and the will should be appropriately focused. To best achieve this, Stanford suggested that other avenues of action must seem unavailable and a supernatural agency must be invoked and appealed to properly, thereby abnegating responsibility to the agency and reducing concern, and focusing the attention prior to releasing it. In magical terms, "The sorcerer should be able to deliberately forget, or at least become consciously detached from, the outcome of the rite" (Humphries & Vayne 2004, p 13).

> "What is there to believe that is free of belief? What is there to wish that is safe from reaction?" (Spare 1921, p 10)

Whatever the formula, conscious manifestation requires a belief system upon which to hang it and the manipulation of the delicate intricacies inherent within its technique, so the PMIR model indicates that unconscious focus itself works best, freeing the agent from some of the paradoxical pitfalls that arise when desire encounters belief. For example, as Lee (2003 p 108) notes, the path of belief, intrinsic in attempts of conscious manifestation, can be a sceptical *cul-de-sac*, because "the whole game of questioning reality, if taken as a game of doubting, puts the issue of belief in the foreground." Indeed, Spare (1913/1975) rather suggested that belief is merely counterproductive and that even to have need of belief diminishes the purpose.

"Every man is a God, in whatsoever he will his belief."

(Spare 1921, pp 13-14)

Regardless of belief factors, Stanford has offered a set of principles for the realisation of the magical will, dressed as it is in the cloak of psychic expression, and spoken in the language of academic psychology rather than an occult dialect. In its inception PMIR is a means of explaining psi and delineating its contours, and in doing so it paints an image of psi as an everyday ability that most often secretly serves the unattended-to desires of the individual, and in quite subtle and sublime ways. As Dukes (2000 p 84) notes "…the modern Magician can hope for runs of luck or some 'amazing coincidences', but he should not expect too many gold coins to materialise from thin air." It is rather a hidden angel than a rowdy demon doing one's bidding. Yet it is clear that there are also a number of limiting factors to the true expression of the will, preventing this conceptual guardian angel from always creating a perfect environment for the unknowingly blessed. Yet, in PMIR most of these limitations are actually eliminated when the will acts without the observer, making the somnambulist potentially omnipotent and omniscient, so Stanford has been judicious in noting other factors that obstruct the free expression of unconscious psi.

Given that PMIR most often functions through the ready responses of the individual, particularly with receptive psi, then these responses must be suitably flexible to allow for the subtle, implicit redirection of the agent towards its goal. The principle is, again, simply one of expressive economy. If the behavioural repertoire of the individual is overly restricted or determined, then the expression of unconscious goal-directed mistakes, mistimings, associations, and memory omissions or triggers become much less fluid or available. Examples of this restrictive behaviour include the use of rigid schedules and plans; rational, determined, and un-impulsive actions; and repetitive responses, which Stanford respectively termed behavioural- rigidity, inhibition, and stereotyping. Response chaining, the tendency to follow familiar events with habitual actions, was also noted as being restrictive, as were strong preoccupations, which suppress the expression of the sublime will. Taken together these factors form the model's supposition numbered by Stanford (1974a) as the eighth PMIR component, which, appropriately, relates it to the mercurial nature of Hod in kabalistic terms.

> "Chaos magic is results magic, designed to get you what you need" (Ellwood, 2004)

Collectively these psi-inhibitive behaviours and compulsions are antithetical to what Braud (1980) termed psi-conducive 'lability', which may be seen as the desired personality substrate of chaos that lurks within the magical current of that name. To the discordian, this translates into the Church of the Subgenius' power of slack, or more eruditely, this relates to what Weibel (2003) refers to as the disorder intentionally created within situations to make them compatible with the use of magic. It is those ambiguous states of in-between, the undecided conjunction at the crossroads where, in the language of physics, consciousness has not yet collapsed the state vector. And it relates to what Vayne (2001) reminds us is the 'liminal' state. It also vindicates the Spare-ian reasoning behind transmuting the identity into a metamorphic ensemble of effluvious 'selfs'. How better to conduct the chaotic current of Kia? No doubt unwittingly, Stanford (1978) further offered himself as a chaos-magic theorist when he suggested that the body-brain system functions as a random event generator necessary for the reception of psi. He also later supposed that chaotic EEG traces would be psi-conducive, thereby implicating chaos as the primary medium through which magic manifests and announced 'readiness for change' as a central tenet of PMIR (Stanford 1990).

> "One thing is desired, another is thought; and a different becomes. Everything loved obtains an obscene disease."
>
> (Spare 1921, p 8)

While the PMIR model outlined so far is encompassing enough to accommodate the conditions both favourable and anathema to psi, the model also comes equipped with a breakdown feature to account for instances where psi manifests desire counter to the needs of the individual using it. Here Stanford (1990) proposed that when individuals are disposed towards negative self-esteem (or self-concept, or self-image respectively in Stanford, 1974a, 1982), neuroticism, or conflicting needs or desires, then psi may manifest itself in ways counterproductive to the needs of the organism.

> "What man can prevent his belief from incarnating? Who is free of filth and disease? All men are servile to the great unconsciousness of their purpose in desire" (Spare 1921, p 11)

In some instances this counterproductive expression of psi is something like psychic masochism and can occur in combination with guilt and the unconscious desire to be punished. Indeed, as Spare (1921, p 9) intoned "What man prohibits and then commits will certainly cause suffering, because he has willed double. Born of complex desire, results of actions are dual, multitudinous virtue and vice." Such conflicting desires, as when they are prohibited, were clearly unhealthy for William Blake (1994, p 181) when he wrote "He who desires but acts not, breeds pestilence". Similarly, although he speculated upon the precise wording, Stanford was certain of the centrality of negative aspects of 'self' in manifesting maladaptive consequences through psi, just as they would through non-psi behaviour. Extending this notion to desire's opposite pole would then include the metaphor that "Fear attracts bullets" (Levi 1856, p 34), which may be taken quite literally. For as Spare (1921, p 2) asks, "Is fear of desire?"

...et Coagula

> "Will to pleasure is the basic function underlying all activity whether conscious or not, -and whatsoever the means."
>
> (Spare 1921, p 7)

Evaluating the PMIR model, Stanford (1990) was able to report a reasonable body of evidence to support most of his suppositions, although he urged for further research to shore-up these claims. Central to his ideas is the notion that psi is driven by the needs, desires, or dispositions of the individual, and in achieving these aims psi is solely goal-orientated. That is, only the desire and the goal – the object of desire – are in themselves sufficient to cause psi. In terms of receptive psi this means that the need-serving psi-information is automatically sought out and that there is no need to scan the entirety of the information available, and this makes it far simpler than the alternative because, empirically, psi appears to have no outer limits in space or time so the available information is essentially infinite. As such, any 'informational' system of psi would seemingly have problems processing that much data without any known boundaries, so a goal-orientated model is also advantageous. So rather than an informational, or cybernetic model of psi, PMIR is fundamentally teleological, because it is concerned with the direct consequence of purpose. Yet, Stanford also recognised that, once the psi information had actually been received, it was then processed cybernetically, so that it then became subject to all the usual processing trends known to cognitive psychology. Nevertheless, the fundamental process for the occurrence of psi was contingent solely upon teleological factors. In terms of magic, this makes PMIR primarily thelemic, in the true sense of the word as being 'of the will', rather than techgnostic, in the way that Davis (1999) visualises information, or McKenna (1991) visualises language, rather than will, as the official substrate of magical reality.

Yet despite the intuitive appeal of a teleological model Stanford had become slightly suspicious of it by 1990 and, thinking that the definition of 'goal' was a bit vague, he hoped to distance himself from its 'magical' connotations. Added to this, there was some evidence appearing from Vassy (1986) (and more recently from May & Spottiswoode 1998) suggesting that psi was subject to a degradation of the 'signal' in proportion to the informational complexity of the psi transmission. Evidence such as this, indicating that psi exhibited 'Shannon entropy', would imply a cybernetic basis for the transmission of psi. This argument itself becomes quite complex when considering expressive psi (i.e. psychokinesis), but there is a good theoretical argument that all laboratory psychokinesis so far, which is largely demonstrated on a micro rather than a macro level, can be explained conceptually in terms of precognition (e.g. see May, Spottiswoode, & Utts 1995). Precognition, unlike psychokinesis, can easily be conceptualised cybernetically.

> "According to Magical theory, the outcome of an act will be influenced by the intent of the actor, so any Scientific experiment or measurement carried out with a desire to prove something will be affected by that desire…"
>
> (Dukes 2000, p 39)

To make the whole theoretical complication a bit saltier, Stanford's PMIR, like any concept of unconscious psi, implicates the actual experimenter as a cause of the results of psi experiments just as much as the participants, if not more so. As Stanford (1990) noted, in criticism of others' work, it is often the experimenter who has the strongest desire to get positive results. This has rather distasteful implications for any scientist because it means that the desires of the experimenter may be responsible for any results that occur. Mainstream psychology has long been aware of the potential, non-psi, 'experimenter effect' and has often responded to its threat with seemingly adequate blind controls. But its psychic equivalent, experimenter psi, rather upsets any hope of obtaining objective scientific results because blind controls become quite meaningless. This is probably the main reason why parapsychology has long been so unpopular amongst its bigger scientific peers - psychology in particular. The philosopher of science Karl Popper was also unpopular for suggesting that objectivity was a subjective illusion. Returning to the issue of Shannon entropy, because of experimenter psi it may well be that this apparent cybernetic behaviour of psi is, quite literally, just wishful thinking on the behalf of the experimenter.

"…Scientists, understandably, would question this assertion".
(Dukes 2000, p 39)

Devoting an entire paper to the topic of experimenter psi, entitled 'Are we shamans or are we scientists?', Stanford (1981) had already become quite concerned not just with the tacit science of magic, but with the growing implication of science *as* magic. Like most parapsychologists Stanford (1990) has, however, been quite dismissive of experimenter psi. Reviewing the evidence, he invoked the god of Occam's razor and suggested that it was more plausible that experimental psi was due to the participant rather than the experimenter, because of the complexity of psi involved otherwise. While the law of parsimony elsewhere has its elegance, Stanford's (1990 p 98) attempts here to "…put down the myth of almost omnipotent experimenter psi" are reminiscent of Doctor Frankenstein trying to kill his own monstrous creation. It also seems to backfire because issues of psi complexity and parsimony become obsolete when it is remembered that, in PMIR, psi is goal-orientated – the desire manifests *directly* without heed of the process.

> "In the Science sector an open, skeptical mind is a virtue that one aspires to, in the Magic sector it is an inner emptiness one seeks to fill with meaning". (Dukes 2000, p 46)

In the end, Stanford (1990, p 113) finally back-peddled over his reservations about goal-orienated psi but still remained somewhat equivocal of his concept, accepting it for the time being – "It is probably too soon to dismiss entirely the earlier formulation of PMIR that assumes the goal-oriented character of psi…but I confess to uneasiness about the magical quality of such a formulation…". It is here ironic to hear a scientist, in attempting to deny his own model, eventually discuss it less logically and rather more in terms of his 'feeling', a mode of operation which Dukes (2000) has pointed out is definitively magical, not scientific (see also Snell, 2004).

> "In fact a scientific investigation which came to any conclusion in favour of Magic would be as disturbing to me as to other Scientists". (Dukes 2000, p 56)

It is perhaps not surprising that as a scientist Stanford had some difficulty accepting his own model, despite its empirical cohesion, given the intrinsically magical nature of it, as has been shown throughout this essay. Magicians too can be reluctant to accept scientific explanations of magic. Nevertheless, PMIR is based upon the findings of a great wealth of psychological and parapsychological research and has itself been tested empirically to some extent, largely fulfilling all its hypotheses – experimenter psi aside. It is by dint of being empirically testable in this way that makes Stanford's model a genuinely scientific model of psi, and, by extension, of magical reception and expression too. Being empirically testable in this way is what distinguishes a scientific model from a pseudo-scientific theory, which I suspect, is partly what Phil Hine objects to.

> "...magick has become obfuscated under a weight of words, a welter of technical terms which exclude the uninitiated and serve those who are eager for a 'scientific' jargon with which to legitimise their enterprise into something self-important and pompous." (Hine 1995, p 11)

Yet, for all its obfuscation to the scientifically uninitiated, PMIR, as a model rather than a theory, does not attempt to explain *what* psi *is*, merely *why* psi works, and, more importantly, *how* it works psychologically. The *why* – that it is evolutionarily needs-serving – might be wrong, but regardless of this the *how* can only be useful, because, for the magician's purposes, it need not be right if it works. As Dukes (2000, p 34) has pointed out, for the magician "...the theory is being accepted only because it is 'working', not because it is 'true'..."

Nevertheless, it would help to further our understanding and help inspire confidence in those who would choose to use this model magically if scientific 'evidence' can support it. Furthermore, Dukes (1992, p 128) has offered that "...occultists...are still asking permission of science to belief in magic". Apparently, magicians are still experiencing a hangover from the enormous influence of science and its obsession with causality and, particularly, falsification (Dukes 2000). Ideally, magicians are concerned with association not causality, and should only be interested in verifying rather than falsifying their temporary magical beliefs. However, such subjective magical conviction about reality is apparently proving problematic to new-millennium magicians because "Magic…inherits unconscious scepticism from Science. Just as the 'open minded' Scientist is deep down a total believer in material reality, so also the 'gullible' Magician deep down does not really believe in anything." (Dukes 2000, p 45)

> "What so many un-evolved Magical thinkers are trying to do is convince themselves of the reality of Magic which, deep down, they do not believe can really exist" (Dukes 2000, p 46)

If Dukes is right, perhaps PMIR can help the struggling un-evolved magicians, seeking to shed their sceptical skin, to realise that magic can exist and to help them know where to spot it. Having the conviction of empirical reason behind it, perhaps a model such as PMIR can offer aspiring mages a solid scientific basis for belief in magic, as an intermediary part of the process of weaning them onto much more flamboyant modes of thought. As Dukes (2000 p 84) noted "…it is interesting to wonder whether it is the strength of Scientific beliefs which gives them their power to unify our experience". Yet whilst flirting with the power of scientific belief, Dukes also warned that, whilst magical thought is complete, scientific theories all too often become outdated and those 'chaoist' mages who are dressed in a lab coats are left feeling somewhat ridiculous when the science moves on. Nevertheless, new millennium magicians are reminded that 'nothing is true, everything is possible' and that beliefs are there to be borrowed temporarily as befits the purpose. Whether or not science is built upon shifting sands, those with winged feet may find that "…in order to be an effective and practising magician in contemporary times one must utilize the most practical and cutting edge technology and theories of the era" (P-orridge 2003, pp 113-114).

> "...the irrational feeling which haunts some of us – the feeling that Science is shrinking the world and making it more boring and empty – is possibly a betrayal of a suppressed inclination towards the magical way of thought" (Dukes 2000, p. 29)

Regardless of his fears, Dukes suggested that the dominant scientific way of thinking is nevertheless experiencing a fundamental shift towards magical thinking, for reasons too numerous to include in this essay. That this may well be the case has begun to be shown here because, whilst scratching rather covertly at the surface of a science of magic, parapsychology has already unearthed some unpopular signs of science *as* magic, with methodological paradoxes like experimenter psi, for example. Indeed, Roney-Dougal (1991) supposed that the scientific experiment is little different from a magical ritual, with the experimenter as the high priest/ess. This concept is now being taken seriously, as Mario Varvoglis (2003) in his presidential address to the Parapsychological Association suggested that researchers should refine and amplify their experimenter effects, like shamans. So rightly Dukes (2000 p 40), in looking to the future, has predicted that "...it will still be called 'Science' but it will amount to a choice of belief systems, which is pure Magic". However, in the meantime, PMIR can serve as a useful scientific model of the psychology of magical manifestation and divination, offering a usable scientific belief system to those magicians inclined towards science, and a testable model of magic for those scientists inclined towards magic. It is possible that both disciplines may also learn from the other.

> "...early anthropologists tended to overlook the positive aspect of what gets lost in the transition from magic to science...(and that is) the resonating worldview that organically bound the perceptions and procedures of the magician to the holistic web-work of cosmic, animal, and ancestral forces." (Davis 1999, p 173)

Finally, although PMIR might be limited in its conception of conditions favourable to psi, because, for instance, it omits to consider the role of altered states, it is a particularly useful model of the factors *necessary* for psi. Similarly, although psi in no way equates entirely to what may be considered magic, and is actually only considered by some magicians to be an unimportant side effect (e.g. Nema 1995), it relates directly to some of the most basic functions of magic. Psi, in essence, is the anonymous numen of a scientific magic, denied of spirit or personality but still recognised by some by its secret names, such as mana (Winkelman 1983) or Kia, it is the expression of the scientific current of magical thought.

References

Auerbach, Loyd M., 1996, *Mind over matter*, Kensington Books, New York.

Batcheldor, Kenneth J., 1966, 'Report on a case of table levitation and associated phenomena', *Journal of the Society for Psychical Research*, 43, 339-356.

Beirman, Dick J., 2000, 'Anomalous baseline effects in mainstream emotion research using psychophysiological variables', *Journal of Parapsychology*, 64, 3, 239-240.

Blake, William, 1994, *The works of William Blake*, Wordsworth Editions Ltd, Ware, Herts.

Braud, William G., 1980, 'Lability and inertia in psychic functioning', in B. Shapin & L. Coly (Eds.), *Concepts and theories of parapsychology*, Parapsychology Foundation, New York, 1-28.

Braude, Stephen, 1993, 'The fear of psi revisited, or it's the thought that counts', *American Society for Psychical Research Newsletter*, 28, 1, 8-11.

Carroll, Peter J., 1987, *Libernull and psychonaut*, Weiser, Maine.

Davis, Erik, 1999, *Techgnosis: Myth, magic and mysticism in the age of information*, Harmony Books, New York.

Dukes, Ramsey, 1992, *Blast your way to megabuck$ with my SECRET sex-power formula*, Revelations 23, UK.

Dukes, Ramsey, 2000, *S.S.O.T.B.M.E. revised: An essay on magic*, El-cheapo Books, UK.

Ellwood, Taylor, 2004, 'What is chaos magic?', *Razor Smile*, Recidivist Press, Brighton, 3, 4-7

Hine, Phil, 1995, *Condensed chaos: An introduction to chaos magic*, New Falcon Publications, Tempe, AZ

Houtkooper, Joop M., 2004, 'Exploring volitional strategies in the mind-machine interaction replication', *Proceedings of the Parapsychological Association 47th Annual Convention*, 51-65

Humphries, Greg, & Vayne, Julian, 2004, *Now that's what I call chaos magick*, Mandrake, Oxford

Illuminates of Thanateros, 2002, *The Book: The Truth*, self-published, UK

Lee, Matt, 2003, 'Memories of a sorcerer', *Journal for the Academic Study of Magic*, Mandrake, Oxford, 1, 102-130

Levi, Eliphas, 1968 [1856], *Transcendental magic*, Rider & Company, London.

May, E. C., & Spottiswoode, S. J. P., 1998, 'The correlation of the gradient of Shannon entropy and anomalous cognition' *Journal of Parapsychology*, 62, 2, 108-109

May, E. C., Spottiswoode, S. J. P., & Utts, J. M., 1995, 'Decision augmentation Theory: Towards a model of anomalous mental phenomena', *Journal of Parapsychology*, 59, 3, 195-220

McConnell, R. A., 1955, 'Remote night tests for PK', *Journal of the American Society for Physical Research*, 49, 99-108

McKenna, Terence, 1991, *The archaic revival: Speculations on psychedelic mushrooms, the Amazon, virtual reality, UFOs, evolution, shamanism, the rebirth of the goddess, and the end of history*, Harper, San Francisco

Nema, 1995, *Maat magick: A guide to self-initiation*, Red Wheel/Weiser, York Beach, ME

P-orridge, Genesis, 2003, 'Magick squares and future beats: The magical processes and methods of William S. Burroughs and Brion Gysin', in Richard Metzger (Ed.), *Book of lies: Disinformation guide to magick and the occult*, Disinformation Company Ltd, New York, 103-118

Pratt, J. G., & Keil, H. H. J., 1973, 'Firsthand observations of Nina S. Kulagina suggestive of PK upon static objects', *Journal of the American Society for Psychical Research*, 67, 381-390

Radin, Dean I., 1997, 'Unconscious perception of future emotions: An experiment in presentiment', *Journal of Scientific Exploration*, 11, 163-180

Radin, Dean I., & Nelson, Roger D., 1989, 'Evidence for consciousness-related anomalies in random physical systems', *Foundations of Physics*, 19-22, 1173-1175

Roney-Dougal, Serena, 1991, *Where science and magic meet*, Element Books, London

Snell, Lionel, 2004, 'Four glasses of water: Magic considered as a 'culture' distinct from art, science or religion', *Journal for the Academic Study of Magic*, Mandrake, Oxford, 2, 177-205

Spare, Austin Osman, 1921, *The focus of life: The mutterings of AAOS*, published privately by the author (text available on-line at www.hermetic.com)

Spare, Austin Osman, 1975 [1913], *The book of pleasure (self-love): The psychology of ecstasy*, 93 publishing, London.

Stanford, Rex G., 1974a, 'An experimentally testable model for spontaneous psi events: I. Extrasensory events', *Journal of the American Society for Psychical Research*, 68, 34-57

Stanford, Rex G., 1974b, 'An experimentally testable model for spontaneous psi events: II. Psychokinetic events', *Journal of the American Society for Psychical Research*, 68, 321-356

Stanford, Rex G., 1977, 'Conceptual frameworks of contemporary psi research', in B. B. Wolman (Ed.), *Handbook of Parapsychology*, Van Nostrand Reinhold, New York, 823-858

Stanford, Rex G., 1978, 'Toward reinterpreting psi events', *Journal of the American Society for Psychical Research*, 72, 197-214

Stanford, Rex G., 1981, 'Are we shamans or scientists?', *Journal of the American Society for Psychical Research*, 75, 61-70

Stanford, Rex G., 1982, 'An experimentally testable model for spontaneous extrasensory events', in I. Grattan-Guiness (Ed.), *Psychical Research: A guide to its history, principles and practices*, Aquarian Press, Wellingborough, 115-205

Stanford, Rex G., 1990, 'An experimentally testable model for spontaneous psi events: A review of related evidence and concepts from parapsychology and other sciences', in S. Krippner (Ed.), *Advances in parapsychological research Vol. 6*, McFarland, NC, 54-167

Stanford, Rex G., [personal communication], 27-06-2005

Tart, Charles, T., 1984, 'Acknowledging and dealing with the fear of psi', *Journal of the American Society for Psychical Research*, 78, 133-143

Varvoglis, Mario P., 2003, 'Scientists, shamans, and sages: Gazing through six hats', *Journal of Parapsychology*, 67, 3-16

Vassy, Zoltán, 1986, 'Experimental study of complexity dependence in precognition', *Journal of Parapsychology*, 50, 235-270

Vayne, Julian, 2001, *Pharmakon: Drugs and the imagination*, E-Books, London

Weibel, Deana, 2003, 'Controlling chance, creating chance', *Journal for the Academic Study of Magic*, Mandrake, Oxford, 1, 161-178

Winkelman, Michael, 1983, 'The anthropology of magic and parapsychological research', *Parapsychological Review*, 14 2, 13-19

Is Magic Possible Within A Quantum Mechanical Framework?

Steve Ash

In this paper I intend to explore the possibility of a 'theory of magic' within a scientific framework, specifically in a quantum mechanical context, as I do not intend to go too far beyond established science. The term 'magic' as used here can be understood as the craft of those who call themselves 'magicians' or 'witches', professed psychic abilities, or any form of physical modification of the world caused by the mind alone. I exclude the 'evocation of spirits' etc here as outside of current scientific understanding, though not necessarily beyond future scientific interpretation. In doing so I shall be opposing the great tide of philosophical and scientific bias in favour of Realism - the doctrine of a physical, mind independent and causally closed, objective reality - and hope to reveal this as a prejudiced dogma through its exposure to rival possibilities.

The way I shall do this is through an analysis of our present understanding of quantum mechanics, with special reference to magic, and an exploration of those interpretations that might allow magic, or are believed to by those with little knowledge of the subject. I will end with an original examination of the metaphysical possibilities of the best case for a 'quantum mechanical magic'. I do this as a philosopher of science and of mind, rather than as a scientist or mathematician, but will be outlining the basic mathematical formalism and science in the first section, without which no understanding of the subject would be complete.

In the course of the paper I will also be criticizing the misconceptions and misuses of quantum mechanics in the hands of so-called 'New Agers', but also some of the crypto-mystical tendencies found even amongst trained scientists.

Admittedly this is an ambitious task considering the unresolved philosophical problems associated with quantum mechanics, and the innate mysteries inherent in the concept of 'magic'. It will also of necessity touch on the probable relationship between physics and that other great enigma, consciousness. As such this may strike some as worthy of the classic retort of 'attempting to explain one mystery in terms of another'. However I hope to demonstrate that the possible interpretations of quantum mechanics are narrower than many believe, and that its nature might only be regarded as 'mysterious' when viewed within the framework of the current Realist metaparadigm.[1] I conclude magic is indeed possible within a scientific framework and may even be a necessary consequence of the best explanation of quantum cosmology.

What follows is a beginning and should be considered as an opening into a deeper study and possible research project

What is Quantum Mechanics?

Quantum mechanics is essentially a mathematical model for predicting the behavior of subatomic phenomena. It was adopted in the face of a series of bizarre experimental results that could not be understood within the context of any of the existing models of physics, or indeed within that of any rational explanative theory - the famous superposition of particles and a general defiance of the basic 'laws of physics'. It was found, largely through trial and error, that the form of mathematics now utilized in the standard quantum mechanical equations was the only formulation capable of producing accurate predictions. The accuracy of these predictions over the course of nearly a century has since shown to be 100%, an unheard of degree of accuracy within any science. What's more much of our everyday electronic technology has been based on the consequences of these equations. Quantum mechanics, hence forth referred to as QM, has thus been sometimes dubbed the "only true science".

The main philosophical problem with QM is that it appears to make no rational sense whatsoever, and arguably its mathematics can not be visualized. The breakdown of reason inherent is largely due to the fact it uses a different mathematical model to that subconsciously deployed in our intuitive judgments of the world, as well due to the related redundancy of classical concepts, such as position, motion, time and identity, within its domain. This has been often interpreted in the context of a Neo-Kantian notion of the conceptual construction of the world of everyday experience being distinct from a non-conceptualisable underlying reality. The problem is accentuated by our relative inability to visualize what is being represented by the QM equations. Whereas the mathematics of Newtonian mechanics could be visualized in terms of billiard balls no such visualization is possible with QM, again due to its apparent departure from 'common sense' perceptions of 'reality'.

Two approaches have been taken in dealing with this. One extreme is to argue that the formulation is simply a function that outputs results, that is it is not representing anything, in the way geometry is supposed to, it is in essence a kind of 'rule of thumb' for producing results. Any visualization we might achieve in such a scenario is thus at best an explanatory metaphor for understanding the equation rather than a description of reality (something often also held to be the case for General Relativity Theory and its 'curvature of space'). The other option is to argue that the QM formalism is indicative of something ontological, but is enigmatic due to its incompleteness. The amazing degree of predictability it produces is said to mitigate against any 'rule of thumb', and an 'exact model' which 'does not represent anything' might be justifiably regarded as contradictory. I shall be taking the latter perspective in this paper.

There are two forms of mathematics used in QM, one is referred to as Matrix Mechanics, the other Wave Mechanics, both have been demonstrated to be mathematically equivalent and are used interchangeably in standard QM. Wave Mechanics is sometimes represented as 'easier to conceptualize' than Matrix Mechanics, but the latter is easier to describe in my view and appears to be more fundamental. In very simple terms Matrix Mechanics represents a simulation of the world in which all the possible states of an object or system under investigation are represented as vectors (often used to represent forces in classical physics) within an abstract state space, which includes a representation of normal space-time (using the Four Dimensional Space Operator). This is formulated as a series of coordinates for each vector visualisable as a graph-like map, in which four axes represent space-time referents and the rest the possible states of a system. Most of the oddities of the model occur due to the fact that the apparent properties of the object are not representable within vector space at all, but only within variables representing the operations that alter that vector space - the primary operation actually being the measurement of the property. That is the perceived 'redness' of a 'red object', to use a simple archetype, is not the state 'red' recorded in vector space but is given by the operation that measures that property of the object. The operation is represented by a matrix of numbers that represent the operational 'influences' on the vectors, and the properties of the object have to be coded here in order to match experimental data. This seems to imply that the act of measurement, and possibly other operations on the object, are required for it to actually have any observable properties at all! Note this is not saying that these cannot be measured without measurement, which would be trivially true. It is saying there are no properties without measurement or some similar operation. That is, the operation profoundly changes and defines the state of the object. No other form of mathematical representation fits the experiments. Another oddity is that only so called 'eigenvectors' within vector space have fixed values in relation to an operation, such as measurement. To understand what this means we can propose a 'hand rule'. Hold your hand out and point forwards with your index finger while your thumb is vertically raised, then rotate your thumb to a horizontal position on the axis of your index finger. If your fingers were the vector axes of the vector space, your index finger would be an eigenvector (it is unchanged) while your thumb is not (it changes). Now rotate your index finger up or down vertically on the axis of your thumb. In this operation your thumb is now an eigenvector (it is unchanged) and your finger not (as it moves). The motion of your hand is an operation, measurement is an operation in which only the 'stationary vectors' have fixed measurable values, while the moving vector does not. The direction of the index finger up or down is a random event and defines the outcome of the measurement as say 'up spin' or down spin'. This is the core of what the maths of Matrix Mechanics is describing. The rest basically consists of a more detailed description, one that dovetails into that large array of equations that constitute physics as a whole. This core formulation describes why a particle whose momentum is measured has no position until a position measurement is made. It also describes how the measured position will have a random outcome based on a probability formula. Wave mechanics essentially describes the same thing, but actually represents the probability curve in a mathematical wave description. A wave that has direct correlations with the electromagnetic waves involved, being based on a probability that is objective or deterministic, rather than subjective or epistemic. Finally we need to mention the phenomena of entanglement, where the operational result on one object simultaneously affects the another in the same complex system or two 'linked systems'. This can be demonstrated by performing the hand maneuver with two hands, with the thumbs touching and the index fingers pointing in opposite directions. This systemical connection seems to suggest the two objects are interconnected in someway, however they can be light years apart in time and space - a fact that arguably indicates a non-local acausal relation if not a holistic underpinning of the cosmos. That's quantum mechanics in a nutshell, or at least all of it needed for the purposes of this paper (a more detailed but simplified outline of the formalism can be found on by website, see bibliography). The process modeled by Matrix Mechanics is not really a conceptual problem, however what all this actually means ontologically is a huge problem!

Quantum Mechanics and Consciousness

The most obvious response to the so called 'problem of measurement' in QM is to assume that a measurement is an observation or a perception. Indeed this idea was first put forward Eugene Wigner in 1960, "My chief scientific interest in the last 20 years has been to somehow extend theoretical physics into the realm of consciousness — consciousness is beautifully complex. It has never been properly described, certainly not by physics or mathematics" (Cited in Szanton 1992, p 309). He argued that consciousness was the key factor in the act of measurement. That is the effect of measurement on an observed system is the effect of consciousness on it, or that the properties of an object need to be perceived in order to exist. This seems fair enough, how can one measure an event without observing it and so being conscious of it? But we have to be very careful with this as the situation is not as straight forward as this view might imply. For some the basic notion that 'properties require observation' implies the Berkleyan notion that 'to be is to be perceived', and from there leap head long into the absurdities of ontological idealism. Worse still this has been taken onboard by New Agers who believe 'we create our own reality through our perceptions'. The easiest counter argument to such a patently false notion would be to throw its proponents out of very high window and ask them to perceive gravity differently. Fortunately we don't have to take such drastic steps to reveal that this view is misguided. The simple fact is that even objects in superposition are 'real' in some way, as they react with each other and with defined particles according to the same laws applicable to any particle. They just appear to be in a 'ghost-like' state that enables them to be in two places at once, and do apparently impossible things, such as appearing from nowhere and just as mysteriously disappearing again. If consciousness does anything at all it merely modifies the state of the object, fixing it into a definable classical one. But there is no empirical indication that the final results of this 'random fixation' are in anyway influenced by consciousness. Therefore consciousness does not appear to have any influence on the actual outcome, which remains entirely probabilistic. But beyond this it is by no means certain that consciousness is involved in a determinating operation such as measurement anyway, which may be one observed type amongst many other observer less operations. Worse, even if it was we would then be faced by the question of 'whose consciousness and why' which may lead us towards solipsism. The alternative view is that the key factor in measurement is the quantum object's connection with the wider world, by becoming part of an interactive system that includes the measuring device, it's operator and their entire environment. It is quite possible that other operations that involve connecting the quantum system with a larger macro-system might also have the same effect as measurement, even when consciousness is not present. However this is difficult to demonstrate experimentally as all experiments involve observation at one stage or another. Thus the properties of a system would only exist by virtue of a set of holistic relations.

Another closely related idea to this is that of the 'wave function collapse'. As said earlier the wave function is basically a complex variable containing all the possible superimposed states of an object or system, as well as their respective probabilities. When a defining operation such as a measurement is performed the wave function is sometimes said to have 'collapsed', meaning the wave function is no longer applicable to the situation, as the state of the object is now determinate and classical and no longer in superposition. Here the measurement operation, and often consciousness, is typically said to have 'collapsed the wave function'. However what this means is by no means clearly understood. This shift from probability to certainty is sometimes said to simply represent a change in our awareness of the situation, however as we have already observed the wave function only makes sense if it codes an objective probability (the likelihood of an indeterminate situation becoming the case) not a subjective one the likelihood of a belief being true, which implies a determinate situation), so this purely cognitive interpretation of probability does not seem to fit the picture. The mathematics represents actual situations not mere knowledge of situations.

Part of the motivation for this belief in a 'collapse' is the common sense assumption that quantum mechanics (perhaps) applies at the micro-level and classical mechanics definitely applies at the macro-level, with some cut off point between them. Thus either the connection between the quantum system and the wider world brings it into the classical domain, or alternatively consciousness does the trick, and the wave function is no longer representational. However there is nothing in the core mathematical formalism of QM to suggest any demarcation between quantum and classical domains, it is simply introduced as a 'fiddle factor' in the equations, the so called 'correspondence principle' which indexes the wave equation to Planck's constant (which defines the smallest quanta[2]), thus solely linking it to quantum scales. There is no reason why this should be the case however. Thus the principle is quite contrary to the descriptive elements of the equation which attempt to map a bizarre set of data, in that it does the opposite and tries to preserve 'common sense'. Many contemporary interpretations of QM thus reject this and argue that the formalism applies at every scale even the macro-level. The real mystery is in this view why large objects do not behave as weirdly as quanta, and many speculative reasons have been posited. The whole idea of the 'wave function collapse' is now often rejected and rightly in my opinion. If an equation in physics describes an objective situation it always does so, the mathematical laws do not change according to perspective or scale. After all Schroedinger's equation is essentially a variant on Newtonian laws, as is Relativity Theory, and it would be bizarre to say these are changed according to scale, mass or statistics (this should not be mistaken for an ignorance of Relativity Theory, as we are talking of the consistency of the laws themselves not their application or form). Thus the wave function almost certainly constantly applies and never 'collapses'. I would suggest this seems a basic truism from our understanding of the close parallelism between mathematics and physics.

Two closely related interpretations of QM currently incorporate this non-collapse assumption, referred to as so-called Relative State Theories by Hugh Everett.[3] One is the Many Worlds Theory, the other is Decoherence Theory. The way the first model represents this is well known, the wave function always applies to the universe as a whole, but the universe is a multiverse, it branches into alternative possibilities and we can only exist in one. From an internal perspective each of the components of the wave function is instantiated in a world of its own, and we only experience one world. When a measurement is made we thus enter one of several 'parallel alternative worlds'. Whether the universe splits, our minds do, or reality itself does, varies between different versions of this theory. There are several reasons this approach is popular, apart from doing away with wave collapse, one is the potential for bridging quantum mechanics and Relativity, the other is that it is entirely Realist. A Realist metaphysics in which conscious plays no role and the world is entirely physical and causally closed to the mind. Realism is still the dominant metaparadigm amongst Physicists, a paradigm shift from classical to quantum physics is one thing, but a metaparadigm shift in the deepest metaphysical assumptions of science is quite another! The branching of worlds is purely a mechanical process in which all the potential futures split off from each other and our awareness randomly follows one timeline. It is perplexing and not a little irritating to read some New Agers take up this idea of the multiverse and give it their characteristic Idealist spin, as if our minds choose the future world, something very far from the truth. But this theory is not without its problems. What the branching actually means, and how separate branches can interact, and later remerge, is a mystery that seems to add even more confusion to the situation. The popular idea of parallel universes or space-times is totally absurd, and not what any serious physicist believes at all. Interaction across disconnected spaces being impossible as there is no continuum or medium between them. It is rather as if some abyss opens up between the alternative states of a system, and seems to imply some non-space on which the branches supervene, and within which neither classical nor quantum laws could apply. This would obviously seem to make the 'branches' incapable of causally interacting and they most definitely can, as numerous experiments have demonstrated. Another serious misgiving many have with this theory is that it implies an infinite or innumerable number of parallel worlds, something that seems excessive even to the most ardent critics of parsimony and energy conservation!

One thing is certain, 'magic' would not function within its context. This may not be the case with Decoherence Theory however. This second thesis is a little harder to grasp, essentially it says that superposition, and all the quantum weirdness that goes with it, is the normal state of the universe and always remains so. Classical physics is an illusion in this model, but there really is one universe rather than a multiverse as we shall see despite attempts that have been made to make Decoherence a mechanism within one version of the Many Worlds Theory. What happens in the clearest version of this interpretation is that when we make a measurement we simply reduce the superpositional possibilities of the system and make a quasi-classical world more probable. This is because whereas conventional quantum mechanics assigns a unique vector space to each 'isolated' system, the Decoherence model is theoretically rooted in unifiable vector space, where entanglement is the norm, and spaces representing defined systems can fuse together as subspaces of a higher dimensional vector space mutually interacting. Thus when an isolated quantum micro subspace, full of superpositional potential, connects with a measuring device, or any other environmental macro subspace, it merges with it and shifts it into superposition, with all the components of the new vector space combining into a much larger entangled array of superpositions. However the large size of the new space disengages the superpositional elements from each other, 'spreading them out', by entangling them with the more 'separated' elements in the macro space, thus negating their mutual interference, or coherence. This creates a non interfering quasi-classical situation, which is further modified by the history of the macro system it entangles with. That is a consistent history is imposed on the measured superpositions creating the coherent 'classical' world of everyday experience. However all the superpositions still remain but we can only measure one consistent quasi-classical set of them with each measurement. There are an infinite number of such potential sets and so each measurement will be a unique quasi-classical perspective on a single universe in eternal superposition. Whereas the previous interpretation had an observer entering one of many possible 'classical' worlds on each measurement, this one has one superpositional world with several possible 'classical' observations of it, rather like Relativity Theory, with which it is hoped it will merge. All the perspectives are assumed to be ultimately consistent with each other, though simultaneously incompatible, as the quantum mechanical history of the entire universe, its 'quantum cosmology', should be consistent (otherwise we have the possibility of alternative universes again). This is somewhat like a non-collapse version of Bohr's Complimentarity, a singularly incompatible but mutually completing set of situations.

One remaining problem with Decoherence Theory is the absence of a Superselection rule that would predict which one of many possible consistent sets of histories is selected and maintain the overall consistency. In other words why we experience a particular consistent history of the world. Some speculate on a kind of logical essentialism that predisposes the necessity of a coherent and consistent reality, but why this should be so is inexplicable and smacks of a crypto-mystical Platonic 'order' that transcends everyday reality. One interesting alternative possibility however is that this relates to the Anthropic Principle, the idea that our very existence depends on a consistent history in a coherent world which we ourselves thus 'impose' on the universe. Thus it would be the necessity of some future human situation rather than individual observation that figures the human into the equation. This idea currently exists only on the vaguer speculative fringes of theoretical physics however, and so it is at this point we must leave the philosophy of physics and embark on a more metaphysical analysis.

The Metaphysics of Magic?

The Anthropic Pinciple was once thought to be wild speculation in some quarters, but today seems forced on us by another consequence of modern science. This consequence involves the mystery of the initial conditions and precise constants of our universe. It is now widely accepted that the constants of the equations representing natural laws are incredibly finely tuned to form the kind of universe we exist in. A tiny difference in any one of them would make the universe unable to support our existence. Examples range from the charge on an electron to the cosmological constant. This has led to many to argue that such a situation could not have come about through random chance. Solutions to this problem have been sort by invoking parallel universes and the big bang / big crunch cycle, to argue for many sequential universes, with our universe a necessary rarity among a great many possibilities. However from our understanding of objective probability (Popper 1959)[4] we can not really apply what appears to be a particular objective property of our universe, with its own laws, across all the, very different, disconnected universes, any more than we could apply Newtonian Mechanics. The only recourse appears to be Theology or the Anthropic Principle. Personally I am convinced by the many atheistic arguments within the philosophical literature of the absurdity of theism and deism to believe the latter is the only option.

The mystery of the particular consistency in experience posed by Decoherence theory is also found in arguments for Idealism, here some ordering principle is usually posited to solve the problem, be it various God concepts, shared language / narrative or the 'human collective consciousness'. We seem to be faced with a similar situation with the Anthropic solution to the QM Superselection problem. Interestingly within Decoherence Theory it is also said that the initial conditions of the universe at the Big Bang must meet a certain requirement for the consistent history theory to work and perhaps some parallel lies here. With the Anthropic Principle what all this adds up to is the idea that our future or current existance somehow constitutes a telos or goal towards which the past has been drawn. Such teleology has been made unpopular by historicist theories which claim to be able to determine such a telos, however this is not a necessary part of the theory, and I will argue does not apply here. How the telos works depends on the nature of the universe, a deterministic, finite cosmos might have an 'omega point' towards which events are directed, a less deterministic model might have several possible 'omega points' whose probability changes with events, while an infinite cosmos might have many teloi that form a chain of teleological focal points stretched out in time.

Whatever the case, the telos reaches back with reverse causation, a real possibility in a quantum cosmology, to engineer the very events that lead to those existances. Such a state of affairs being perceived by any situated observer as a mysterious historical process leading towards a certain end result. From a magical point of view one necessary component of the world is 'free will' of course, and to account for this a multiplicity of possible time-lines must be taken into account, and the less deterministic variety of the principle adopted. Such time-lines would probably manifest as a series of coincidences, such as the convenient extinction of the dinosaurs, a kind of purposeful synchronicity. With which we seem to already be approaching a magical viewpoint. Whether all this requires the temporary presence of humanity (or any other collective of sentient life forms) at time T, or whether it requires the stronger requirement of a specific historical situation at time T depends how strong the Anthropic Principle is taken to be. For magic to have a place in this hypothesis it would have to be very strong.

One of the problems with such a strong application of the Anthropic Principle is that it seems to imply that certain specific future situations have a high probability of occurring. Which would seem to indicate a very tight net of causal interactions extending in both directions across time, and, given the quantum mechanical aspects, it also indicates a tight net of limited acausal entanglements too. This however is quite likely within the context of a possible form of what I would dub a Hi-Strength Anthropic Decoherence Theory (HADT), that I would suggest may underlie any possibility of magic. Of course this is purely a metaphysical thesis, as such a theory has yet to be devised. Another major problem for this kind of Anthropic Principle is the fact that it not only appears to be having a reverse causal influence, or even just an acausal influence, but rather appears to be influencing the very constants of the universe and therefore the laws of nature themselves. That is the way the pre-geometry of the universe came together to fix the constants is also being influenced - something that seems a lot more than a causal influence or acausal influence. This is not only like building your ship in the middle of the ocean, but even in the absence of any ocean! How could such a thing be possible? What could be the possible position this was performed from?

What would appear to be required would be a continuum of influence between an 'ordered space' and a 'non-ordered space', something outside the range of causation under natural laws of any kind. An obvious answer is a greater dimensionality, a 'higher dimensional space' in which order emerges, a stratification running from the pre-geometry of the universe to the realm of quantum mechanics and the probability laws, down to the quasi-classical level of a unified set of consistent histories and apparent classical reality. Such a dimension might be considered a logoic dimension, one in which order emerges to fit the end result defined by the telos under the control of a logos or ordering principle. The teleological influence would thus be working backwards along the time axis, shaping events and defining the consistent histories, and simultaneously acting along the logoic axis defining the mode of ordering of those events. Including the 'random' structuring of space-time from pre-geometry that defines those mysterious constants and the nature of the ordered universe. Such a higher dimensionality would be visualisable as a projected hypercube (either with the time dimension ignored or the first three space dimensions collapsed into a 2D 'flatland'), in which the 'pre-ordered' domain was the 'outer cube' and the 'inner cube' the realm of ordinary physics. It also likely that this 'pre-ordered' domain also corresponds at least in part to the quantum realm that makes up the universe as a whole. Because what is interesting then is that a hypercube can be more easily analyzed by way of a set of 3D cross sections which produce self contained geometric forms, and such a mathematical approach seems close to the quasi-classical perspectival domains isolated from the quantum universe through measurement. It is also not hard to see a parallel in this with David Bohm's theories (see endnotes), and this approach could be a way of combining Bohmian and Decoherent Models. However there is still a missing factor in all this if the both events and order are shaped by the telos, what is it before these realities are shaped? In imagining a Anthropic universe based on (a)causation alone we can overcome the linear time paradox by positing a bootstrap cosmos within quantum mechanical framework, but when we talk about an influence of a pre-ordered universe we arguably have a completely different situation. One in which at least part of the telos must lie outside of the ordered physical universe of space-time in order to interact in a hypothetical logoic dimension. But what could be the nature of this existance?

The solution I would suggest, is one that also makes a scientific theory of magic possible. That is the extra dimension hypothesized above may be identical to the fourth or fifth dimension suggested by P D Ouspensky in 1912, in his controversial work Tertium Organum - in other words, a dimension of consciousness. Contemporary Philosophy of Mind now takes very seriously the possibility of a non-reductive, panpsychic theory of 'potential awareness' (many of us would in fact suggest this is the only rational possibility given the evidence. See Chalmers 1996). One way of making sense of this would be to posit that the very capacity of objects in space-time ('us' for instance) to have 'qualitative experiences' is through the medium of an extra dimension of consciousness in which such things exist. That is just as within an Einsteinian view of space-time an object can exist in a certain spatial coordinate, but not 'exist for us' until it also exists in our temporal coordinates (the block theory of space-time), so might an object exist in space-time but not 'exist for us' until it exists in our consciousness, that is within our conscious coordinates within an extra dimension. Ouspensky explores such possibilities in the early chapters of his book, as well as relating this to a Neo-Kantian phenomenal conception of reality (though unfortunately he later drifts off into some bizarre speculations based on this insight). But within the context of quantum Physics it could be said that the difference between being or not being in our conscious coordinates is identical to the domains of quantum superposition, i.e. reality, and the quasi-classical domain of consistent history. Thus the idea of a dimension of consciousness begins to sound very much like the logoic dimension postulated earlier. An important note to make here is this is not a conscious coordinate based on perception, as is deployed in the 'observer effect' of a single measurement, it would be based on a collective cognition or awareness of reality based on belief systems. Or to put it another way on the 'information field' of this dimension (akin to the gravity field of normal space). Such a field may correspond to what Bohm called the 'information field' of the super-implicate order. Thus the measurement itself, as Decoherentists rightly claim would not need an observer, and a measurement may be only one form of Decoherence, however the consistency necessary for a HADT type theory would require a shared cognitive information field to order it, and that field could reside in an extra dimension of shared consciousness - the ultimate origin of that information field being the telos of the Anthropic Principle. Empirical indications that this might be the case range from the effects of mind on probability distribution recorded by the famous MIT experiment and the alleged effect of scientific consensus on the 'impossible' crystallization of glycerine.[5] It should be noted that with this hypothesis we might also close the gap between subjective and objective interpretations of probability, where subjective belief includes conceptual and cultural 'possibilities', as the gap between belief and actuality narrows to a hair's breadth in this model.

Admittedly this is a bold hypothesis and as yet underdeveloped, however it may be a fertile starting point for a more detailed scientific research program. One of the interesting and testable things about is that it perhaps also facilitates a bridge between a Decoherence Theory, firmly rooted in the quantum mechanical formalism, and the more speculative insights of David Bohm with his Implicate and Explicate Orders. For it to be a serious theory of course it would need to be formalized. This poses a serious problem however with the full extent of the hypothesis, in that how could the content of a dimension of consciousness be represented? It is not hard to see how the mysterious subspace base shift in Matrix mechanics could be tied into an entanglement with another subspace in a higher dimensional vector space, but the exact result of the entanglement remains random in this formalism. It may be that this would be the limit of science a mysterious pseudo-randomness that actually masked a hidden order that could not be represented in any formalism. Even if we extended the Four Dimensional Space Operator from a 4 x 4 array to a 5 x 5 array it is hard to see how this could help. In theory there may well be a way of codifying the effects of the extra dimension on the mechanics but the system would be so complex as to be incalculable. A typical chaos / complexity theory situation. Normally when this situation is met science turns to modeling and simulacra rather than calculation, but here we may have to model the entire timeline of the universe which would be quite hard to say the least. Science may have to eventually accept its limits and embrace an essential mystery. A possible limited formulation might involve subteloi however. Given that there will be an indefinite number of paths between now and any final telos, or teloi, we might speculate that a number of subteloi may exist along these paths. This would be like the various routes we could take between say Charing Cross (now) and Kings Cross (the telos) on the London Underground with a variety of lines used and stations (subteloi) passed through. We could project a range of possible future subteloi say a fraction of a second in the future and formalize these through a fifth Dimension, however this would still be a probabilistic solution.

But how does all this relate to magic? Well in terms of cosmology it is not hard to imagine the extra dimension of consciousness as being equivalent to the entity Occultists have poetically referred to as the Astral Plane, the Imaginal or the Dreamworld etc. It is highly tempting to equate the quantum realms of this dimension with these occult ideas, as well as with the more modern concept of the Collective Unconscious. Of course such imaginative speculations, though fascinating, would have to be constrained to fit the logical consequences of any more developed HADT formulation. Given this speculation however a more practical explanation of magic arises, one in which the teleology of a

HADT model was being exploited. If as seems likely one or more teloi in history are shaping and drawing events in particular directions, perceived as synchronicities by participants in these timelines, and that this influence is operating in part through an extra dimension of consciousness, than any manipulations of this extra dimension would modify the directions such timelines take. In other words we may have the ability to generate subteloi that steer events in a certain direction, that is create synchronicities, within the context of the overall telos. This raises problems for the testability of magic however, as from an experimental perspective any 'magical effect' would appear as a set of random coincidences and the causal factors themselves would be entirely explicable by relatively conventional physics. A testable consequence of this theory however might be the failure of magic to avert a major historical event, if we commited to the hypothesis of 'real magic' as an experimental stance. The deviation from the primary teleology might be too great. Given known magical techniques it seems likely that subteloi might be generated by the imagination but need some form of 'mental energy' to actualize them. This could be compared with the indentation of space-time by gravity and the amount of energy required to do this. Images in the fifth dimension might be understood as an equivalent 'indentation' or 'impression' in a malleable medium requiring energy. The energy concerned from studies of magic (Austin Osman Spare's orgasmic sigils and abstinence practice, and the infamous black fast of witchcraft) seems to be one of great psychological tension or will, and often is linked to a necessity for survival, the black fast being an obvious example, but addiction might be another (one ponders on the potential of 'crack magic'!). This might indicate that the driving force of the teleology is indeed the necessity of survival however perceived. Such an idea would not be far from the necessary human existence postulated by the Anthropic Principle, which if taking the form of a particular outcome, as necessary in this theory, might well require the existence of a certain pre-existence of precursor events and ancestors. Such metaphysical speculation could go on and on, but it would be folly to get too far ahead of the useful limits of our, lagging but crucial, experimental physics.

In conclusion I would sum up the essence of this paper by saying contrary to popular philosophical prejudices there is really nothing 'impossible' about magic within the context of modern science. Whether the thesis outlined here is true or partly true or false, it at the very least demonstrates a possible mechanism for magic within contemporary physics and a starting point for a more detailed philosophical analysis, within what might be dubbed the Philosophy of Magic, and perhaps an eventual scientific research program.

Endnotes

1. The term Metaparadigm, or Metadigm in popular usage, refers to the more stable paradigmal assumptions shared by different Kuhnian paradigms. For example both the Newtonian and Einsteinian Physics paradigms are Classical in nature, while both Relativity Theory and the Many Worlds Interpretation of quantum mechanics adopt a Realist metaphysical foundation. It is much harder for Scientific Revolutions to shift metaparadigms than paradigms.

2. Planck's Constant is a consequence of early Quantum Theory, the discovery that energy was not emitted continuously from objects but rather in continual quantifiable bursts of radiation. The smallest burst being the size of this constant, and all other values being multiples of it. This was explained in terms of EM energy particles, or photons. It was subsequently found the subatomic particles also correspoded to this scale, which was thus defined as the smallest possible size for any entity.

Planck' Constant thus featured legitimately in many subatomic and electromagnetic equations.

3. I have excluded one other possibility here the Implicate Order Theory of David Bohm, as like many I feel its significance is as yet unclarified, and following Bohm's death such clarification may be a long time coming. Though reference is made to it in conclusion so a basic understanding will be useful. Essentially Bohm argues that the probabilistic wave function describes an ontological wave of propensity, a 'force' which governs the distribution, movement and localization of particles. Moreover such 'waves' are manifestations of a universal 'field' that governs such probabilities in the same way light waves are an oscillation in an electromagnetic field. Beyond this the particles that are determined by this field are in fact a localized 'unfolding', or manifestation, in what Bohm calls the explicate (directly connecting causal) order, of an 'enfolded' or hidden holistic order, universally extended in spacetime as an implicate (indirectly connecting acausal) order, that is experienced as non-local relations of entanglement and propensity. The 'universal field' is regarded as a way of modeling how the implicate order unfolds as the explicate order. Bohm thus appears to imply that each photon is a local manifestation of a universal electromagnetic field, and all photons essentially manifestations of that one field, and so universally interconnected through it, and that electrons have the same relation to a universal electric field, and so on into unified field theory. With the 'implicate field' being the primary foundation of these, as well as the source of propensity. He describes how particles unfold from this field through metaphors of vortexes and most detailedly through the example of an ink drop suspended in a container of glycerine, that can be stirred anti-clockwise, thus defusing the drop and making it disappear into the glycerine, but can also then be stirred clockwise making the inkdrop reappear, its order or structure having been secretly 'preserved' diffusely in the solution. These ideas are fascinating and arguably aesthetically appealing, however Bohm fails to explicitly relate these metaphors to the formalism of quantum mechanics, the core of the the physics, or any other foundational model, other than to say that the wave function refers to the implicate order and classical physics to the explicate order (and perhaps to imply the vortex of unfoldment is related to the rotational parallels of measurement. Remember the hand rule). He does say that the idea was inspired by

Green's Function, an acknowledged part of quantum mechanics, however inspired and derived are too different things. Instead he merely uses them to describe his intuitive understanding of quantum phenomena. Where he does use mathematical formalization to describe his theory the maths just appear to be algebraic definitions of his metaphors, notably the defusing inkblot. For this reason he has had little impact on mainstream physics and more importantly what all these metaphors are supposed to actually represent within established physics is very unclear.

4. Karl Popper demonstrated that Physics required a singular objective measure of probability to completely model events. Before this probability was either measured in terms of subjectivity (how certain we were in our knowledge) or objectively, but collectively, in the Frequency Theory (which formulated the 'rules' of probabality, i.e those stating the familiar averaging of heads and tails for large numbers of coin throws). But Physics required individual probabilities for singular 'random' events, to explain which required the concept of Propensity. That is for example a coin has a 'tendency' to be either heads or tails and this manifests evenly over time. Popper argued if this theory matches reality, as it appeared to, this propensity was very much like any force of nature that determined a physical result. Thus Probability had 'natural laws'.

5. The mystery around the crystallisation of glycerine is still controversial. The phenomena was first popularly reported in the book *Lifetides* by Lyall Watson. In this account liquid glycerine was regarded as uncrystalisable until 1923, when it was found in crystalline state by chance in various locations, Watson highlights a dramatic tale of a ship carry liquid glycerine being caught in storm which seemed to catalyze the crystallization. On the news of this reaching other scientists, and in particular of crystal samples reaching them, Glycerine suddenly becomes crystalisable, despite previously failed attempts, Watson claims in one case, "that soon after their first crystals arrived in the mail and were used successfully for inducing crystallization in an experiment on one sample of glycerine, all the other glycerine in their laboratory began to crystallize spontaneously, despite the fact that some was sealed in airtight containers" (p 47). This story has been used to support claims such of those made by Rupert Sheldrake in his now discredited Morphogenetic Fields theory, however the key point is that it is the knowledge of and belief in the crystallization that triggers the possibility of crystallization.

However things are not this simple, skeptics have pointed out that the crystallization could have easily occurred through the seeding of glycerine by microscopic fragments of the mailed crystals, whether purposefully or accidentally. The issue turns on the details of the events, and unfortunately Watson relies on an ambiguous paper in a rare Journal of Chemistry published in 1923 as his only factual source (this was formerly available on the Internet but no longer seems to be available). The sober paper roughly corresponds to Watson's more dramatic account, but simply says glycerine crystallized within 'sealed containers'. No reference is made to their air tightness or whether they had been previously opened. Read through a conservative mindset this is not a conclusive case therefore. Though does correspond to less dramatic and scientifically documented anecdotes of a similar nature. The case is thus still open. The MIT experiment is well known and involved a cascade of ball bearings being allowed to freely drop one at a time and form a physical even probability curve within a precisely engineered sealed mechanism designed to create this effect. Experimental subjects were asked to concentrate on the mechanism and attempt to change the probability curve. According to the experimenter's conclusions a very slight shift was detected.

References

A Popular Science Essay on Anthropic Principle and Constants, 2005, [On-line], http://www.2001principle.net/2005.htm

Albert, D.Z. ,1992, *Quantum Mechanics and Experience*, Harvard University Press, Cambridge, MA.

Ash, Steve, 2006, *Matrix Mechanics for Dummies*, [On-line], http://blackcatpress.co.uk/QM/QMintro.htm

Barrow, John and Tipler, Frank, 1986, *The Anthropic Cosmological Principle*, OUP, Oxford.

Bohm, D.,1980, *Wholeness and the Implicate Order*, Routledge, London.

Chalmers, D., 1996, *The Conscious Mind*, OUP, Oxford.

DeWitt, B. S. and N. Graham (eds), 1973, *The Many-Worlds Interpretation of Quantum Mechanics*, Princeton University Press, Princeton, NJ.

Everett, H, 1973, 'The Theory of the Universal Wave Function,' in DeWitt and Graham (eds).

Everett, H, 1957, '"Relative State" Formulation of Quantum Mechanics', *Reviews of Modern Physics*, 29,454-462.

Ouspensky P.D., 1923, *Tertium Organum*, Kegan Paul Trench Trubner, London.

Popper, K R, 1959, 'The Propensity Interpretation of Probability', *British Journal for Philosophy of Science*, OUP, Oxford.

Szanton, Andrew, 1992, *Recollections of Eugene P. Wigner*, Plenum Press, New York.

Angels with Nanotech Wings: Magic, Medicine and Technology in *The Neuromancer* and *Brain Plague*

Catherine M. Lord

Angels with Nanotech Wings

How many angels can dance on the head of a pin? This question perplexed medieval scholars. For them, the fantastic was not a matter of science fiction, but science fact. There was much debate as to whether angels were material or occult. The unseen and enigmatic have always provoked scientific hypothesis. Quantum mechanics asked whether the building blocks of matter form particles or waves. The miniature threatens to be everywhere but nowhere. Nanotechnology, or the art of engineering miniature assemblages that can transit our bodies, could soon produce the equivalent of guardian angels with silicone wings. These might watch over cells tempted to turn cancerous. Science tests changes through hypotheses and measurement. Mysticism requires speculation, faith and the unknown. We fancy that Arthur C. Clarke's famous dictum that "Any sufficiently advanced technology is indistinguishable from magic" (Clarke's *Third Law* 1962) has done away with the mystical. But like the Freudian repressed, it returns.

Only more recent studies of the life work of Isaac Newton have uncovered the relationship between his practice of magic, or alchemy, and the enlightenment rationality of his scientific discoveries (Golinski 1988). For Newton, one did not preclude the other. Alchemy provided him with what today, we might call a space for lateral thinking. This led to the creative break-throughs of his major works in optics and gravity. One of the many enduring purposes of alchemy has been medicinal. Newton's alchemy, unwittingly medical, came to reveal colour spectrums and the laws of gravity. Without the latter, no rocket could have reached the moon. Magically (because technologically), there is a longstanding tradition in which medical explorations, however crude, lead to the development of technologies at both the cutting and bleeding edges.

What then, does medical engineering have to do with discourses of magic and theology in contemporary science fiction? William Gibson's celebrated cyber-punk classic *The Neuormancer* (1984) and Joan Slonczenski's *Brain Plague* (2001), a novelistic 'buddy movie' about the relationship between a struggling artist Chrysoberyl and an accelerated culture of sentient cells, both confront forces neither entirely human nor scientifically verifiable. The microbes, which trespass into Chrysoberyl's body, summon her neurally in the voices of Old Testament supplicants praying to their god. In Gibson's novel, one manifestation of the cyberspace system's artificial intelligence, or AI, calls itself 'Neuromancer.' The word itself conjures a configuration of discourses – neurology, romance and necromancy. Necromancers like the 17th century John Dee, claimed to raise demons. Artificial intelligence is a force which science has confidently predicted or denounced as impossible. AI remains the stuff of science fiction, and in Gibson's novel, its connection to evil spirits is made explicit in the novel's title. Indeed, both novels dramatize the less explored edges between mysticism, theology, and the discourses of medical engineering that are at present in development.

The technologies that pose the potential to take us into a medical revolution are neural-enhancers and nantechnological robots. An associate professor of molecular and pharmacology and toxicology, Dr. Roberta Dia Brinton is developing a "neurochip" (Networker@USC, Jan./Feb 1999). This silicone device can be planted into the neural connections of the brain, and compensate for basic genetic dysfunctions in neural tissue. Nanotechnology also works at the micro-level. Molecular-sized robots can now mark cells, so that doctors can track fluctuations in a medical condition. The next frontier will involve nanomachines that repair damaged cells.

Both *The Neuromancer* and *Brain Plague* seize every opportunity to throw their characters into countless situations of neural damage and drug addiction. In a time when 'mad cow disease' still haunts, and SARS terrifies, readers can readily identify with Chrysoberyl's risk venture. Allowing her brain to become the Promised Land for a culture of religiously minded microbes, Chrys gains their powers off immunization, but also team-mates to help her build a commissioned city, Silicone. Jonquil, one of the leader cells, declares the human project to be completely in line with that of the miniature world (chapter 13). Similarly, in Gibson's novel, Neuromancer implies that Case's role requires that he learn the correct codes to call up a burgeoning artificial intelligence (chapter 21). Case may be *posthuman* in his connection to cyberspace, but his contribution to the system - chemical, emotional and unpredictable - cannot be dispensed with. Both novels explore what happens when medical interventions tread into terrains beyond the scope of healing, where creativity is pursued for creativity's sake.

Creativity is a concept that calls for clarification and attracts censure. In a now famous essay, entitled "The Work of Art in the Age of Mechanical Reproduction" (*Collected Essays*, Hannah Arendt), celebrated writer and scholar Walter Benjamin (1892-1940) wrote about how the 'work of art' undergoes transformation through reproduction. Photography and film provided two key examples. The 'aura' around a painting fades when reproduced through catalogues, photographs and copies. Benjamin argues that words such as "creativity" and "genius" have become outmoded. The model of the powerful and solitary creative spirit becomes discarded in an age where reproduction begins to produce a technology of creativity.

Both Chrysoberyl and Case, the protagonist of *The Neuromancer*, do not operate as even independent beings. They can only perform creatively with the aid of prostheses, pharmacological drugs and, in Chry's case, microbes. For Case, super-hacking requires learned competence from systems with vast and already formulated rules. He can only outface his AI opponents Wintermute and the Neuromancer through spontaneity. Case is the rightful precursor of Neo, from the blockbuster movie *THE MATRIX* (1999). Played by Kenau Reeves, Neo learns that his only advantage against the 'Matrix', or the vast AI network, is the act of breaking rules. AIs cannot improvise. Humans can. With an ability to play the system brilliantly, but also be unpredictable and emotional, humans can overwrite the apparently triumphant cybernetic system and its agents. Gibson's novel and its successor *The Matrix*, provide what I have termed elsewhere (1999) a theoretical fiction for analyzing how a system can be transversed and transformed through an act of creativity. Such fictions are more than 'objects' that give us ethical or scientific insights into our current practices. These fictions act as bridges between systems from the past and those in the future. That bridge requires innovative thinking, and this requires more than a solitary human working from inspiration.

A relatively young field devoted to the topic of how individuals interact with domains of knowledge has helped our understanding of creativity. The cliché that creativity is an aggressively individualistic act has been subverted. Creative work is rarely left touched by culture and its collective concerns. One of the field's pioneers, Mihaly Csikszentmihalyi, has provided a definition of creativity which resonates uncannily with *The Neuromancer*, *Brain Plague*, neurochipping and nanotechnology. A domain of practice, be this the visual arts or biology, has its own fields, such as multimedia design or neurobiology. "Creativity occurs" clarifies Csikszentmihalyi, when

> …a person using the symbols of a given domain…has a new idea or sees a new pattern, and when this novelty is selected by the appropriate field for inclusion into this relevant domain. The next generation will encounter that novelty as part of the domain they are exposed to, and if they are creative, they in turn will change it further. Occasionally creativity involves the establishment of a new domain (1996, p 28).

Take for example, the neurochips being developed by Dr. Roberta Diaz Brinton and her colleagues (Online, Networker@USA, Sep/October,

1999). Miniature chips can be connected into brain synapses. Once the bar on the high jump of the technology is raised several more notches, the benefits for stroke victims will be awaited. Such technology and its modern alchemists have formed a new domain. They have sutured the areas of microbiology and computer engineering. The results of these creative collaborations appear in business and marketing. One company specializing in the development of neural microchips dubbed itself, not surprisingly, "Neuromancer Consulting: Your Telemedicine Partner." This example resonates with Csikszentmihalyi's concept of creativity as a third term working between the already established and the future of research and business. Science fiction inspires representations of medical application and the domains of future research. The sci-fi narrative may be regarded as the 'fuzzy logic' between what can be identified and quantified, and what can be qualitative and ineffable.

The Medieval mind embraced the spiritual dimension of angels in unpredictable numbers. Despite the wish to quantify the angel, many acknowledged the angel as numinous and beyond measurement. Perhaps the metaphor of the angel persists because we know that in the creative enterprise, be it scientific or artistic, resides in the ephemeral. Biomedical science will quantify and control, but when the angel of unpredictability shakes its wings, the chaos of weird science will out. Science fiction analyses such chaos. It pursues sociological and aesthetic critiques of biomedical interventions, their uses and abuses. Such applications take off into the future on wings of technological achievement. These will be the wings of flight for angels with glue on their horns.

Angels With Glue Horns

Horns conjure the devilish side. Equal amounts of 'good' and 'evil' might keep the cosmos in balance. Though a matter of irrelevance to hard-core science, tiny left-overs of shattered theologies hurtle into our medical and aesthetic futures. The interaction between science and art produces an ethical minefield. Dr. Brinton treads carefully. The nanochips she is developing interconnect with brain tissue. They do so though an interface that would allow the chip to absorb human tissue would be the next gigantic step for pharmacology. However, as Brinton underlines: "It is possible to encode information into the neurochips. Those signals can be devised for good or evil – that's a possibility" (Networker@USA). While Brinton refers to societal consequences, she nonetheless uses theological terms.

I am using the terms angels and demons as metaphors. I intend to tread the opposition. Angels can have horns and pointed tails, just as demons of revolt can bestow on us powers of creative thought. By using angels and demons I maintain their magic, in Arthur C. Clarke's sense. But I depart from his formulation by arguing that the magical, angelic or demonic side of the technology defines the unforeseen consequences of its application. One could characterize science fiction as both a mode of sociological critique and a reminder that science will confront us with bolts from the blue.

As yet, we can only speculate how technologies such as neurochip and neural-chemical interventions will affect consciousness. Nor do we have concrete examples of how though biomedical engineering can be put to uses beyond the medical. In *The Neuromancer*, the neurologically debilitated protagonist Case can only 'jack' back into the giant 'matrix' through receiving a neural re-wiring, both organic and synthetic. This is paid for by his self-appointed and enigmatic boss Armitage, himself more construct than human, well-oiled on countless prostheses. Armitage ensures Case's loyalty by inserting hidden toxin's into his employees new nervous system. Disloyalty would mean re-debilitation. Such handicaps would deprive Case of the creative life, which for him is the cowboy life of Cyberspace. In the world of *The Neuromancer*, experimental technologies are applied to extreme limits. Gibson's novel warns of how medical technology will always provide the next innovation, and offer the human the next Faustian temptation. And as Dr. Faust discovered, the dynamics of self-empowerment demand dependency.

In fact, *The Neuromancer* is a world characterized by the one underlying fact: there is no creative life, no possibility of making a difference, no path to a colourful existence, without prostheses and medication. Dermatrodes link Case into his adventures and benthylmethane (a fictional drug) control the emotional perils of his virtual life. In his battle with AI life, the enigmatic enigmatic Neuromancer and his sidekick Wintermute, Case tackles products of the system that have developed their own agenda. In Gibson's novel, the relationship of cause and effect between creative thinking and medical cures, becomes inverted and diversified. The macabre alliances between electrodes, medication and human tissue are what produce AI. And here is the rub: the AIs have not been birthed from intention, but are the results of endless collisions by trial and error. The survival of the fittest is a lottery born from endless interactions. It is these endless algorithms of connect, disconnect, failure and success, which are the material procedures of science. Medical engineering can spawn technologies which create their own systems of cause and effect. And it is this 'created' that the scientific creators might never have intended.

The potential creations of medical technology are more pervasive than a single Frankstein's monster running wild on a backward clock. Today, be it through the prostheses of nanotechnology, medication or neurochipping, we could soon be living on miniscule pieces of monster. The parts are expendable, multiple, aesthetic and fractal. Any pattern, natural or synthetic, can be broken down, re-produced, disseminated. The smaller versions iterate the larger structure. Nanotechnology can explore and compute the natural fractal landscape of the human body in quest of disease. K. Eric Drexler, who coined the term nanotechnology, has written about the 'tiny machines' of DNA/RNA protein cells. Star-studded with exotic atoms, these contraptions make 'assemblers.' These miniscule miracles can re-programme bacteria and blood cells. Inevitably, they should be able to make semiotics with brain cells. Roberta Brinton identifies the next threshold of her field's research. It will occur when microchips and neurons can 'talk to each other.' Here would be the moment when the organic and inorganic glue together like never before. They would make a consciousness which as yet, no one has sampled. The miniature worlds might become a source of dependency to the macrocosm of daily, human consciousness.

Brain Plague examines the problems dependency between macrocosms and the monads within. Between the cities of arteries and stem cells, and those of human civilization, is the glue, or interface of Chrysoberyl's consciousness. It is tough being a local deity. For her, the tiny microbes, some angelic, priest-like, or unholy experimental, become indispensable and omniscient to their heroine. Without the rise and fall of their nano civilizations, Chrysoberly would lose her muses, and her success. Without them and her expanded neural abilities, she could not take on an ambitious architectural project. But the dramas of worldly success at the macrolevel, become challenged by the spiritual ambitions of dissenting microbes. One 'nano-being' Rose, wants to improve her condition inside Chry's brain. Rose wants to "enlighten" the protagonist's mental centers in "small, subversive ways, feeding the brainless, tending the sick. Yet its seductions tempted her more than she cared to admit. The host's doses of AZ gradually sapped one's will" (2001, p 242). Rose would like to knock some sense into her Great Host. Angelic in their quest for social improvement, demonic in their defiance, Rose wishes to change the shape of microbe destiny to come. Revolt produces creativity in its host.

Yet the resulting glue of medical interventions produces a dangerous reliance, that Chrysoberyl witnesses in a fellow host, Daeren. She notices that he has acquired the "shifting eyes of a slave." The implication is that the price of creative excellence is slavery to a domain. This domain is not static. It is undergoing its own evolution. There are winners of the freedom of the fittest race, and losers.

Both *Brain Plague* and *The Neuromancer* may be a warning that the price of developing medical technologies that can advance consciousness, creativity and our capacity to self-reflect upon the tensions between both, may exact the dangerous price of our dependency. That weakening reliance may produce unseen diseases and neurological conditions, which, in turn, demand, further interventions. Throughout Gibson's novel, Case is constantly in need of medical attention and medication.

Chrysoberyl does not receive a cure so much as an ongoing medical condition which predicates her as an artist. Angels and demons are metaphors for a spiritual, non-materialist excess which pervades both novels, and the contemporary technologies who 'magic' is an unknown quantity. The mysterious excesses of what we cannot predict from the fruits of our scientific adventures, become the technical visions of a fictional genre that cannot rid itself of ancient spirits.

The Memes in the Machine

While not the genes themselves, memes are their powerful relatives. As a metaphor for genes, the meme swims around in the pool of information and ideas which jump from one generation to the next. Richard Dawkins lists many items that can jump, from catch phrases and techniques of building arches to broader bodies of (*The selfish gene*, 1976, qtd. and expanded on in Drexler, p. 35-38). Just as genes compete, replicate, copy then deviate from each other in the journey of transformation, so do memes. In terms of contemporary evolutionary biology, particularly in the recent work of Stephen Pinker, memes and genes are inextricably linked. To read the interaction between the gene and the meme as comparable to that between a switch and a light, would be to simplify a problem of oceanic proportions. How the 'hard wiring' of the neurological brain and its genetic codings process memes will underline the work of this century. Yet the frontiers of medical research will provide us with many cutting edge examples. The goal of medical technology is to find ways of making synthetic units to heal damaged tissue and genes. When the healing process has consequences for meme pool, our relationship to creativity and identity becomes transformed.

Both *The Neuromancer* and *Brain Plague* examine how drugs, brains wired enmeshed in a virtual matrix, and humans soaring on the wings of microbe imagination, are all propelled by the memes in our heritage machines. Both science fiction novels critique how our memes rely on the history of medicine, and suggest how creativity will miscode or misread medical interventions. According to Dawkins, it is the competition and collisions between different memes, the way in which one 'incorrectly' imitates and replicates another that evolution (or devolution, according to some) takes place.

The Neuromancer attempts to dramatize a life in which posthumanity can control their all too human side; but it is precisely this flesh-ridden burden, forever in want of medical attention, that remains stamped on the novel's players. Gibson's matrix of names bears testament to the fate of medical bodies in perpetual crisis. Take the protagonist Case, who in every chapter, experiences the vicissitudes of being a medical 'case'. His helper, Dixie Flatline, has a surname suggestive of emergency resuscitation equipment. Case's boss Armitage has a bodily 'arm' in his name, and is discovered to be much older than expected. (Note the 'age' in last suffix). Armitage is a sum-total of his prostheses, through which one replica has replaced yet another. The 'original' Armitage is but a simulacra. One of the two AIs, Wintermute, manifests virtually as 'Finn.' Perhaps the reference to the fin of a fish harks back to the first creatures of evolution. The more complex the interaction with virtual reality, the greater is the tendency of images from prehistory to stalk the hard-wired future. The novel's climax brings home how the coded, molecular level of information, that is the meme, makes the apparently cybernetic Case unavoidably human.

> His [Case] vision crawled with ghost hieroglyphs, translucent lines of symbols arranging themselves against the neurtral backdrop of the bunker wall. He looked at the backs of his hands, saw faint neo molecules crawling beneath the skin, ordered by the unknowable code (1984, p. 241).

The ghosts cause a physiological effect, as though Case is in the lure of a drug. Thus, the shifting, nanotechnological interactions below the surface of the skin, which suggest a primeval stirring in the undergrowth, act medicinally, and most unpleasantly. The 'ghost' and the 'hieroglyphs' conjure ancient knowledge, and make its particles capable of tracking Case's bloodstream. The memes of ancient and primeval times meet those of our futurity. Indeed, creativity, from the evolutionary point of view, is linked to dissemination of memes, which will not dispense with the human body as a medical entity or, in contrast to evolutionary theory, as that set of codes which is constantly re-written by environmental factors: a technology that feeds on the unpredictable edges between health and sickness.

In *Brain Plague*, the microbes debate questions of theology and creativity on a platform along brain capillaries. Revolutionary microbes worship lesser gods or none at all. One microbe Rose reminded me of a religious Quaker. So often, she turns within for inspiration. The old cliché that artists in a creative struggle need to "go inside and ask the big questions" is not a decision Chrysoberyl needs to make. The life and death of microbe nations, cultural inheritances religious and technological revolutions at the monadological level, permit Chrys no sleep. In the cities of Chry's mind, the meme-like microbes develop their fields of knowledge at alarming rates. One microbe - Saf, ironically, less than safe - learns how to build the first microbe space-ship. While the miniature populations can be transported from one human host to another through injections, the space ship is a sign of the memes ability to make a giant, and above all, self-motivated leap for 'meme kind.' Its quest for outer space is both religious yet infectious. In the wrong mixtures, these disease protecting microbes can themselves become the disease. Hence, this comical aspect of *Brain Plague* uses the miniature narrative of microbe evolutionary leaps, to bring together three discourses – that of creativity, memes, theology and the spread of disease.

Multiplying through both *The Neuromancer* and *Brain Plague* the discourses of mysticism, theology, innovation and biomedicine dissolve, separate and intercut, making myriad patterns. These intimations of posthumanity are not fantasies based on fanciful expectations about the future of neural programming or nanotechnology. Nor can the fiction of sci-fi be held responsible for making inaccurate or partial predictions from the multiple pathways of now. The cybernetic system of *The Neuromancer* conceives of a metaphorical and exaggerated version of the Internet, which is not the Internet itself. Gibson's novel hypothesizes that which has not happened; but this prediction may be a prescient metaphor for that we cannot envisage. When Neuromancer appears as a boy doing somersaults in the cyber system, he explains to Case that stating and calling the correct computer codes is the equivalent of raising demons.

Neuromancer has given us piece of advice about interpreting works of sci-fi in an age of neural pharmacology. Neuromancer gives us a code for reading, with and against the grain of science. Science fiction conjures untested moral, ethical and creative ciphers in technologies full of untapped demons and angels. Neuromancer warns us that no biomedical intervention can provide an innocent panacea. Humans seize hold of one intention, to turn or pervert it to another. They do so in an attempt to escape from the human into the *posthuman*. Yet our fleshy, meaty, crude chemicals, full of emotion and fury, smoulder out. Towards the end of Gibson's novel, Case realizes that he cannot escape "the old alchemy of the brain and its vast pharmacy" (1984, p 262). When Chrysoberyl credits the "brain in the back" for her work, she refers to technologies of the future. But in *Brain Plague*, the nano-beings are based on a model as old as Leibniz's monads, and his concept of worlds within worlds. What makes the new biomedical interventions intimidating is that our humanness and its unpredictability show no signs of disappearing. We are our angels and demons. And as science fiction warns us, there are few places where either party will fear to tread.

References

Benjamin, Walter, 1984, 'The work of art in the age of mechanical reproduction', in H. Arendt (Ed) *Illuminations*, Schocken Books, New York, 217-252.

Brinton, Roberta Diaz, 1999, 'A Chip on Her Shoulder', [Online] *Networker@ USA. Sep/October*, 1999.

Clarke, Arthur C, 1984, 'Third law', *Profiles of the future: an inquiry into the limits of the possible*, Henry and Holt Company, London.

Csikszentmihalyi, Mihaly, 1996, *Creativity: flow and the psychology of discovery and invention*, Harper Collins, London.

Dawkins, Richard, 1978, *The selfish gene*, OUP, Oxford.

Drexler, K. Eric, 1990, *Engines of Creation: The Coming era of nanotechnology*, New York: Anchor Books.

Gibson, William, 1984, *The neuromancer*, New York, Ace Books.

Golinksi, Jan, 1988, 'The secret life of an alchemist' in John Fauvel, Raymond Flood, Michael Shortland, & Robin Wilson (Eds.), *Let Newton be! a new perspective on his life and works*, OUP, Oxford, 169-185.

Lord, Catherine M, 1999, *The Intimacy of Influence*, ASCA University Press, Amsterdam.

Slonczewski, Joan, 2000, *Brain plague*, A Tor Book. New York.

Wachowski Andy, Larry, 1999, *The Matrix*, Warner Bros.

Rowling's Devil: Ancient Archetype or Modern Manifestation?

Lauren Berman

The abundance of folkloric references in J. K. Rowling's *Harry Potter* novels has contributed significantly to the series' success. Consequently, this study examines the manner in which traditional demonic conventions associated with the devil have influenced Rowling's formation of Lord Voldemort. These well-established themes are manipulated and combined with innovative concepts in order to construct a unique version of the ultimate personification of evil.

The term *devil* designates the personification of absolute evil found in a variety of cultures. For instance, the ancient Egyptians, Norse and Greeks conceptualized evil in the form of wicked deities while Christians and Muslims speak of the actions of disobedient angels. Embodiments of evil also exist in Eastern societies such as the mythological figure of Mara in the Buddhist tradition, the malevolent forms of Parvati in Hinduism, as well as malicious spirits known as the 'peey' in Madras and the 'buta/kala' in Bali (Parkin 1985, p 19). Although the specific details of this phenomenon including name, gender and number, may vary from one society to another; it traditionally exhibits two universal functions as an explanation for the origin and the essence of evil (Russell 1977, p 35).

J. K. Rowling, the author of the *Harry Potter* series, has expertly crafted her own version of this ancient enemy, Lord Voldemort, whose very name evokes a threatening atmosphere of fear and frenzy from the moment Professor McGonagall first mentions it in the darkness outside number four, Privet Drive. The six novels written thus far clearly indicate that Rowling's Dark Lord incorporates many of the devilish traits common to the personification of evil in numerous cultures around the world. For instance, Lord Voldemort possesses a sadistic disposition akin to that of the evil antagonist in Egyptian myth known as Set or Seth. Once a beneficent deity, Seth gradually degenerated into a vindictive god of evil and darkness due to his vicious, cruel and jealous nature. He tried to steal the throne belonging to his brother, Osiris, by tricking his sibling into a chest and sinking it in the Nile, but Osiris was resurrected and his son, Horus, eventually defeated the wicked god of darkness (Gordon 1993, p 614; Russell 1977, p 80).

In addition, Rowling's villain also exhibits duplicitous behavior comparable to the Norse trickster god, Loki. According to Scandinavian folklore, this wicked deity possessed a beautiful exterior but a foul and corrupt spirit, and was described as "foe of the gods" and "forger of evil" (Russell 1984, p 65). Loki's chief talent was shape shifting, which is also a sign of the Christian devil's duplicity (Gordon 1993, p 424).

The ancient Greeks did not have a being that personified the principle of evil (Russell 1977, p 144). However, Greek religion, legend and mythology produced a number of concepts and symbols that were influential in shaping Rowling's version of the devil. One malevolent figure was Typhon, a monster associated with fiery volcanic eruption (Gordon, 1993 p 698), as well as serpents, which formed his lower body and emanated from his shoulders (Russell 1977, p 136). Similar to this grotesque creature, Lord Voldemort is a destructive entity with a certain affinity for snakes. Moreover, the description of the Dark Lord's resurrected body reinforces this connection as the potion containing venom milked from the giant snake, Nagini, contributed to his snake-like features: "Harry stared back into the face that had haunted his nightmares for three years. Whiter than a skull, with wide, livid scarlet eyes, and a nose that was as flat as a snake's, with slits for nostrils… (*Goblet of Fire* 55[1]).

Notwithstanding these obvious similarities, the personification of evil in the *Harry Potter* books most strongly resembles the Christian devil as he appears in the New Testament and in medieval folklore. Voldemort's selfish disregard for the lives of others, his willingness to manipulate the truth, his penchant for tempting the innocent and his obsessive desire to destroy humankind and rule the world leave no room for doubt that he is anything but a malevolent incarnation of diabolical evil functioning in the work as a perfect example of the satanic destroyer.

In Judeo-Christian demonology, the traditional opponent of God has many names, including Apollyon, Beelzebub, Semihazah, Azazel, Belial, and Sammael, as well as nicknames such as the Tempter, Evil One, God of This World, Father of Lies, and Prince of Darkness. Despite these numerous designations, the name Satan with its Greek equivalent *diabolos* (the Devil) dominates as the leading manifestation of personified evil, displacing or demoting other names and figures (Russell 1977, p 189; Pagels 1995, p 47).

In the Hebrew bible, 'Satan' meaning *adversary* is not a monster but a being of superior intelligence and status in God's heavenly court. He appears in the Old Testament as one of God's obedient servants functioning as an accuser of men whose duty it is to test a person's faith in God (Taylor 1985, p 34). Thus, contrary to Western Christianity, Satan does not appear as the leader of an "evil empire," or as the head of an army of hostile spirits who make war on God and humankind, but as a messenger sent by God for the specific purpose of blocking or obstructing human plans and desires. The messenger is not necessarily malevolent, but merely performs a task that human beings may not appreciate (Pagels 1995, p 39).

In later Jewish and Christian writings, Satan gradually developed into an independent adversary and rebellious angel who personified the origins of evil. He turned into a malicious figure and was demonized as the proud angel who instigated a revolt against God. This rebellion resulted in his transformation into the prince of a host of evil spirits, who may be viewed as fallen angels or as demons (Russell 1977, p 236; Taylor 1985, p 35). In his demoted and disgraced state, Satan became God's antagonist, enemy, and rival in the eternal contest for human souls (Pagels 1995, p 47). Thus arose the myth of Eve's seduction in the Garden of Eden, where Satan tempted the first woman to eat from the Tree of Knowledge and then persuaded her to give a piece of the fruit to Adam (Gordon 1993, p 187).

In Islam, the devil is known by two names, Iblis (perhaps derived from the Greek *diabolos*) and 'Al-Shaitan' (influenced by the Jewish and Christian *satan*) (Russell 1984, p 54). The Muslim devil is described in the Qur'an as an evil Jinn who disobeyed God by refusing to prostrate himself before Adam, and was therefore expelled from heaven. According to Islamic belief, God allowed Iblis respite from punishment till an appointed time and gave him the authority to use his wiles and forces to tempt humanity and to destroy those who yield to temptation. However, Man has free will and cannot use Satan as an excuse by arguing that the devil forced him to sin, as the Muslim devil has the power to tempt but never to compel (Russell 1984, p 57; Hassan 1997, pp 86-87).

It should be noted that in addition to these biblical and folk motifs, the construction of Lord Voldemort's demonic character was also influenced by the evil figures depicted in J. R. R. Tolkien's *Lord of the Rings* trilogy and C. S. Lewis's *Chronicles of Narnia*. Rowling has expertly manipulated several cultural and literary motifs in order to create a uniquely modern incarnation of absolute evil well suited to the hostile environment of the late 20th and early 21st centuries in which ethnic conflict and wars between nations are prevalent.

The first point of comparison between Rowling's devil and the aforementioned sources pertains to his physical appearance. Lord Voldemort began life as Tom Marvolo Riddle, a handsome teenager and brilliant scholar, who concealed an enormous potential for hostility, brutality and megalomania behind his mild-mannered façade. In *The Chamber of Secrets*, Dumbledore explains how Tom's sinister quest for immortality and his manipulation of the Dark Arts led to a physical transformation during which his external appearance was adapted to suit his internal iniquity: "Very few people know that Lord Voldemort was once called Tom Riddle … He disappeared after leaving school … travelled far and wide … sank so deeply into the Dark Arts, consorted with the very worst of our kind, underwent so many dangerous, magical transformations, that when he resurfaced as Lord Voldemort, he was barely recognisable. Hardly anyone connected Lord Voldemort with the clever, handsome boy who was once Head Boy here." (*Chamber of Secrets* 242[2]).

In addition, Voldemort's physicality deteriorated all the more when he was unable to murder little Harry Potter despite the strength and skill he had accumulated during the years in which he terrorized the wizard and Muggle communities in an obsessive desire to become mightier than any living wizard. Instead, the Dark Lord was deprived of his body and reduced to a horribly disfigured state lacking corporeal form, "I was ripped from my body, I was less than spirit, less than the meanest ghost … but still, I was alive. What I was, even I do not know …" (*GF* 566). This physical loss may signify that the final vestiges of Voldemort's humanity vanished together with his body, as implied in book I when Hagrid says: "Dunno if he had enough human left in him to die" (*Philosopher's Stone* 46[3]), and in book IV where the Dark Lord is portrayed as more of a "thing" than a person, "It was as though Wormtail had flipped over a stone, and revealed something ugly, slimy and blind – but worse, a hundred times worse" (*GF* 555). Furthermore, when Voldemort does eventually reacquire a body, his physical appearance does not improve and he is described as having hands like pale spiders, gleaming red eyes with split pupils and a face like a snake's with slits for nostrils.

This description of the Dark Lord's physical appearance differs significantly from those of the characters embodying absolute evil in the bible and in the works of Lewis and Tolkien. For instance, contrary to Voldemort's repulsive features, the biblical devil is portrayed as a being 'of perfect beauty'. This description stems from passages in the books of Isaiah and Ezekiel. The passage in Isaiah, "How you have fallen from heaven, bright morning star, felled to the earth, sprawling helpless across the nations" (Isaiah 14:12), describes a magnificent fallen angel, Lucifer [Hebrew: *Helel ben-Shahar*; Latin: 'light bearer'], who becomes synonymous with Satan in the medieval tradition (Gordon 1993, p 187; Russell 1977, p 197), and is used interchangeably with Satan to designate the devil. The passage in Ezekiel reinforces the devil's splendor as it specifies that the fallen angel was covered in every precious stone and gold: "You have been in Eden the garden of God. Every precious stone was your covering, the sardius (ruby), topaz, and the diamond, the beryl, the onyx, and the jasper, the sapphire, the emerald, and the carbuncle, and gold. The workmanship of your tabrets and pipes was prepared in you the day that you were created" (Ezekiel 28:13).

The hideous descriptions of the devil only appeared during the Middle Ages, and many of his grotesque attributes, such as the cloven hooves and horns, goat's legs and hair, beast's ears, and saturnine features, can be traced back to pre-Christian fertility deities including the two-headed god Janus and the Greek nature god, Pan (Russell 1977, p 125, Rudwin 1973, p 38). The medieval Church based their notorious visual images of the devil on ancient folk-belief and superstition in order to manipulate devil-worship as a weapon against dissidents (Barrett 2000, p 61). The monstrous symbolism was intended to deprive the devil of his biblical beauty and portray him as a twisted, ugly distortion of the angelic being he was before the fall. According to Jeffrey Burton Russell, the didactic purpose of this manipulation was to frighten sinners with threats of torment and hell (Russell 1984, p 131). It is therefore apparent that

Voldemort's monstrous features have more in common with the hideous creature depicted in medieval folklore than with the radiant image of the biblical devil.

Tolkien's personification of a malevolent and corrupting force against which man is doomed to fight, Sauron the Great, Lord of the Rings, is also depicted as a fallen angel similar to Lucifer. His history as provided in Appendix A of *The Return of the King* corresponds, point by point, with that of the biblical Satan, and even his name resonates with a serpent-like quality, probably derived from the Greek word *sauros* meaning 'lizard'. At first, Sauron was an attractive being endowed with supremacy in Middle-earth. Then toward the end of the Second Age, he persuaded the Númenoreans, or original men, who were forbidden to enter the Undying Lands, that they would have everlasting life if they disobeyed the Ban of Valar. Thus, the Númenoreans committed Middle-earth's Original Sin and their kingdom was destroyed. As a punishment, Sauron's physical form perished and he was never able to regain an appealing visage but became hideously grotesque (Helms 1974, pp 75-6). Conversely, Tom Riddle, the Dark Lord's alter ego may have been attractive in his youth, but his transformation into the repugnant Lord Voldemort is the product of his own choices and not as the result of a specific punishment as in the cases of Satan and Sauron. The changes in his appearance after leaving Hogwarts were caused first and foremost by a conscious decision to dabble in the dangerous Dark Arts and the subsequent decay of his physical form was triggered by a curse he had intended for another. These facts may be connected to Rowling's conception of moral justice in the sense that evil is often self-destructive and as a result Riddle's internal iniquity may ultimately lead to Voldemort's eventual demise.

Concerning C.S. Lewis's work, the indisputable figure of evil in *The Chronicles of Narnia* is Jadis, otherwise known as the White Witch. In *The Lion, the Witch and the Wardrobe*, she is depicted as a person with human features including great height, a deathly pale face and a crimson mouth, but it is later revealed that she has no human blood (Ford 1980, p 307). She is also clearly linked to two demonic manifestations: Lilith and Iblis. As Mr. Beaver explains, "her they call Lilith. And she was one of the Jinn." (*The Lion, the Witch and the Wardrobe* 88[4]). According to ancient Semitic legend, Lilith is an evil female spirit who allegedly murders newborn babies, harms women in childbirth, and haunts deserted areas in search of children (Ford 1980, p 189). Moreover, in Muslim demonology, the Jinn are a class of spirits that inhabit the earth, assume various forms, and exercise supernatural power. One of the Jinn mentioned in the Qur'an is Iblis, the Muslim devil. It is apparent from this information that although Jadis and Voldemort differ with regard to their physical attributes, their malicious natures and their obsessions with controlling others indicate that they are both marked by an innate inhumanity. While Jadis's demonic heritage plays a more significant role in her characterization than her physical features, Voldemort's characterization is derived from a combination of corrupt physicality and inherent evil.

Despite these obvious differences, Lord Voldemort has much in common with the literary villains in these classic fantasy novels. For example, the evil sorcerers in both Tolkien's *Lord of the Rings* and Rowling's *Harry Potter* series are often referred to indirectly, as if they are too terrifying to name. This is illustrated in Tolkien's epic when two valiant men from Gondor, Boromir and his brother Faramir, call Sauron "him that we do not name" while other characters refer to him as "The Nameless One", as well as in *Harry Potter* where one of the most prevalent codes among magical folk is that Voldemort should be called, "You-know-who" or "He-Who-Must-Not-Be-Named". The prohibition on Voldemort's name functions as a technique for keeping the wizard world intact by not invoking the name of its primary threat (Schafer 2000, p 43). It is possible that this practice is grounded in the religious superstition that one must refrain from saying the devil's name as he may hear and answer the call (Russell 1984, p77), or it may have its origins in Greek mythology according to which Hades, the Greek god of the underworld, was so feared that both mortals and gods seldom used or spoke his name for fear they might attract his attention (D'Aulaire & D'Aulaire 1962, p 56). Moreover, the 17th century English proverb, 'talk of the devil and he's bound to appear' has its roots in this ancient belief as do the numerous euphemisms for the devil such as "Old Harry" and "Old Scratch".

Another significant feature that Sauron and Voldemort share is their lack of physical form, which is analogous to the disembodied depiction of Satan in the Gospels (Pagels 1995, p 100). Notwithstanding the correlation between these two characters in this respect, the presentation of their physicality differs in accordance with the aims of each author. For instance, the greatness of Tolkien's terrifying adversary lies in his concealment (Torre 2002, p 66). For this reason Sauron is never really seen nor heard and his hidden essence contributes to the perception of his overwhelming and seemingly omnipotent power. In contrast,

Voldemort's physical presence is initially obscured but eventually resurfaces in the fourth and fifth books suggesting that he is not an invincible being. In *The Philosopher's Stone,* he is glimpsed only fleetingly when he appears as a hooded figure emerging from the shadows of the Forbidden Forest to drink the blood of a unicorn, which he desperately needs in order to stay alive, and then at the end of the book, when Harry discovers that his evil nemesis has taken possession of Quirrell's body because he lacks one of his own, "I have form only when I can share another's body" (*PS* p 213). The Dark Lord is also elusive in *The Chamber of Secrets*, but eventually materializes as a memory of his younger self contained inside a diary given to Ginny Weasley. He is kept hidden in the third book but reappears in *The Goblet of Fire* as a disembodied voice in the first chapter, and then at the end of the book where his putrefied remains are finally exposed: "The thing ... has the shape of a crouched human child ... hairless and scaly-looking, a dark, raw, reddish black" with weakened limbs and a "flat and snakelike face, with gleaming red eyes" before his true physical form is resurrected in a mystical ritual (*GF* pp 555-6). To conclude, Voldemort physical presence is fully affirmed at the end of *The Order of the Phoenix* when he materializes once again to kill Harry: "Tall, thin and black-hooded, his terrible snakelike face white and gaunt, his scarlet, split-pupilled eyes staring ... Lord Voldemort had appeared in the middle of the hall, his wand pointing at Harry.... 'I have nothing more to say to you, Potter'.... 'You have irked me too often, for too long. AVADA KEDAVRA!'" (*The Order of the Phoenix* pp 716-7[5]).

Accordingly, the initially cryptic physical and verbal descriptions of Rowling's demonic villain may seem to cast him in the role of an unstoppable satanic force (Schafer 2000, p 41), however, as the series progresses the impact of this effect is diminished when Voldemort's seemingly triumphant return to physical form actually turns him into a tangible entity capable of being defeated rather than someone who, as Dumbledore puts it is not "truly alive" and therefore "cannot be killed" (*PS* p 216). This possibility is strengthened in the sixth book with the description of the Horcruxes, objects containing portions of Voldemort's soul that if destroyed would nullify the Dark Lord's immortality, as "[w]ithout his Horcruxes, Voldemort will be a mortal man with a maimed and diminished soul'" (*The Half-Blood Prince* p 475).

An additional aspect of the Dark Lord's formlessness, namely his physical suffering despite the absence of a corporeal body, is elucidated in Jeffrey Burton Russell's book, *Lucifer: The Devil in the Middle Ages*. Russell sheds light on this issue by explaining that even though the devil lacks flesh he can still experience excruciating pain (Russell 1984, p 98), which clarifies Voldemort's description of the tremendous pain he felt at the time the Avada Kedavra curse backfired, "Aaah ... pain beyond pain ... nothing could have prepared me for it" (*GF* 566). Similar is Quirrell's inability to restrain Harry in *The Philosopher's Stone*: "Quirrell couldn't touch his bare skin, not without suffering terrible pain" (*PS* 214). There are two problems with this scene. First, it is Quirrell who touches Harry and not Voldemort, and second, Quirrel was able to touch Harry during their first encounter at the Leaky Cauldron without blistering his fingers, "P-P-Potter, stammered Professor Quirrell, grasping Harry's hand ..." (*PS* 55). The explanation for these seeming inconsistencies lies in the fact that Voldemort invaded Quirrell's body following the meeting with Harry and after the failed robbery at

Gringotts, "When I failed to steal the stone from Gringotts, he was most displeased. He punished me … decided he would have to keep a closer watch on me …" (*PS* 211). Thus, it is in fact Voldemort who touched Harry's skin and suffered the painful consequences.

Another parallel with the devil pertains to the close connection between Rowling's satanic villain and the threatening figure of Death. According to Jeffrey Burton Russell, this link is grounded in the medieval tradition where the devil is often depicted in association with Hell and Death. For example, the devil's head is often depicted as a skull to indicate this affiliation, and at times the devil is portrayed as livid or pallid, a hue related to illness and death (Russell 1984, pp 210-1).

The first indication of the Dark Lord's association with death is his name, 'Voldemort', which has several possible derivations. The Latin root for "death" is *mort* and *de* means "of". *Vol* may stem from the French *voler* (to fly), and as such *Voldemort* means "Flight of Death", or it may be from the Latin *volo* (to will or be willing), thus the name means "Will of Death". *Vol* also suggests the German verb *wollen* (want, wish, desire) and so Voldemort is he who has a "Wish of Death". In any event, there is a clear connection between the threat of death and Rowling's archetype of evil.

Voldemort's link with death is also illustrated by the effect he has on Harry. In each novel, Harry has a near death experience initiated by the Dark Lord or one of his allies. For example, during his struggle with Professor Quirrell in *The Philosopher's Stone*, he feels as if "all was lost, and fell into blackness, down … down … down … (*PS* p 214). Then in *The Chamber of Secrets*, Harry almost dies from the venom of Voldemort's pet basilisk: "Harry slid down the wall. He gripped the fang that was spreading poison through his body and wrenched it out of his arm. But he knew it was too late … (*CS* p 236), and in *The Prisoner of Azkaban*, he narrowly escapes a dementor's 'kiss'. This natural ally of the Dark Lord tries to deprive Harry of his soul, resulting in a fate worse than physical death - living death and a soulless existence: "A pair of strong, clammy hands suddenly wrapped themselves around Harry's neck. They were forcing his face upwards … he could feel its putrid breath … his mother was screaming in his ears … she was going to be the last thing he ever heard" (*Prisoner of Azkaban* p 414[7]). Next in *The Goblet of Fire*, Harry is saved from Voldemort's killing curse when their wands neutralize each other while in *The Order of the Phoenix* his body is taken over by his nemesis and he "[knows] that he [is] dead" (*OP* p 719). Finally, in *The Half-Blood Prince*, he is saved from the apparently evil Professor Snape by Buckbeak the Hippogriff: "Harry felt a white-hot, whiplike something hit him across the face and was slammed backwards into the ground. Spots of light burst in front of his eyes and for a moment all of the breath seemed to have gone from his body, then he heard a rush of wings above him and something enormous obscured the stars: Buckbeak had flown at Snape, who staggered backwards as the razor-sharp claws slashed at him" (*HBP* p 564).

Voldemort's followers, the Death Eaters, also represent the power and nature of death. Their designation is an indication of immortality owing to the belief in a number of cultures that eating death equals defeating death, and that when one person kills another the killer absorbs his victim's life-force so that feeding on his or her death increases his own power. As Reay Tannahill expounds in her book, *Flesh and Blood: A History of the Cannibal Complex*: "When a man killed an enemy, it was believed he could take possession of that enemy's life essence and vitality by the simple expedient of swallowing part of him . . . . the Aborigines of Australia, the Maoris of New Zealand, the Hurons and Iroquois of America, the Ashanti of Africa and the Uscochi of the Balkans are only a few of the many peoples who have been reported as absorbing strength from their enemies through the medium of blood, flesh, heart or broth" (Tannahill 1996, pp 15-6).

Two additional motifs associated with the devil that Rowling incorporates into the *Harry Potter* books are demonic possession and temptation. According to Christian belief, the devil is capable of attacking a person's body by entering into it (Russell 1981, p 40; de Tonquédec 1952, p 44). For example, in the scriptures Satan is said to have entered Judas before he betrayed Jesus: "Then entered Satan into Judas surnamed Iscariot …" (Luke 22:3), and "[h]e it is, to whom I shall give a sop … he gave it to Judas Iscariot, the son of Simon. And after the sop Satan entered into him" (John 13:26-27). This particular mode of attack is made against an unwilling victim and as such cannot corrupt the soul because the victim does not voluntarily surrender to the enemy (Russell 1981, p 40). Contrary to the purpose of this technique in the New Testament as an indication of Satan's ability to control the thoughts and actions of others, in Rowling's series it has two different functions. Its primary objective is to sustain Voldemort's life as he has no body: " 'See what I have become? … Mere shadow and vapour … I have a form only when I can share another's body…but there have always been those willing to let me into their hearts and minds …" (*PS* p 213). Thus, the Dark Lord is compelled to inhabit the bodies of animals, and on at least one occasion he commandeers the body of another wizard: "I sometimes inhabited animals - snakes, of course, being my preference ... Then ... A wizard wandered across my path ... he was easy to bend to my will ... and after a while, I took possession of his body, to supervise him closely as he carried out my orders" (*GF* p 567). The invasion of Quirrell's body reveals the second use of this motif in the *Harry Potter* series, namely that the Dark Lord takes possession of others in order to carry out his nefarious plans, which in this case is for Quirrell to steal the Philosopher's Stone, first from Gringotts and when that fails from the secret room at Hogwarts.

Another example of this aim is Voldemort's possession of Ginny Weasley in *The Chamber of Secrets*. In this book Voldemort describes how he took control of the girl using Tom Riddle's diary so that she would open the chamber and release the Basilisk: "Ginny Weasley opened the Chamber of Secrets. She strangled the school roosters and daubed threatening messages on the walls. She set the serpent of Slytherin on four Mudbloods, and the Squib's cat ... Of course, she didn't know what she was doing ... It was very amusing" (*CS* p 228). In accordance with the Christian belief that possessed individuals are not responsible for their actions, Dumbledore excuses the terrible behavior Ginny exhibited while under the Dark Lord's influence by explaining that she was a helpless victim and that "[o]lder and wiser wizards than she have been hoodwinked by Lord Voldemort" (*CS* p 243).

Finally, Voldemort's objective when he possesses Harry for a short time at the conclusion of *The Order of the Phoenix* is to force Dumbledore's hand, as the latter explains to Harry: "Voldemort's aim in possessing you, as he demonstrated tonight, would not have been my destruction.

It would have been yours. He hoped, when he possessed you briefly a short while ago, that I would sacrifice you in the hope of killing him" (*OP* p 730).

The second motif, temptation, involves an assault on the individual's free will as opposed to possession, which entails the assimilation of a person's body. In order to tempt an individual, the devil manipulates his or her very human desire for pleasure, and uses deceit, violence and fear in an attempt to disrupt reason and lead that person to stray from his or her faith (Russell 1981, p 115; de Tonquédec 1952, p 42). Regardless of the devil's intervention, those who give in to temptation remain responsible for the sins they commit. Lewis expresses this motif in his *Chronicles* through Jadis's temptation of Digory in *The Magician's Nephew* and of Edmund in *The Lion, the Witch and the Wardrobe*. In the former, Jadis's role as a satanic figure and a symbol of evil is emphasized when, like the serpent in Genesis 3, she tempts Digory to eat the forbidden apple: "Do you know what that fruit is? ... It is the apple of youth, the apple of life ... Eat it, Boy, eat it" (*Magicians Nephew* p 192). Then in the latter, she exploits Edmund as the White Witch by offering him a warm drink and his favorite candy, Turkish Delight. From the first bite, he is hooked, for each "piece was sweet and light to the very center and Edmund had never tasted anything more delicious." (*LWW* p 38). Driven by an insatiable hunger for more and more of the delectable sweet, Edmund eagerly replies to the witch's questions regarding his siblings.

Rowling follows in Lewis's footsteps when she integrates this motif into her *Harry Potter* novels. Her first example is Professor Quirrell who is led astray by his naiveté and curiosity and falls prey to Voldemort's deceitful explanations of good and evil: "A foolish young man I was then, full of ridiculous ideas about good and evil. Lord Voldemort showed me how wrong I was ... Since then, I have served him faithfully ..." (*PS* p 211). Then Voldemort makes an attempt to lure Harry over to the dark side. His initial plan is to threaten the boy: "Don't be a fool ... Better save your own life and join me ... or you'll meet the same end as your parents ...", and then he tries emotional blackmail, "... your mother needn't have died ... she was trying to protect you ... Now give me the stone, unless you want her to have died in vain" (*PS* 213). However, Harry's strong sense of morality and his ability to see through the tempter's deceitful lies help him resist the Dark Lord's enticements.

Lord Voldemort's next and most satisfying conquest is Peter Pettigrew, a former schoolmate and close friend of Harry's father, whose treachery is revealed in *The Prisoner of Azkaban*. Pettigrew, aptly nicknamed Wormtail owing to his dual nature as a rat whether in human or animal form, is the double-crossing wizard who betrayed Harry's parents in order to prove his allegiance to Lord Voldemort. When confronted regarding his treacherous past, Pettigrew argues that Voldemort would have killed him if he had refused, but Sirius Black knows him well enough to see beyond this excuse to his real motivation: cowardice and self-interest. He accuses Pettigrew of standing in the shadow of "people who were stronger and more powerful" than himself (*PA* p 397), and of "never [doing] anything for anyone unless [he] could see what was in it for [him]." (*PA* p 399). Furthermore, Pettigrew was easily corrupted due to his low self-esteem. For instance, Sirius believed he would be the best secret keeper for the Potters precisely because "Voldemort ... would never dream they'd use a weak, talentless thing" (*PA* p 398), but the Dark Lord took advantage of this weakness and provided Pettigrew with a sense of self worth, as Black says, "… it must have been the finest moment in your miserable life, telling Voldemort you could hand him the Potters." (*PA* p 398).

Voldemort's "faithful servant" in *The Goblet of Fire* is another of the Dark Lord's conquests. The servant turns out to be Barty Crouch, Jr., a man motivated by his intense hatred for his father, a ministry official, who allowed his son to be sent to the horrific wizard prison rather than risk his reputation by attempting to defend him. Given the difficult relationship between father and son it is not surprising that Crouch, Jr. turned to evil for consolation and revenge. He willingly joins the Dark Lord so that he can have "the pleasure … the very great pleasure … of killing [his] father" (*GF* p589).

Regardless of motivation, each of these characters, Quirrel, Wormtail and Crouch, voluntarily succumbs to Voldemort's seductive power and forceful will, which bends weak and power hungry wizards to his pernicious bidding. However, the Dark Lord's power is not without restrictions. Similar to the biblical devil whose power to harm humanity is great but limited and held in check by an omnipotent God who has the power to destroy him (Russell 1981, p 32; Farrell 1952, p 5), the devil in Rowling's works is powerful but not invincible. Professor McGonagall verifies this when she relates the rumor, later corroborated by Voldemort, that the Dark Lord's powers were destroyed when he failed to kill baby Harry: "He couldn't kill that little boy. No one knows why, or how, but they're saying that when he couldn't kill Harry Potter, Voldemort's power broke – and that's why he's gone" (*PS* p 15).

Moreover, Voldemort fears and despises Albus Dumbledore, the soft spoken and kindhearted headmaster at Hogwarts, who is almost universally revered in the wizarding world as "the greatest wizard of modern times" (*PS* p 77). Dumbledore is the antithesis of Lord Voldemort, but despite his gentle exterior the headmaster has a backbone of solid steel, which is overwhelmingly evident at the end of *The Goblet of Fire* when he realizes the extent of Barty Crouch Jr.'s treacherous duplicity. "At that moment, Harry fully understood for the first time why people said Dumbledore was the only wizard Voldemort had ever feared. The look upon Dumbledore's face … was more terrible than Harry could ever have imagined … There was cold fury in every line of the ancient face; a sense of power radiated from Dumbledore as though he was giving off burning heat" (*GF* pp589-90).

The Dark Lord's apprehension regarding Dumbledore is similar to the Devil's fear and hatred of God and is also reminiscent of Jadis' fear of Aslan in *The Lion, the Witch and the Wardrobe*. "A howl and a gibber of dismay went up from the creatures when they first saw the great Lion … for a moment even the Witch herself seemed to be struck with fear (*LWW* p 166). However, despite her anxiety, the White Witch is determined to destroy the source of her trepidation and gloats over her victory in the moment before slaying her nemesis: "Understand that you have given me Narnia forever, you have lost your own life and you have not saved [Edmund's]. In that knowledge, despair and die" (*LWW* p 170). It should be noted that the witch's victory is short lived as at the end of the book Aslan is resurrected and Edmund is morally saved.

Tom Riddle behaves in a similar manner at the end of *The Chamber of Secrets* before he sets the Basilisk on Harry. "Now, Harry, "I'm going to teach you a lesson. Let's match the powers of Lord Voldemort, heir of Salazar Slytherin, against famous Harry Potter, and the best weapons Dumbledore can give him" (*CS* p 233). Despite the danger, Harry confirms that the Dark Lord's fear of Dumbledore is still a significant weakness when he threatens his enemy by evoking the headmaster's name: "the greatest wizard in the world is Albus Dumbledore … [he] saw through you when you were at school and he still frightens you now … [Dumbledore's] not as gone as you might think!" (*CS* p 232). At this point, all Harry wants is to stand up to Voldemort, though it immediately becomes clear that his threat has teeth when the words herald the arrival of Dumbledore's pet phoenix, Fawkes, without whom Harry would be unable to defeat Tom Riddle.

In addition to the biblical motifs already mentioned, the Christian conceptualization of the devil has also been significantly influenced by folkloric elements from numerous cultures (Russell 1984, p 62), and Rowling has successfully integrated a number of these demonic symbols into her series including colors associated with the devil, the Devil's Mark, the satanic black mass, and the concept of secret societies.

The colors traditionally linked with the Devil are black, red and green. For example, in many folk sources the Devil's skin or clothes are black, and he appears in the form of a black animal, or as a black rider on a black horse. He is also associated with red, the color of blood and fire, and is often presented with flaming red hair, beard or clothes. Furthermore, the Devil is occasionally depicted in green due to his image as a hunter with souls as his prey (Russell 1984, p 69), and the color green is most emphasized in the *Harry Potter* series. The novels contain numerous examples indicating a strong connection between this color and the Dark Lord's malicious powers. To begin with, green is the color adopted by Lord Voldemort's house, Slytherin, which admits the power hungry and ambitious students who are not above using the dark arts to achieve their aims. Second, the Chamber of Secrets, which houses a horrific monster programmed to eradicate the 'unworthy students' at Hogwarts, has many 'green' characteristics. The wall-like door to the chamber has "two entwined serpents … their eyes set with great glinting emeralds" (*CS* p 225), and inside the room there is an "odd, greenish gloom that fill[s] the place". Moreover, the creature that inhabits the chamber, the Basilisk, is an "enormous serpent, bright, poisonous green" (*CS* p 234). Third, the Avada Kedavra curse emits a blinding flash of green light, which is apparent during Harry's flashbacks of his parents' murder, when Voldemort kills the Riddles' gardener, while Moody aka Crouch Jr. enacts the killing curse in a Defense Against the Dark Arts class, when Wormtail kills Cedric in *The Goblet of Fire* and during Voldemort's battle with Dumbledore in *The Order of the Phoenix*. To end with, Voldemort's satanic sign, the Dark Mark, is also green: "something vast, green, and glittering erupted from the patch of darkness … it was a colossal skull, comprised of what looked like emerald stars … it rose higher and higher, blazing in a haze of greenish smoke, etched against the black sky like a new constellation" (*GF* p 115).

This fear-provoking sign is Rowling's version of the "Devil's Mark" (*stigmata diabolic*), also known as the "Devil's Seal" (*sigillum diabolic*). According to theories current in the sixteenth and seventeenth centuries, the devil affixed this brand of ownership on his followers at their initiation to designate the formation of a pact between the Evil One and his devotee (Colbert 2001, p 55; Ogden 1997, p 49). The medieval demonologist, Ludovico Maria Sinistrari, described the mark in his book, *Demoniality*, as varying in shape and size. It is usually in the form of an animal such as a hare, spider, puppy, dormouse or toad's foot, and is commonly imprinted on a secret part of the body. For instance men may have it under an eyelid or armpit, on the lips or shoulders while women generally have it on their breasts or private parts (Sinistrari in Ogden 1997, p 55).

In the fourth *Harry Potter* book, Lord Voldemort's Dark Mark is in the shape of a "skull ... with a serpent protruding from its mouth like a tongue" (*GF* p 115). Worn by the Evil One's disciples, the Death Eaters, the brand is imprinted on its bearer's forearm but can also be conjured out of thin air as it is at the Quidditch World Cup. This indicates that even though the symbol has its roots in folk belief, Rowling's Dark Mark has several unique features as well. For instance, Snape explains that in addition to its original application as a sign of the bond between Lord Voldemort and the Death Eaters, the mark also functions as a means for fellow Death Eaters to identify each other and as a way for the Dark Lord to summon his followers. "When he touched the Mark of any Death Eater, we were to Disapparate, and Apparate, instantly, at his side" (*GF* p 616). Furthermore, the mark evokes anxiety, panic and terror owing to the fact that the Dark Lord and his minions launched it into the air whenever they killed someone, as Mr. Weasley explains, "[t]he terror it inspired . . . . Just picture coming home, and finding the Dark Mark hovering outside your house, and knowing what you're about to find inside . . . . Everyone's worst fear ... the very worst ..." (*GF* p 127).

Former Death Eaters react strongly to the re-emergence of the imprint on their arms. Karkaroff is profoundly alarmed at its intensification because he realizes that it is a sign of the Dark Lord's return, and he will surely be punished for his cowardice and treachery. Snape is equally troubled as his life may be in jeopardy for rejoining Dumbledore and spying on his former master (Killinger 2002, p 173).

The lightning bolt scar on Harry's forehead is also connected to the folklore surrounding the devil. For instance, Satan's fall from heaven is associated in the New Testament with lightning: "And he said unto them, I beheld Satan as lightening fall from heaven" (Luke 10:18) while Harry's original wound is described as "… a curiously shaped cut, like a bolt of lightning" (*PS* p 17). Harry later learns from Hagrid that the lightening bolt scar is a remnant of the powerful Avada Kedavra curse used by the dark wizard, Lord Voldemort, against Harry and his parents: "Never wondered how you got that mark on yer forehead? That was no ordinary cut. That's what yeh get when a powerful, evil curse touches yeh …" (*PS* p 45). This is not to say that Harry's scar is a sign of his satanic nature, rather that Lord Voldemort who inflicted the curse upon an innocent infant and caused the scar is a new incarnation of the devil. Moreover, the thunderbolt shape of the scar calls to mind the stylized "SS" tattoo of Hitler's special forces and is similar to the "mark of Cain". Thus, the scar may function as a means of setting Harry apart or perhaps to reinforce his opposition to Lord Voldemort on a moral level as the scar is a sign of the latter's evil.

Another folk element appearing at the end of *The Goblet of Fire* is a ritualistic ceremony similar to a satanic black mass, which is used to raise the Dark Lord's new body. The black mass is a parody of the

Roman Catholic liturgy, ascribed to worshipers of Satanism, and it is also fitting that Voldemort's demonic resurrection occurs in a graveyard, among the dead, where he feels most at home. As a black priest, Voldemort concocts a magical potion and orchestrates a diabolical ceremony that nullifies the traditional Christian sacraments. For example, the potion's ingredients: the bone of the father, flesh of the servant and blood of the enemy invert the Eucharist sacrament consisting of the blood of the Savior, flesh of the Master and Spirit of the Father (Granger 2002, p 236).

The third and final element is that the Dark Lord's followers, or Death Eaters, can be compared to different secret societies such as the Knights Templar, the Illuminati and the Ku Klux Klan, groups that have often been connected with the occult, devil worship and satanic rituals.

The Templars were founded by a French knight, Hugues de Patan, during the crusades for the expressed purpose of protecting pilgrims traveling to Jerusalem. However, their reputation as harsh and exceptional fighters did not prevent mounting suspicion resulting from their religious independence and financial power (Barrett 2000, p 51). The charges against the order included a secret alliance with the Saracens, acts of debauchery and other recognized abominations such as homosexual behavior; scorning the sacraments; trampling, spitting or urinating on the cross; blaspheming against Christ, and worshiping the head of a demon named Baphomet (Barrett 2000, p 53). The fact that meetings and initiation rites were held in secret counted against the Templars as they were unable to prove, through outside witnesses, that they were innocent of the charges brought against them (Barrett 2000, p 54). Similarly, the Death Eaters are powerful men in the wizard community who seem to worship Voldemort as their spiritual master. For example, the Dark Lord's disciples gather in a graveyard when the Evil One summons them, and they pledge their continued allegiance to him. "Voldemort stood in silence, waiting for them. Then one of the Death Eater's fell to his knees, crawled towards Voldemort, and kissed the hem of his black robes … The Death Eaters behind him did the same …" (*GF* p 561).

The Death Eaters can also be compared to the Order of Perfectibilists, also known as the Enlightened, or the Illuminati. The order, founded in 1776 by a Bavarian named Adam Weishaupt, was overtly political and declared its aims to eliminate monarchies, abolish the clergy, eradicate private ownership and create a Utopian state in which all men were free and equal. As a result of their revolutionary ideas, the Illuminati were outlawed, and according to conspiracy theorists, disappeared underground only to reappear from time to time under assorted names in order to reassert their political and financial influence in the world (Barrett 2000, p 86). Similarly, the Death Eaters support their master's political agenda, which, according to Rowling, consists of Lord Voldemort's obsession with the idea of having complete and unopposed supremacy in the Wizard world. As she stated in a live interview, he intends to dominate Europe and will then turn his attention to the rest of the world (Scholastic chat[8]). In this respect, the Dark Lord is comparable to Tolkien's villain, Sauron, whose zeal to obtain the One Ring and dominate everything and everyone in Middle-earth is supported by the servile Nazgûl, and to Lewis's selfish, cruel and merciless witch, Jadis, who is fixated on bending others to her own will and is determined to keep Narnia under her thumb with the help of her eager admirers, the Black Dwarfs, Ghouls and Boggles (Ford 1980, p 307).

Finally, the Death Eaters' racial prejudices lend credence to a comparison with the Ku Klux Klan. A Confederate Army general, Nathan Bedford Forrest, established the Klan, a group opposed to the abolition of slavery and angered at the interference of northern Republicans in the internal policies of southern states (Barrett 2000, p 182). The resemblance between the Klan and Voldemort's Death Eaters is especially obvious at the end of the Quidditch World Cup, with the latter's torture of a Muggle family invoking images of a Ku Klux Klan rally. Other similarities include their menacing robes and hoods, flaming wands (torches) and destructive behavior.

It is important to note that even though Voldemort shares many qualities with the devil and other literary characters such as Tolkien's Sauron and C.S. Lewis's Jadis, he is ultimately the embodiment of Rowling's conception of evil. Consequently, Voldemort possesses some character traits that have been exclusively constructed to suit Rowling's idea of the devil. One of these constructs is the Dark Lord's obsession with immortality, which stems from his belief that "[t]here is nothing worse than death" (*OP* p 718). Voldemort's lust for eternal life signifies the essence of his depravity as it violates the laws of nature decreeing that in order for new lives to begin old lives must end. For example, in *The Philosopher's Stone* Voldemort wishes to possess the "Elixer of Life", (*PS* p 213), which will not only restore his physical form but will help him elude death as well, and in *The Chamber of Secrets*, he is immortalized within the pages of Tom Riddles's diary. Then, in *The Goblet of Fire*, he reminds his supporters of his evil intentions: "You know my goal – to conquer death" and claims to have taken "the steps … to guard [himself] against mortal death", which explains how he managed to survive the ricochet of his seemingly fatal curse: "it appeared that one or more of my experiments had worked … for I had not been killed, though the curse should have done it" (*GF* p 566). Finally, *The Half-Blood Prince* clarifies the heinous steps the Dark Lord has taken to ensure his longevity, "Voldemort . . . . particularly wanted . . . . an opinion on . . . . what would happen to the wizard so determined to evade death that he would be prepared to murder many times, rip his soul repeatedly, so as to store it in many, separately concealed Horcruxes" (*HBP* p 467).

Moreover, it appears that the Dark Lord's insane quest to ensure that his power goes on forever has destroyed the basic human traits that make life worth living (Bridger 2002, p 110). Consequently, in *The Philosopher's Stone* when Voldemort slays a sacred unicorn in order to drink its blood, he commits a truly heinous act that curses him forever. As Firenze the centaur explains, "[o]nly one who has nothing to lose, and everything to gain, would commit such a crime. The blood of the unicorn will keep you alive, even if you are an inch from death, but at a terrible price. You have slain something pure and defenseless to save yourself, and you will have a half-life, a cursed life, from the moment the blood touches your lips" (*PS* p 188).

Another original aspect of Lord Voldemort's demonic nature is his racist hatred for Muggles, which was influenced by the despicable deeds of one of history's most diabolical tyrants, Adolf Hitler. Rowling's evil antagonist shares many of the same qualities as the leader of Germany's Third Reich including an obsession with racial purity as well as feelings of inferiority resulting from his own mixed heritage (Nel 2001, p 44).

Analogous to Hitler's ethnic cleansing of the Jewish race, Voldemort and his Nazi-like loyalists promote a racial ideology and plan to exterminate the wizards of Muggle extraction. The plot of *The Chamber of Secrets* makes it clear that Harry and his friends are on the verge of witnessing an ethnic war, which may result in genocide against Muggles and half-Muggles similar to the Holocaust. For example, Draco Malfoy and his father Lucius, a faithful supporter of the dethroned Dark Lord, employ a racially charged vocabulary, referring to themselves as "pure bloods" and to the mixed-blood students at Hogwarts with denigrating epithets like "filthy Mudblood" (*CS* p 86). Moreover, Draco introduces Harry to the racial politics of the wizarding world early in the first book when he warns him about associating with the right people: "You'll soon find out some wizarding families are much better than others, Potter. You don't want to go making friends with the wrong sort" (*PS* p 81), and later during the Sorting Ceremony, Draco is appropriately placed in Slytherin house, which has a nasty reputation for devious members who dabble in the dark arts and believe in the importance of racial purity, a belief that goes back the house's founding member, Salazar Slytherin. As the ghostly Professor Binns explains, "'Slytherin wished to be more *selective* about the students admitted to Hogwarts. He believed that magical learning should be kept within all-magic families. He disliked taking students of Muggle parentage, believing them to be untrustworthy'" (*CS* p 114). Thus, Voldemort's eagerness to destroy anyone standing in the way of his power-hungry plans for world domination, namely Muggles and those who support them, is in line with the racist ideology developed by his spiritual father, Salazar Slytherin.

Furthermore, in an online interview Rowling likened the Dark Lord's fanatical obsession with racial purity to "Hitler and the Aryan ideal to which he did not conform at all, himself". Thus, "[Voldemort] takes what he perceives to be a defect in himself, in other words the non-purity of his blood, and he projects it onto others" and in doing so "attempts to exterminate in them what he hates in himself" (Solomon interview[9]). This point is most apparent in *The Chamber of Secrets* where Tom Riddle reveals that he is part Muggle and that he despises his Muggle heritage because his father deserted his mother: "You think I was going to use my filthy Muggle father's name for ever? … I, keep the name of a foul, common Muggle, who abandoned me before I was born, just because he found out his wife was a witch? No …" (*CS* p 231), and in *The Goblet of Fire*, where Voldemort describes how he took his revenge on the man who condemned him to a bleak future within the walls of a Muggle orphanage, "… I vowed to find him … I revenged myself upon him, that fool who gave me his name … *Tom Riddle* …" (*GF* p 561). Consequently, Voldemort's determination to retaliate against all 'Mudbloods' stems from his own self-hatred, and his belief in the superiority of wizards with purely magical bloodlines is parallel to Hitler's position that people of pure Aryan descent are perfect examples of humanity.

In sum, the ultimate personification of absolute evil in Rowling's series appears in the form of Harry Potter's nemesis, the malignant Lord Voldemort. This character constitutes a new incarnation of the conventional figure of the devil as it combines numerous religious, cultural and literary resources with modern traits well suited to the author's progressive vision. Moreover, the folk traditions included into the construction of this character reveal Rowling's considerable knowledge of original demonic motifs as well as her skillful manipulation of these themes.

For instance, the devilish qualities integrated into the Dark Lord's character are representative of several mythological deities. These characteristics include Voldemort's brutality and cruelty which are reminiscent of Set, the Egyptian god of darkness; his deceit and treachery which suggest the involvement of Loki, the Scandinavian trickster, and, of course, his kinship with snakes, which evokes associations with the Greek monster, Typhon. Despite these similarities, Rowling's Dark Lord parallels the Christian devil more than any other demonic entity as indicated by his selfish disregard for the lives of others, his willingness to manipulate the truth, his penchant for tempting or possessing the innocent as well as his obsessive desire to destroy humankind and rule the world. Moreover, several historical and literary figures such as Sauron in J. R. R. Tolkien's *Lord of the Rings* trilogy and Jadis in C. S. Lewis's *Chronicles of Narnia* as well as Adolf Hitler contributed to the depiction of the Lord Voldemort's demonic nature.

Notwithstanding the similarities between Voldemort and the aforementioned literary and cultural 'devils', Rowling has endowed her demonic creation with a number of unique constructs such as his desire for immortality as well as his obsession with racial purity. These imaginative conceptions function in conjunction with the more traditional themes to form a character that encompasses every conceivable aspect of evil, thereby representing all that is depraved and vile in our times.

Notes

1. Additional references to this novel will be noted in the text as GF.
2. Further references to this work will be noted as CS.
3. Quotations from this book will be indicated in the text as PS.
4. Additional quotations from this book will be indicated as LWW.
5. References to this text will be noted as OP.
6. Further quotes from this text will be marked as HBP.
7. Subsequent references to this novel will be noted as PA.
8. Scholastic Interview, October 2000. http://www.scholastic.com/harrypotter/author/transcript2.htm
9. Solomon, E. "J.K. Rowling Interview" Hot Type. CBC, 2000. http://www.cbc.ca/programs/sites/hottype_rowlingcomplete.html

References

Barrett, David. V., 2000, *Secret Societies: From the Ancient and Arcane to the Modern and Clandestine*, Blandford, London.

Bridger, Francis, 2002, *A Charmed Life: The Spirituality of Potterworld*, Image Books, Doubleday, New York.

Colbert, David, 2001, *The Magical Worlds of Harry Potter: A Treasure of Myths, Legends and Fascinating Facts*, Puffin Books, London.

D'Aulaire, Ingri & D'Aulaire, Edgar Parin, 1962, *D'Aulaires Book of Greek Myths*, Doubleday, New York.

de Tonquédec, Joseph, 1952, 'Some aspects of Satan's activity in the world', in *Satan*, Sheed & Ward, New York, pp 40-51..

Farrell, Walter, 1952, 'The Devil Himself, in *Satan*, Sheed & Ward, New York, pp 3-18.

Ford, Paul F., 1980, *Companion to Narnia*, Harper & Row Publishers, San Francisco.

Gordon, Stuart, 1993, *The Encyclopedia of Myths and Legends*, Headline Book Publishing, London.

Granger, John., 2002, *The Hidden Key to Harry Potter*, Zossima Press, Port Hadlock, WA.

Hassan, Riffat, 1997, 'Feminist theology as a means of combating injustice toward women in Muslim communities and culture', in William Cenker (Ed), *Evil and the Response of World Religion*, Paragon House, St. Paul, MN, pp 80-95.

Helms, Randel, 1974, *Tolkien's World*, Thames and Hudson, London.

Killinger, John, 2002, *God, The Devil, and Harry Potter*, Thomas Dunne Books, New York.

Lewis, C. S., 2002 [1955], *The Chronicles of Narnia: The Magician's Nephew*, Harper Trophy, New York.

Lewis, C. S., 2002 [1955], *The Chronicles of Narnia: The Lion, the Witch and the Wardrobe*, Harper Trophy, New York.

Nel, Philip, 2001, J.K. *Rowling's Harry Potter Novels: A Reader's Guide*, Continuum, New York.

Ogden, Tom, 1997, *Wizards and Sorcerers: From Abracadabra to Zoroaster*, Facts on File Inc, New York.

Pagels, Elaine H., 1995, *The Origin of Satan*, Random House, New York.

Parkin, David, 1985, *The Anthropology of Evil*, Basil Blackwell Ltd., Oxford.

Rowling, J. K., 1997, *Harry Potter and The Philosopher's Stone*, Bloomsbury, London.

Rowling, J. K., 1998, *Harry Potter and The Chamber of Secrets*. Bloomsbury, London.

Rowling, J. K., 1999, *Harry Potter and The Prisoner of Azkaban*, Bloomsbury, London.

Rowling, J. K., 2000, *Harry Potter and The Goblet of Fire*, Bloomsbury, London.

Rowling, J. K., 2003, *Harry Potter and The Order of the Phoenix*, Bloomsbury, London.

Rowling, J. K., 2005, *Harry Potter and The Half-Blood Prince*, Bloomsbury, London.

Rudwin, Maximilian, 1973, *The Devil in Legend and Literature*, Open Court Publishing Company, La Salle, Ill.

Russell, Jeffrey Burton, 1977, *The Devil: Perceptions of Evil from Antiquity to Primitive Christianity*, Cornell University Press, London.

Russell, Jeffrey Burton, 1981, *Satan: The Early Christian Tradition*, Cornell University Press, London.

Russell, Jeffrey Burton, 1984, *Lucifer: The Devil in the Middle Ages*, Cornell University Press, Ithaca, NY.

Schafer, Elizabeth D., 2000, *Exploring Harry Potter*, Beacham Publishing Corp., Osprey, FL Osprey, FL.

Sinistrari, Ludovico Maria., 1927, *Demoniality*, translated by Rev. Montague Summers, The Fortune Press, London.

Tannahill, Reay., 1996, *Flesh and Blood: A History of the Cannibal Complex*, Abacus, London.

Taylor, Donald, 1985, 'Theological thoughts about evil' in David Parkin (Ed), *The Anthropology of Evil*, Basil Blackwell Ltd., Oxford, pp 26-41.

Torre, Michael, 2002, 'The portrait of evil in *The Lord of the Rings*: Reflections personal, literary, and theological', *Logos*, 5, 4, pp 65-69.

"Delivered From Enchantment": Cotton Mather, W. B. O. Peabody, and the Struggle against Magic

Carl Sederholm

Recent studies of magical traditions and their impact on American culture suggest that the questions we have asked about religion, culture, literature, and personal identity need to be largely rethought. David Hall, for example, recently argued that "the people of seventeenth-century New England lived in a world that had not one but several different meanings" (1989, p 3). Such heterodoxy, while not completely surprising, challenges the long-held notion that seventeenth century religion, particularly in New England, all stemmed from a common way of thinking and believing. Part of the "several meanings" these people enjoyed, Hall suggests, includes those that developed through the persistent belief in the reality of the supernatural, whether based on Christian tradition, magic, or folklore. Moreover, Jon Butler's own *Awash in a Sea of Faith* argues further that scholars of early American history and religion need to "attach less importance to Puritanism as the major force in shaping religion in America and more importance to the religious eclecticism that has long been prominent" (1990, p 2). The result, Butler argues, will be a new series of questions, ones that will lead to a completely new understanding of the development of religion in America. Finally, Arthur Versluis recently argued that the study of Western esoteric beliefs will demonstrate that they are "intimately woven throughout the American Renaissance, and were much more widespread in America before this period than many scholars have cared to acknowledge" (2001, pp 6-7).

What such claims hold in common is that the study of magical beliefs and practices will generate a new series of interpretations about the general nature of American culture. Nevertheless, the challenges posed by these studies continue to lack strong discussion, particularly in literary studies. Indeed, the study of American literature has mostly been hindered by a lack of interest in exploring the deep interconnections between the two subjects. My own view is that we ought to respond to Versluis' claim by studying to what extent magical beliefs and practices were intertwined in American culture in the past and, from there, attempt to explain the significance of those deep connections. In this paper, I examine how two very different individuals — Cotton Mather and W. B. O. Peabody — attempted to deny the place of magic in their lives. What they discover, however, is that there is an irreplaceable tension between belief in magic and belief in some form of orthodoxy, whether religious or scientific. The result of this tension suggests that there can be no simple dividing line between religion and magic, science and faith, and reason and belief.

Cotton Mather often expressed a desire to become one of God's most powerful servants; he was especially interested in receiving the kind of grace that would "make [him] a Man of an *excellent Spirit*, one whom God could "make a singular Use . . . in the *Awakening* of my people" (1957, pp 146-7). So strong was this desire that Mather began to see himself as a specially chosen messenger of God's future kingdom on the earth, a kind of Puritan John the Baptist who would help prepare the way for the coming of God. As he expresses it, "This Day, I likewise obtained of God, that Hee would make use of mee, as of a *John*, to bee an Herald of the Lord's Kingdome now approaching. and *the Voice crying in the Wilderness*, for Preparation thereunto" (1957, p 147).

Armed with this sense of mission, Mather quickly turned his attention against what he defined as the powers of the Devil as they manifested themselves in Salem Village. In particular, Mather cried out against what he called the "horrible *Enchantments*, and *Posessions*" that he witnessed during his services there (1957, p 147). Mather's use of the term "enchantments" to describe the workings of Satan in Salem Village is hardly surprising. After all, Mather believed that Satan would stop at nothing to destroy the New England Puritan settlement in America; enchantments would serve well, particularly because of their ability to mesmerize people with their charms and their almost miraculous feel. But there is another element to Mather's use of the term "enchantments" that is significant. Indeed, by drawing on a word long known for its associations with magic, Mather suggests that Satan's power is not only real, but that it can be used to deceive members of the church away from their true quest for grace.

Mather was no stranger to the influence of magic and the occult, even among his fellow Puritans. As Jon Butler demonstrates, Mather "ruefully acknowledged the commonality of occult practice in New England, including the use of charms, enchantments, and most dangerous of all, witchcraft" (1990, p 72). Indeed, despite his complaints against enchantments, some of Mather's writings reveal that he was not only familiar with the language of magical practices but that he sometimes used them in his teachings. Butler argues further that Mather sometimes "borrow[ed] subtly from the vocabulary of magic to describe Christian defenses against their temptations and effects" (1990, p 72). Consider Mather's use of the term "amulets" in his book *The Angel of Bethesda*. In this text, Mather transforms concept of a magical amulet into a metaphor for Christian practice. He explains that in times of crisis, people can draw on the "amulets" of prayer, faith, and holiness in the healing process (cited in Butler 1990, p 72). In this sense, Mather wants to persuade his readers that Christian practices hold the source of true magic and that the best amulets they can use are those already prescribed by the church. Mather suggests that there is an easily identifiable difference between Satan's magic and God's grace even though he draws on the same vocabulary to describe each one. Mather hoped that by recasting faith, prayer, and holiness as "amulets," his audience would understand that to petition the invisible world, one must employ study, fasting, and prayer rather than charms, amulets, and spells. But Mather was mistaken. When he used the term "amulets" to describe Christian practice, he invited the language of enchantments a place within the very theology he hoped to purify from error (cited in Butler 1990, p 72). Faced with a people openly interested in enchantments, Mather and others attempted to instruct them that, despite the efficacy of some enchantments, their spiritual dangers were not worth the occasional positive result. His father Increase Mather explains that even though magical practices may heal a person of illness, "it were better for a Man to remain sick all his dayes, yea . . . he had better die than go to the Devil for Health" (cited in Butler 1990, p 73).

My discussion of Cotton Mather so far focuses mainly on his sense of enchantments as a kind of decoy of true religious faith. Indeed, his descriptions of enchantments suggest that they are something external, something that can be easily exorcized from the community. In his December 1692 diary, however, Mather described the enchantments as something that comes from within, almost as if they were a kind of personal sin. Mather begins his comments with a description of what he referred to as his "Hearty Wishes" (1957, p 158). Throughout his description of these wishes, Mather again stresses his desire to serve God and to free himself from the kinds of things that would hinder this service. As I suggested above, such hopes were common for a man with Mather's aspirations; indeed, he often proclaimed his religious commitment (and his anxieties) in his personal writings. Moreover, his "Hearty Wishes" only make up less than a page of text, hardly the stuff that warrants close examination. Yet, Mather's comments may be more crucial than we suppose, particularly because they help demonstrate that his own relationship with magic and the occult may be much more embedded in his sense of religion than we previously supposed.

Mather's "Hearty Wishes" reflect not only his spiritual hopes, but also his doubts and fears concerning his future spiritual state (1957, p 158) In particular, Mather expresses his wish to be personally free of "Enchantments" (1957, p 158). Whereas before he applied that term to the people of Salem Village, he now sees it as something more personal. As Mather expresses it:

"I have ever now and then gone to the Good God, with the most solemn Addresses, *that I may bee altogether delivered from* Enchantments; *that no* Enchantment *on my Mind, may hinder mee from seeing or doing any thing for the Glory of God, or dispose mee to any thing whereat God may bee displeased.* The Reason of this Wish is, because I beleeve that a real and proper *Enchantment*, of the *Divels*, do's *blind*, and *move* the Minds of the most of Men; even in Instances of every sort. But I remember, that much *Fasting* as well as *Prayer*, is necessary, to obtain a Rescue from *Enchantment*" (1957, p 158).

Mather's comments are notable primarily because of their repeated emphasis on the term 'enchantment.' What does Mather mean by his repeated use of this word? Moreover, what is the relationship between enchantments and sin?

Whereas Mather formerly believed enchantments to be a kind of external torment for others, he now sees them as an internal threat to himself. Returning to his December 1692 comments on enchantments, we see that Mather uses the term to describe incidents in his own life. In fact, he writes, though his words clearly form a kind of prayer, that he would be "altogether delivered from Enchantments" (1957, p 147). As a minister, Mather was bound to recognize the presence of enchantments in others, but now he faced the possibility that he, too, struggles with enchantments. Mather suggests that his own struggle against enchantment is so strong that he can do nothing to alleviate it. Mather would resist enchantments, yet he recognizes that they have so many manifestations as to be nearly impossible to categorize and control. Mather therefore links his prayer to be "altogether delivered from Enchantments" to the theological staple of deliverance. As in most

Puritan captivity narratives, Mather uses the notion of captivity to signify a spiritual challenge from which only God can "altogether deliver" (1957, p 158). Mather's phrase evokes the tone and the mood of a captivity narrative, only here he believes himself the captive and Enchantments the captor. Mather's "most solemn Addresses" toward "the Good God" therefore represent his wish to be personally free from the effects of enchantment (1957, p 158). As long as he is under the influence of enchantments, Mather feels a breach in his faith, a breach that signifies a different relationship to the invisible world than Puritanism ought to provide. In short, so long as Mather remains under the spell of enchantments, he cannot develop the kind of faith in the "Good God" that he hoped to obtain through his "hearty wishes" (1957, p 158).

By applying the term "enchantments" to himself, Mather creates an analogy between the force of enchantments and the temptations of Satan. His claim that he wanted to be "delivered from Enchantments," then, suggests that he would be free of the regular and consistent presence of Satanic influence (1957, p 158). Mather underscores this point when he notes that the Devil employs "a real and proper Enchantment" to "blind" and "move" the hearts and "minds of most men" (1957, p 158). As a minister, Mather frequently wrote and taught concerning the fallen nature of mankind and the sinful effects of Original Sin. Moreover, he recognized that human beings deserved the punishment of eternal damnation and that there was nothing anyone could do to merit the rewards of heaven. As in the case of temptation, enchantments can occur in every setting, every condition. According to Mather, Satan's brand of enchantments, just as with temptations, covers "instances of every sort" (1957, p 158). The problem, Mather suggests, is that "enchantments" are beyond his immediate control. They are so frequent and recurring, in fact, that only "much fasting as well as Prayer" can overcome them (1957, p 158).

Some readers may argue that Mather's association between freedom from enchantments and release from Satanic influence is so obvious and generic that it hardly warrants comment. After all, Mather was not alone in praying for deliverance from sin, the devil, and hell; in fact, other Puritan writers were much more interesting, if not eloquent, in their own pleas for deliverance. Why spend all this time on Mather's complaint against enchantments? The answer to this question lies in Mather's implication that enchantments are so deeply embedded in his life that he will likely never be free of them. Indeed, Mather's comments seem to beg God to allow that "no Enchantment on my mind may hinder me from seeing or doing anything for the Glory of God, or dispose mee to any thing whereat God may bee displeased" (1957, p 158). Here, Mather seems to define enchantments in terms of his personal fear of doing anything that would be deliberately or even unconsciously sinful. Because Mather was a Puritan minister, his public confession was that God may be found at the heart of everything good. What bothered him, however, was the recognition that there could be moments, perhaps even while confessing God's Sovereignty, where there would remain in his own heart an inclination to deny Him and to sin against Him.

Mather's plea against enchantments, then, reflects his desire to be freed from any tendency to sin or to doubt in any way. In other words, Mather suggests that enchantments themselves may be understood in terms of his own mortal weaknesses. Though Mather is certainly not the first to wish for freedom from mortal drives and ambitions, his request seems odd in the face of Puritan belief of innate depravity. After all, the *sina qua non* of New England Puritanism is that humankind is depraved and therefore incapable of becoming permanently free of the tendency to sin. By pleading for release from enchantments, Mather seems to be realizing that not even he can control his sinful and fallen state; the means of committing sin are simply too numerous. To hope for freedom from this state, then, is to commit an awful act of presumption—one that assumes God will grant him power over his own fallen state. One of the firmest tenets of Puritanism is that God alone chooses from among his fallen people who will be the subjects of salvation. Nowhere does that suggest that election will bring perfection. If God were to grant his request, Mather would be free from the very nature that compels him to worship and to pray in the first place. Though sincere in his wish, Mather's hope to be free of enchantments indicates that he wants to develop a different relationship to the invisible world than that suggested by the orthodox teachings of his faith. What Mather really means by his request is that he wants to obtain freedom from the challenges of life itself. Such freedom can only be seen as a kind of Faustian bargain, one that will increase his power at the cost of an even greater distance from God.

According to Mather, then, the state of being enchanted refers to the state of having a different relationship to the basis of faith than orthodoxy teaches, and this is why they recur in "instances of every sort" (1957, p 158). Enchantments are so inveterate, Mather suggests, that one cannot resist them without a significant effort that must include much fasting as well as prayer. As long as mankind remains subject to sin, Mather suggests, they will remain subject to enchantments. Mather's

"Hearty Wishes," then, reflect both a personal effort to be free from enchantments and a recognition that such freedom may never be possible. Even his assertion that "much Fasting as well as Prayer" could lead to a "rescue from Enchantment" seems like a thankless task that may never bring about the desired results (1957, p 158).

One hundred forty years later, the literary critic W. B. O. Peabody amplified Mather's complaint against enchantments into his own argument against superstitions. Some readers may wonder why I would draw a comparison between two very different men who seem to be arguing against different things. While it is true that these men have little in common, it is Peabody himself who largely urges the comparison to be made. Throughout his article, he frequently uses Cotton Mather as a foil to suggest how far New England has come since the Puritan settlements. Significantly, Peabody urges his readers to consider the ways in which nineteenth century scientific thought starkly contrasts with the opinions of the past. But, like Mather's comments, Peabody's article, entitled "New England's Superstitions," attempts to argue against superstitions but ends up proving that even the most rational arguments can do little to eradicate superstition from culture. The essence of Peabody's article is that the powers of reason, if used correctly, will swiftly erase all forms of superstition from American culture. Indeed, Peabody claims to be offering the reader an "intellectual history of Superstition," one that will conclude with the dismissal of superstition altogether (1833, p 139). As if to underscore this point, Peabody insists that writing about superstition alone is largely beneath him. As he writes, "the subject is one which I should hardly think of introducing here were it not connected with other subjects of great importance" (1833, p 139). Peabody implies that these "other subjects" are the larger themes of reason and intelligence that he hopes will triumph over superstition. In nearly every paragraph, Peabody attempts to demonstrate how every superstition may be explained through appeals to reason. He argues that "Ignorance is the cause of superstition," and the only defense against such ignorance is the development of a superior intellect, one that has the capacity to repel the possibility of superstitious belief (1833, p 139). As he puts it, "In all ages of the world the most intelligent men seem to have been most exempt from superstition" (1833, p 153). Those who are not "exempt," Peabody argues, "rest satisfied with absurd explanations of things which they might understand with a little attention" (1833, p 153).

One implication of Peabody's screed against ignorance is that his notion of superstition may be seen as having a similar rhetorical value to Cotton Mather's argument against enchantments. Unlike Mather, however, Peabody expresses little interest in religion in this article. Instead, he worries that belief in superstition opposes scientific thought. To put it bluntly, Peabody believes that those who believe in superstition are not only ignorant, they are unenlightened and uncultivated. Peabody claims that if "any thing remarkable" appears to such individuals, ignorant persons rely on their overly developed imaginations to explain what they see (1833, p 146). According to Peabody, it is this combination—imagination and ignorance—that causes superstition.

To illustrate, Peabody draws on Cotton Mather's writings about witchcraft. Peabody writes that, during the Salem Witchcraft scare, Mather exhibited too much belief in superstition, a trust that undermined his ability to explain the causes of witchcraft itself. In fact, he faults Mather for his description of witchcraft as something "stupendous," a word that, Peabody implies, reveals his lack of willingness to employ reason carefully. Even worse, Peabody complains, Mather passed his belief in witches on to the thousands of American readers who turned to *The Wonders of the Invisible World* for a kind of sanctioned analysis. For Peabody, belief in superstition signifies both a willful ignorance and inveterate desire to share it with others. To believe in superstition, he implies, is to place oneself outside of cultural conventions and orthodox belief.

Peabody's argument suggests that superstitions thwart scientific thought because they invite heterogeneous modes of explanation for natural phenomena. Although Peabody agrees that some things are more difficult to explain than others, he deplores the tendency to use the imagination to explain natural phenomena. Peabody turns his attention to the various means people use to explain the appearance of a comet. In Cotton Mather's day, for example, comets usually signified some kind of Divine sign, perhaps of God's anger, or a warning. As Peabody writes, "A comet was formerly thought to be the cause of war; why? For no reason, but that this remarkable appearance came before the war in the order of time" (1833, p 153). In other words, some American colonists saw comets as causal signs and used those signs to explain particular effects. Peabody rejects this practice. He writes that the appearance of a comet must not signify war because it can only signify a scientific, not a religious, phenomenon. To claim otherwise, Peabody writes, is to misuse reason and to fall into the heterogeneous realm of fancy and superstition.

Lost in his self-importance, Peabody boasts that the rise in scientific though in America will dispel all superstitions within the nineteenth century. In fact, he describes rational thought as a kind of mental juggernaut, one that will send everything fleeing from its destructive force. As Peabody puts it, "Superstition is every where giving way before [intelligence and reason] and where they prevail, superstition will perish from the world" (1833, p 153). In fact, Peabody confidently asserts that New England already serves as a shining example of a place where "superstition does not now generally prevail" (1833, p 139). Although Peabody was clearly wrong to make this claim, he defends his point by remarking that ghost stories are no longer very popular in New England and that even "accounts of witchcraft no longer find credit any where" (1833, p 139). Where such stories are heard, they are head with minds "entirely free from superstition;" some listeners, in fact, listen to ghost stories only to use the occasion to explain away the source of the delusion they contain (1833, p 139). In a rational community, Peabody argues, supernatural tales stimulate the intellectual need to seek the rational explanation for things. Superstition therefore functions exactly like science once people understand how to undermine stories of witchcraft, ghosts, and demons. The appearance of "any thing remarkable" Peabody writes, can be fully explained if only one will "look round for an explanation" (1833, p 139). The enlightened will find that "their minds are set at rest at once; they wonder no longer, and ask no further questions" (1833, p 139). To illustrate the point, Peabody returns to the notion of the sudden appearance of a comet. Most people, Peabody suggests, tend to rely on superstition to explain the appearance of a comet. The result, he continues, is the needless igniting of "anxiety and alarm" (1833, p 143). By contrast, a scientific explanation will result in people viewing the comet as an interesting, but not necessarily threatening, manifestation of nature.

Though Peabody asserts the triumph of science, he notes that superstition, if allowed to triumph, could lead to a "wild play of the imagination," particularly in cases of persons who lack the requisite intelligence to control their thoughts (1833, p 139). For Peabody, an active imagination risks transforming the unknown into the superstitious, thereby making "any thing remarkable" subject to non scientific explanations (1833, p 139). Such an "inventive power," Peabody continues, may "bring images before the mind" that will impair one's use of reason (1833, p 139). Once reason fails, Peabody concludes, superstition prevails. It is precisely on this point that Peabody's article connects to Cotton Mather's own arguments against enchantments. Both Peabody and Mather recognize that to accept "superstitions" or "enchantments" risks placing oneself outside of cultural conventions and therefore weakens the place of orthodoxy in culture. Superstition replaces reason just as enchantment weakens faith. The result, Peabody warns, is that the language of enchantment will infiltrate everyday speech. Like Mather, Peabody would disassociate enchantment from quotidian life. They recognize, however, that Enchantment, or superstition, usually appears to be an inverted version of the orthodox.

Just as Cotton Mather realized the inveterate nature of enchantments in his struggle against enchantments, Peabody also realizes that superstitions cannot be easily removed. The reason for this, Peabody suggests, is that superstitions persist in language, whether we mean to speak of them or not. Indeed, Peabody realizes, to his dismay, that supernaturally influenced idiomatic expressions and the mental associations they trigger survive in daily speech and cannot be challenged by reason. As Peabody himself puts it, "superstitions are now nearly perished from the world—but the language still remains" (1833, p 143). Typically, Peabody privileges his belief that superstitions must fail in the wake of scientific rationalism. Nevertheless, Peabody's remark that "the language still remains" suggests that reason will never prevail (1833, p 143). Even Peabody's sentence structure demonstrates the effect of language. His use of the dash to separate the triumph of science from the idiomatic survival of superstition signifies the continued force of magical traditions in New England. To illustrate, we turn to Peabody's own example of persons who refer to their "unlucky stars," an expression clearly "borrowed from the old profession of astrology" (1833, p 143). The consequence of such language, in short, is that it keeps people aware of the power of such expressions even if science argues that there are no lucky stars. According to Peabody, culture can never be free of superstition so long as individuals use idioms steeped in magical traditions. To his dismay, Peabody recognized that he could not change people's minds without changing their language. It is language, therefore, that enchants human beings — not superstition, not witches, and not Satan. When Peabody claims that "the language still remains," his article shares with Mather's own writing, an awareness that certain phrases, idioms, and usages will outlast the so-called triumph of science and religion. The recurrence of enchantments or superstitions challenges the supposedly rigid lines that people draw between science and magic, reason and faith, visible and invisible, and orthodox and heterodox. To put it another way, enchantments and superstitions infuse language to such an extent that they form an essential part of how we understand ourselves, whether we accept that influence or not.

Both Cotton Mather and W. B. O. Peabody attempt to argue against the effects of enchantments or superstitions on language, thought, and behavior. But they eventually come to recognize that their efforts will largely fail. Magic, whether in the form of "enchantments" or "superstitions," their arguments ultimately suggest, is more than just an aberration of reason; instead, they signify a very real tension most human beings have in their understanding of themselves, their communities, and each other. Allusions to magical idioms, assumptions, and beliefs demand careful attention, therefore, because of their implications to the cultural tensions involved in ascertaining notions of meaning, identity, and community. What is more important, magic, whether in the form of enchantments or superstitions, signify a particular way of seeing the world, one that provides an analogical means of interpreting the world, even the cosmos. As Arthur Versluis suggests, "literature is not merely a means to communicate date, but also a vehicle to transmit means of spiritual understanding. Inherent in this recognition is the view that the entire cosmos emerges out of the combination of divine letters" (2001, p 4). Through arguing against magic, both Mather and Peabody come to realize that they can't conveniently separate binary opposites such as reason / superstition, religion / magic, and so on. The result is a new understanding that, despite our best efforts, we will always be subject to the enchantments of life.

References

Butler, Jon, 1990, *Awash in a Sea of Faith: Christianizing the American People*, Harvard University Press, Cambridge, MA.

Hall, David D, 1989, *Worlds of Wonder, Days of Judgment: Popular Religious Belief in Early New England*. Harvard University Press, Cambridge MA.

Mather, Cotton, 1957, *Diary of Cotton Mather, Vol.2 1681-1709*, Frederick Ungar Publishing Co, New York.

Peabody, W. B. O. (1833), 'New England Superstitions', *New England Magazine*, 4, 139-53.

Versluis, Arthur, 2001, *The Esoteric Origins of the American Renaissance*, Oxford University Press, Oxford.

In a Mirror, Darkly : A comparison between the Lovecraftian Mythos and African-Atlantic mystery religions

David Geall

Introduction

In a previous article (*Journal for the Academic Study of Magic*, # 3, 2005: 'A half-choked meep of cosmic fear': Is there esoteric symbolism in H.P.Lovecraft's *The Dream-Quest of Unknown Kadath*?) I suggested that there might well be evidence of conscious esoteric symbolism in H.P.Lovecraft's 1926 story *The Dream-Quest of Unknown Kadath*. In this article I take another 1926 story, *The Call of Cthulhu*, as a starting point for an investigation of the so-called *mythos*, the pantheon (or pandemonium) of entities in the fiction of Lovecraft, which has since been augmented and elaborated by other authors, including some who are practitioners of magic.

My earlier article suggested that the action of *The Dream-Quest of Unknown Kadath* was consciously mapped onto the Tree of Life glyph of the Cabalah; in this paper I shall continue to refer to the Tree of Life, but I do not claim that Lovecraft was consciously using it to create the Mythos pantheon. If my earlier suggestion has any merit, then it would have been in his mind anyway, and so it may well have become involved in the subconscious imaginative creation of his fictions. In any case, it is a useful model of aspects of the divine (or their inverse, demonic counterparts) on which we can attempt to locate the entities of the Mythos.

The Call of Cthulhu begins with a so-called *voodoo* ceremony near New Orleans, and, as we shall see, the African-Atlantic mystery religions seem to shed a revealing light onto the Mythos. These religions originated in sub-Saharan Africa and were exported via the slave trade to the New World. *Voodoo* is the anglicised form of the Haitian Creole word, variously spelt as *vodoun, vodou*, etc., which derives from the Dahomeyan word *vodun*, meaning "mysteries", that is, of the gods. I have decided to keep to the form *Voodoo*, except when referring specifically to Haitian Voudoun, as the anglicised form used by Lovecraft and other writers of his time. In any case, by *Voodoo* I mean not just the *vodoun* of Haiti, but to some extent the ancestral *vodun* of Dahomey, and the *orishas* of Yorubaland too; and not just them but their descendants in Cuban *Santeria*, Brazilian *Candomble* and so forth.

There are therefore three points of reference which will help us to triangulate the enduring fascination of Lovecraft's fictions:

- the Mythos itself: stories by Lovecraft, his collaborators and circle of literary friends
- the Sephiroth of the Tree of Life of the Cabalah
- Voodoo, i.e. the African-Atlantic mystery religions

A fourth element which is sometimes relevant is Classical mythology, a subject in which Lovecraft and some of his friends were surprisingly erudite; and a fifth aspect is the literary development of some Mythos entities (for example, Hastur) by various authors. However, for reasons of space and relevance, these aspects have been kept to a minimum.

Where possible, then, we shall compare the figures of the Mythos to the *loa* of Voudou and the equivalent *orishas* of Santeria, a comparison which quite often also sheds light on the relationship of the figures to the Tree of Life and thus other symbol systems. We shall locate the *loa* and *orishas*, together with the Mythos entities, on the sephiroth or other sites on the Tree of Life, as have others: Kenneth Grant has placed both Mythos entities (1992, p 124) and West African orishas (1975, p 9) on the Tree of Life, for example. As Denning and Phillips (1988, p 148) say, 'The fundamental Archetypes are discerned in images which are so true to their respective Sephiroth that the principal Loa (Voudoun deities) correspond very closely to concepts associated with the better known Western pantheons'. Just as I do not claim that Lovecraft was consciously mapping the Mythos onto the Tree of Life, neither am I suggesting that he was necessarily consciously borrowing from Voodoo to create it. Nevertheless, even if there was no direct influence from Vodoun or Santeria on Lovecraft, such a comparison is still illuminating enough to be drawn on its own merits.

There are some general similarities: the distinction between Lovecraft's Elder Ones and Great Old Ones, for example, is paralleled in Haitian Vodou by the distinction between the different *nanchons*, i.e. nations or pantheons of deities deriving from different parts of Africa. The Rada (Dahomean) divinities are usually perceived to be more benevolent than their Petro (New World, Haitian) or BaKongo (Central African) equivalents, who are usually perceived to be more malevolent; while his Other Gods are paralleled by the independent or ambivalent deities of Vodou (Deren 1953, pp 82-5). While some Vodou deities may seem more benign than those of the Mythos, we should remember that most of them have their *Ge-Rouge* forms - i.e. *yeux rouge*, or red-eyed, and their potentially more malevolent Petro avatars; and that human sacrifice was also not unknown in the past.

The Call of Cthulhu

In *The Call of Cthulhu*, Inspector Legrasse of New Orleans brings to the attention of eminent archaeologists a

> statuette, idol, fetish ... captured some months before in the wooded swamps of New Orleans during a raid on a supposed voodoo meeting; and so singular and hideous were the rites connected with it, that the police could not but realise that they had stumbled on a dark cult totally unknown to them, and infinitely more diabolic than even the blackest of the African voodoo circles.

To be more precise,

> On November 1, 1907, there had come to New Orleans police a frantic summons from the swamp and lagoon country to the south. The squatters there ... were in the grip of stark terror from an unknown thing which had stolen upon them in the night. It was voodoo, apparently, but voodoo of a more terrrible sort than they had ever known ...

When the surviving participants were examined, it was found that

> Most were seamen, and a sprinkling of Negroes and mulattos, largely West Indians or Brava Portuguese from the Cape Verde Islands, gave a colouring of voodooism to the heterogeneous cult.

(Brava is one of the Cape Verde Islands, situated off the coast of Guinea; contacts with American whalers led to immigration by these Portuguese West Africans into the USA in the nineteenth century).

Later the narrator's uncle, the eminent archaeologist Professor Angell who had followed up Legrasse's discovery, dies in his home town of Providence 'after having been jostled by a nautical-looking Negro'. Although he also referred in the story to Inuit, Polynesian and other cults, Voodoo was clearly in Lovecraft's mind when he composed *The Call of Cthulhu*.

Yog-Sothoth

> Yog-So-thoth knows the Gate. Yog-So-thoth is the Gate.
>
> Yog-So-thoth is the Key and Guardian of the Gate.
>
> Past, present, future, all are one in Yog-So-thoth ...
>
> Yog-So-thoth is the Key to the Gate, whereby the Spheres meet.
>
> **Necronomicon**, quoted in *The Dunwich Horror*

The lines from Lovecraft's fictional tome, the *Necronomicon*, quoted above may sum up the main attributes of Yog-Sothoth, but we can also find them applicable to the Voudoun loa of Legba and the equivalent Santeria orisha of Eleggua. They both derive from the West African deity Legba (which is the Fon name; Eshu is the Yoruba name, which is also used, spelt Exu, in the Brazilian religion of Candomble). As the gate-keeper, Legba is always invoked first in any ceremony, and much the same seems to be true of Yog-Sothoth's role in the Mythos, as evidenced by *The Case of Charles Dexter Ward* and *The Dunwich Horror.*

> 'Legba ... is the guardian of the sacred gateway, of the Grand Chemin, the great road leading from the mortal to the divine world ... "Papa Legba, open the gate, Attibon Legba, open the gates so that we may pass through ..." "Legba, who sits on the gate, Give us the right to pass". Indeed, in Haiti it is now Legba's major function to guard the gates'. (Deren 1953, p 98)

If Yog-Sothoth is assigned to the central position of Tiphereth on the Tree of Life, thus connecting it with every other Sephiroth, light is shed on these lines from the *Necronomicon*, especially the last: it is indeed 'the Gate, whereby the Spheres meet'. One could even argue that the descriptions found in other, later authors' 'quotations' from the *Necronomicon* - 'As a congeries of shining Globes is He' (Carter 1996, xiv), '& Yog-Sothoth ... shall bring his globes' (Derleth 1945, pp 112-3)) - are to be explained by a glance at the diagram of the Tree of Life, dominated by the central position of Yog-Sothoth. Legba / Eleggua can likewise be assigned to this Sephira, as he has been by Louis Martinie and Sallie Ann Glassman (1992) in their *New Orleans Voodoo Tarot.* 'Eleggua is syncretized as the Holy Guardian Angel' (Wippler 1992a, p 112), which is also usually assigned to Tiphereth.

Moreover, 'In Santeria Eleggua/Eshu is said to have 101 "paths" or manifestations, but of these 21 are best known' (Wippler 1992a, p 15). Applied to the Tree of Life, this would mean that the avatars or other forms of Eleggua / Eshu can occupy the other 21 Sephiroth and Paths in addition to Tiphereth, which would thus account for his omniscience, for he is everywhere. A "tree-of-life" with eight side-branches - i.e. with ten extremities, as in the Cabbalah - is a symbol of Legba painted upon tombs in Haiti (for an example, see Seabrook 1936, p 292).

Yog-Sothoth, to whom all space is as one, is thus all-seeing; Yog-Sothoth is also lord of time, in whom past, present and future meet and are one.

> He knows where the Old Ones broke through of old,
>
> and where They shall break through again.
>
> He knows where They have trod earth's fields,
>
> and where They still tread them …

Lovecraft collaborated with E.Hoffman Price - whom he visited in New Orleans in 1932 - on the story *Through the Gates of the Silver Key* (1932), a sequel to Lovecraft's own *The Silver Key* (1926). Carter performs 'the rite of the silver key ... in that black, haunted cave', the Snake Den:

> A gate had been unlocked - not, indeed, the Ultimate Gate, but one leading from Earth and time to that extension of Earth which is outside time, and from which in turn the Ultimate Gate leads fearsomely and perilously to the Last Void which is outside allearths, all universes, and all matter. There would be a Guide - and a very terrible one.

The Guide is 'the Most Ancient One', who is usually taken to be an aspect or avatar of Yog-Sothoth. Having passed through the First Gate, Carter saw the Ancient Ones, apparently seated upon 'gigantic hieroglyphed pedestals more hexagonal than otherwise', the six-sided hexagon suggesting the sixth Sephira, Tiphereth. Then he met the 'frightful Guide and Guardian of the Gate ... the Most Ancient One', who sent Carter through the Ultimate Gate, whereupon he lost his sense of self and identity and was subsumed into a larger entity:

> It was an All-in-One and One-in-All of limitless being and self ... It was perhaps that which certain secret cults of Earth had whispered of as *Yog-Sothoth*, and which has been a deity under other names ...

Legba is introduced by Maya Deren under the name of *The Old Man at the Gate*, and is connected by her with the Sun, which of course is related to Tiphereth. 'Legba ... who was the Sun, itself destined to descend from the noon of each year, from the zenith of its ardent fire, has become an old tattered man shuffling down the road ...' (Deren 1953, pp 96,99). He is often depicted as such on the walls of Vodou temples. Similarly, an important aspect of Eleggua/Eshu in Santeria is Eshu Elufe, who is the oldest, and represented as an ancient old man (Wippler 1992a, p 17).

It is also often useful to envisage Yog-Sothoth as able to move anywhere along the Middle Pillar of the Tree of Life (see Grant 1992, pp 124, 214, 265), and this again parallels Legba:

> 'Legba ... is the link between the visible, mortal world and the invisible, mortal realms. He is the means and avenue of

communication between them, the vertical axis of the universe which stretches between the sun door and the tree root. Since he is the god of the poles of the axis, of the axis itself, he is the God of the Cross-roads, of the vital intersection between the two worlds'. (Deren 1953, p 97).

The Old Ones were, the Old Ones are, and the Old Ones shall be.

Not in the spaces that we know, but **between** *them,*

They walk serene and primal, undimensioned and to us unseen ...

Past, present, future, all are one in Yog-So-thoth. He knows ...

The words above quoted from the *Necronomicon* are again echoed in Deren's discussion of Legba:

Since he stands at the cross-roads, he has access to the worlds on either side ... Therefore it is of Legba that one may enquire: "Papa Legba, we ask you, What do you see there?" ... And at the same time, "Alegba watches me. We do not see him, he sees us ... He is there, he listens ..." Indeed, his knowledge comprehends the whole universe ... ... his omniscience, which was the result of his central supreme position in the centre, from which all could be seen, becomes the omniscience of one who, being below earth, is of all parts of it.

(Deren 1953, pp 98-100).

At this point we seem to be leaving the fairly benign *Rada* divinity Legba for his *Petro* equivalent Carrefour, who might seem closer to Lovecraft's Yog-Sothoth:

> Legba is the divinity of the cardinal points; Carrefour is the master of *the points between.* If Legba commands the divinities of the day, Carrefour commands the daemons of the night ... Thus, as ... Legba, the sun, droops towards the cosmic horizon ...so ... it is Carrefour, the moon, who has the greater immediate power. Daily, at the hour of midnight, his noon, he is at the zenith of his vigour ...(Deren 1953, p 101 – my italics).
>
> .. of Their semblance can no man know,
>
> saving only in the features of those
>
> They have begotten on mankind.

Yog-Sothoth is sometimes known to look favourably upon the daughters of men: for example, fathering upon Lavinia Whateley her son Wilbur and his twin the Dunwich Horror in the story of that name. There is a similarity here with the African original, Legba, routinely described by earlier writers as the Priapus of Dahomey, with his main attribute coyly described by means of euphemisms: 'Dahomeans knew him mainly as the cosmic phallus, and the statue of Legba, squatting, staring at his own enormous symbol and source of generation, was everywhere ...' (Deren 1953, p 97).

Dancers possessed by Legba mime coitus with a large wooden phallus. Photographs of both ithyphallic and non-phallic images of Legba may be seen in Muller (2000, pp 152, 153, 168, 267), for example.

Similarly, dogs are sacred to the West African Legba / Eshu; and the role of dogs is not insignificant in *The Dunwich Horror*, although in this case it is because the animals abhor the presence of Wilbur and his twin, the campus watch-dog finally putting paid to the former. Both these aspects go back to Dahomean originals: see for example the stories *How Legba became guardian of men and gods: Why the dog is respected*, and *Why Legba may take all women* (Herskovits 1958, pp 36-46, 142-9).

The voodoo ceremony with which *The Call of Cthulhu* opens takes place on the night of October 31 - All Souls' Eve, or Hallowe'en. The following day, November 1, All Saints' Day, was sacred in the eyes of the *vodouisants* of Haiti to Legba - and there were often emigres from Haiti in Louisiana. The reaction to the ceremony reported (and felt?) by Lovecraft – 'a dark cult … infinitely more diabolic than even the blackest of the African voodoo circles' – recalls attitudes to Legba / Eshu which are perhaps more in keeping with Lovecraft's Yog-Sothoth.

For example, the West African Legba - a trickster - has often been equated in the past with the Devil: 'Because of his provocative nature, Eshu has been characterized by missionaries and Western-minded Yoruba alike as "the Devil".' (Thompson 1984, p 19) To illustrate the truth of this statement with evidence from earlier writers, one need only read the following:

> The nature of this spirit has very commonly been
> misunderstood, and the people of our area (West Africa)
> called 'devil-worshippers'. Farrow roundly calls Eshu 'the

devil', 'the prince of darkness', 'he is emphatically the supreme evil spirit'. Johnson, who was a native of Nigeria, though a Christian convert ... yet attributes to Eshu or Elegbara the specific characteristics of Hebrew-Christian mythology, and calls him 'Satan, the Evil One, the author of all evil'. (Parrinder 1949, pp 67-8)

Gorer, too, wrote that in West Africa each individual had his own Legba, or *devil*: 'The Legba is a completely personal devil; each person has his private altar to it, and if a man does not keep his legba permanently appeased with offerings of food and so on things will go badly for him.' (Gorer 1945, p 124) In Brazil Exu is associated with the devil's horns and pitchforks, 'particularly in the Yoruba-influenced religious life of Rio, where a kind of meta-literature has arisen in his name, incredibly creolized and inventive ...' (Thompson 1984, p 273) The horned Exu, brought to New Orleans by Brazilian immigrants, has been adopted into Vodou there (see illustration in Haskins, 1978, of an example in the Voodoo Museum of New Orleans). This inventive literature growing from American soil (i.e. creolised) is an interesting parallel to Lovecraft.

Shub-Niggurath

The name first appeared - in the familiar ejaculation, *Ia! Shub-Niggurath!* - in *The Last Test,* written with de Castro in 1927, presumably based on the similar name, also of a forest deity, in Lord Dunsany's story, *Idle days on the Yann.* Shub-Niggurath appears in other revisions of tales by collaborators: in *The Mound* (1929-30) Shub-Niggurath is described briefly as 'the All-Mother and wife of the Not-to-Be-Named One. This deity was a kind of sophisticated Astarte, and her worship struck the pious

Catholic as supremely obnoxious'. As the pious observer in question was a sixteenth-century Spanish conquistador, it may not have been all that bad. In *Out of the Aeons* (1933) she is again described as 'the Mother Goddess', and seems relatively benign. Shub-Niggurath is clearly a fertility figure, a sort of female Pan, and as such she may be compared to goddesses of fertility and generation such as Aphrodite, Astarte and Ashtaroth. She is also invoked in other revisions of other authors' work such as *Medusa's Coil* (1930) and *The Man of Stone* (1932).

Such goddesses are to be assigned to Netzach, the Sephira related to the planet Venus. The metal associated with Venus is copper, so when Lovecraft and Hazel Heald, in their collaboration *Out of the Aeons* (1933), write of 'the copper temple of the Goat with a Thousand Young', and when Lin Carter, a faithful disciple of Lovecraft, writes that 'The copper gates of the temple of Shub-Niggurath were sealed' (Carter 1980), they are quite correct – how cannily or uncannily is an interesting point.

In Lovecraft's own writings, as opposed to his revisions, Shub-Niggurath tends to have less pleasant connotations; in a letter he describes her as *an evil cloud-like entity*. She is often associated with, but should perhaps not necessarily be identified with, the *Black Goat of the Woods with a Thousand Young*. Shub-Niggurath is invoked in the fragmentary recording made by Akeley of a May-Eve forest ritual in *The Whisperer in Darkness* (1928-31):

> Ever Their praises and abundance to the Black Goat of the Woods.
>
> Ia! Shub-Niggurath! The Goat with a Thousand Young!

A Lord of the Wood(s) is also mentioned here, suggesting that Shub-Niggurath's gender could vary, or that she had an un-named consort.

A connection to Haitian Vodoun is made in Ramsay Campbell's Shub-Niggurath story *The Moon-Lens*, in which a character mentions 'the Haitian goat-girl ritual', almost certainly a reference to the *Goat-cry Girl-cry* chapter of William Seabrook's book on Haiti, *The Magic Island* (1929): 'Into this little temple lost among the mountains came in answer to goat-cry girl-cry the Shaggy Immortal One *of a thousand names* whom the Greeks called Pan. The goat's lingam became erect and rigid, the points of the girl's breasts visibly hardened ... Thus they faced each other motionless as two marble figures on the frieze of some ancient phallic temple'. (Crowley and his followers attempted a similar ritual at their Cefalu retreat in Sicily).

The equivalent Voudoun loa is the goddess of femininity, seduction and fertility, Erzulie, whom Deren introduces as *The Tragic Mistress*, whose devotees weep unconsolably when possessed by her, and who also appears 'in that combined rage and despair which is Erzulie Ge-Rouge. With her knees drawn up, the fists clenched, the jaw rigid and the tears streaming from her tight-shut eyes, she is the cosmic tantrum' (Deren 1953, p 143). Maya Deren herself was possessed by Erzulie, as told in *The White Darkness* chapter of *The Divine Horsemen* (1953).

Ezili Je Wouj *(Erzulie Yeux Rouge, of the red eyes)*, or Ezili Danto, is also discussed in the *Ezili* chapter of *Mama Lola*, a biography of a present-day Vodou priestess in Brooklyn:

> anger and even rage ... also appear in the Petwo spirit Ezili Danto ... Danto's anger ... [at times] explodes from her with an irrational, violent force ... A gentle rainfall during the festivities ... is readily interpreted as a sign of her presence; but so is a sudden deluge resulting in mudslides, traffic accidents, and even deaths. (Brown 1991, p 231)

Some manifestations of Ezili Danto are considered evil, going wild at the sight of blood when an animal is sacrificed. The Santeria equivalent is Oshun, among whose attributes is copper. Like Shub Niggurath and Erzulie, she has less benign avatars, such as Ibu Kole: 'Identified with the vulture ... She is a ferocious witch who feeds only on what the vultures bring her' (Wippler 1992a p 106).

Yig

The figure of Yig, 'the half-human father of serpents', first appeared in Lovecraft's revision or collaboration with Zealia Brown Reed Bishop, *The Curse of Yig* (1928). In a further collaboration, *The Mound* (1929-30), in the subterranean world of K'n-yan there were to be found 'the cryptic shrines of Yig, the principle of life worshipped as the Father of all Serpents'. The "days" of K'n-yan were 'timed by the tail-beats of Great Yig, the Serpent', while the "year" was 'measured by Yig's annual shedding of his skin'. Rather like a Voudoun loa, he was of a 'highly arbitrary and capricious nature ... and was usually quite well-disposed towards those who gave proper respect to him and his children, the serpents ...'.

Yig - 'presumably the primal source of the more southerly Quetzalcoatl or Kulkulcan' - obviously resembles other cosmic serpents of myth, such as the primeval Greek Ophion, the Rainbow Serpent of the Australian Aborigines, the serpent of Eden, the serpent hanging upon the Tree of Life of the Qabalah, and the West African originals of the Vodoun loa, Damballah.

> Damballah Wedo is the ancient, the venerable father ... He comes as a snake ... and then writhes ... upon the ground, or mounts a tree, where he lies in the high branches, the primordial source of all life wisdom ... when he speaks, it is a barely intelligible hissing ... He is shown as a snake ... [sometimes with] his female counterpart, Ayida, the rainbow ... Damballah and Ayida, who together represent the sexual totality, encompass the cosmos as a serpent coiled about the world ... (Deren 1953, pp 114-6)

A nineteenth-century folklorist cited by Deren provides an example of the sort of link possible between Vodou and Lovecraft and / or his collaborators:

> At the International Folklore Congress in Chicago in 1893 a Mary Alicia Owen reported on 'Voodooism' as if it were fairly prevalent in that area and cited the following 'Voodoo' myth of origin: That 'Old Sun' (the first divinity) 'squatted down on the bank of a great river ... and tore a fragment from his body and flung it into the weeds ... where it became the Great Rattlesnake' ... there is no doubt but that the stories she quotes are accurately reported, and the incident cited above gives a logical connection to Legba and Damballah. (Deren 1953 p 267, note 52)

The Midwest location – 'in that area' is intriguingly vague - and the figure of the Great Rattlesnake are strikingly reminiscent of *The Curse of Yig*.

Nyarlathotep

Nyarlathotep first appears in the prose text *Nyarlathotep* (1920), written after a dream. The text begins in a modern period of global crisis: 'And it was then that Nyarlathotep came out of Egypt ... he was of the old native blood and looked like a Pharaoh ... swarthy, slender and sinister.' Nyarlathotep can be compared with the Hellenistic-Greek Hermes Trismegistus and the Latin Mercurius of the Hermetic alchemical tradition: he was 'always buying strange instruments of glass and metal and combining them into instruments yet stranger. He spoke much of the sciences - of electricity and psychology ...' Mercury is identified with the Sephira of Hod, and it seems that Lovecraft may have left a clue confirming the connection - which I suggested in my previous article - of Hod with Ulthar in *The Dream-Quest*. He wrote in *The Cats of Ulthar* (1920):

> It is said in Ulthar, which lies beyond the river Skai, no man may kill a cat ... For the cat is cryptic, and close to strange things which men cannot see. He is the soul of antique Aegyptus, and bearer of tales from forgotten cities in Meroe and Ophir.

Ulthar may thus be linked with ancient Egypt, where it was also illegal to harm a cat. 'Nyarlathotep came out of Egypt' too, as his name shows, that legendary land where cats were sacred, of Thoth and Hermes

Trismegistos, 'antique and shadowy Khem', 'the country where all magic arts were known'.

Nyarlathotep is described in *The Dream-Quest of Unknown Kadath* as 'the dread soul and messenger of the Other Gods', which identifies him with the messenger of the gods, Hermes in Greece, Mercury in Rome, Thoth in Egypt, located on the Tree of Life at the Sephira of Hod. As Lovecraft put it elsewhere (in *The Dreams in the Witch-House*, 1932): 'There was the immemorial figure of the deputy or messenger of hidden and terrible powers ... the 'Nyarlathotep' of the *Necronomicon*'. But he is also described in *The Dream-Quest* as 'the crawling chaos Nyarlathotep'.

Just as Nyarlathotep is the soul and messenger of the Other Gods, so the loa Simbi 'shares characteristics and functions ... with all the major deities, of Vodou, both Rada and Petro. Like Hermes Trismegistus and the alchemical Mercury, he is the patron of magicians: 'All magic is perfomed under his patronage' (Deren 1953 p 117). Martinie and Glassman (1992, pp 161-2) agree with Deren:

> The Western counterpart of Simbi is Mercury. Mercury, like Simbi, is a spirit that has great knowledge of magick ... Simbi manifests itself in New Orleans in a unique
>
> form. Voodoo rites often make use of Le Grand Zombi. This is a force called through a snake, at times a rattlesnake ... In New Orleans, the power that is Simbi rides within Le Grand Zombi.

Like the alchemical Mercury, then, he is sometimes envisaged in the form of a snake, as a cosmic serpent similar to but distinct from

Damballah. 'In Vodou art, he is often depicted as a powerful snake who inhabits the rivers, one who shows his strength by uprooting trees and rocks and carrying them downstream during tropical storms' (Desmangles 1992, pp 128-130). There is perhaps even some similarity with Nyarlathotep's characterisation as 'the crawling chaos', in the sense of entropy: 'Vodouisants believe that Simbi is a lazy lwa ... Simbi counteracts Damballah's creative momentum by always struggling to instill within the cosmos a lingering, static quality' (Desmangles 1992, p 130).

The Santeria orisha who may be compared to Nyarlathotep is perhaps Orunla, also known as Orunmila and Ifa, whose attributes and character are reminiscent of the Hermetic Mercury: 'Orunla is the symbol of wisdom ... he is the holy diviner, the owner of the mystical oracle known as the Table of Ifa ... he is the patron of the babalawos, the high priests ...' Like Nyarlathotep, 'Orunla is envisioned as a young man, attractive and self-possessed ... Orunla represents those people who are in constant search for knowledge, who are fascinated by the mysteries of the universe and are always trying to uncover them. He is also a symbol of everything that is hidden and forbidden ...' (Wippler 1992a, pp 44-5).

Cthulhu

In the following lines from *The Call of Cthulhu*, written in 1926, the same year as *The Dream-Quest of Unknown Kadath*, Lovecraft started his own undying cult, devoted to the most famous figure of his mythos:

> They worshipped, so they said, the Great Old Ones who lived ages before there were any men, and who came to the young world out of the sky. These Old Ones were gone now, inside the earth and under the sea; but their dead bodies had told

their secrets in dreams to the first man, who formed a cult which had never died ... and would always exist, hidden in distant wastes and dark places all over the world until the time when the great priest Cthulhu, from his dark house in the mighty city of R'lyeh under the waters, should rise and bring the earth again beneath his sway. Some day he would call, when the stars were ready ...

R'lyeh is located at the bottom of the Pacific Ocean - or, symbolically, in the depths of the subconscious mind. Cthulhu's undersea prison of R'lyeh recalls *Zilet en bas de l'eau* - the isle beneath the water in Vodoun where the souls of the dead go.

My previous analysis of *The Dream-Quest* suggested that Inquanok represents the Sephira of Binah, which is traditionally associated with the planet Saturn; and the late Classical Saturn (in some variants of his myth) anticipated Cthulhu as an imprisoned Titan on an island in the sea. Binah is known as the Great Sea, and in Inquanok, in the garden of the 'great central Temple of the Elder Ones there are fountains, pools and basins ... having in them small luminous fish taken by divers from the lower bowers of ocean'.

The Santeria *orisha* Olokun parallels Cthulhu in several ways: he was chained to the sea-bed by the godhead Obatala, who created land from the waste of waters ruled by Olokun. Occasionally Olokun will attempt to reach the surface, and thus cause tidal waves. Olokun is depicted as sometimes male, sometimes female, perhaps androgynous, and as half-human and half-fish, wearing a mask - 'Whenever he manifests he wears a mask' (Wippler 1992a, p 100) - a fair description of Cthulhu, who is part humanoid and part sea-beast, his face masked by tentacles. The Santeria *orisha* Olokun derives from the Yoruba orisha of the same name, whose attributes are reminiscent of Cthulhu and his retinue of "deep ones":

> Olokun is believed to live in a palace under the sea ... and to have his attendants and mermaid wives, lesser divinities, human and fish-like. Rough seas are attributed to the anger of the god, and propitiatory sacrifices are thrown into the sea for him, generally fowls and animals; formerly, human beings on special occasions. (Parrinder 1949, p 45)

Although Olokun's usual consort is Olosa, he is linked or even combined with the great goddess Yemaya. 'Olokun Yemaya is the deity of the ocean depths', and is treated with great respect, born of fear, by the *santeros*:

> In this aspect, she does not take possession of her omo-orishas [santeros dedicated to her service] because, according to the santeros, "the vastness of the seas cannot fit into a human head". Very seldom, a santero will dare to do her ritualistic dance, with his face covered with a veil or a painted mask. But immediately afterward he must say a special prayer so that the goddess will not kill him. Yemaya Olokun can be seen only in dreams (Wippler 1992b, p 119).

Cthulhu, of course, also communicates only by means of dreams:

> When, after infinities of chaos, the first men came, the Great Old Ones spoke to the sensitive among them by moulding

their dreams; for only thus could Their language reach the fleshy minds of mammals ... In the elder time chosen men had talked with the entombed Old Ones in dreams, but then something had happened. The great stone city R'lyeh, with its monoliths and sepulchres, had sunk beneath the waves ...

In Migene Gonzalez Wippler (1992b) there is a photograph (#18) of a woman celebrant personifying Yemaya-Olokun, with a beaded veil over her face which is suggestive of Cthulhu's facial "tentacles".

Nath-Horthath / Nodens

Lovecraft had written of Celephais and its wise ruler, King Kuranes, both in *Celephais* (1920) and in *The Dream-Quest of Unknown Kadath* (1926). In both he mentions the turquoise temple of the deity Nath-Horthath; turquoise is one of the gem-stones attributed to Chokmah, the Sephira with which I identified Celephais in my previous article. Nath-Horthath has been neglected by later authors, perhaps because Lovecraft left little more than a name, but the name may be significant: the Romano-Celtic name Nodens is cognate with Nuada in Irish and Nudd (pronounced Nuth) in Welsh (Tolkien, in Wheeler 1932) and Nuth is virtually the same as Nath ... The symbolism of the colour turquoise, of the Sephira Chokmah, and the details of Celephais, Ooth-Nargai and Serannian in the *The Dream-Quest*, all suggest a deity who presides over the sea and the sky. As imagery from his temple at Lydney in Gloucestershire shows, the original Romano-Celtic Nodens would fit this role suitably enough, particularly the marine aspect, so Nath-Horthath is perhaps a 'Great One' who is an avatar of Nodens:

> On the following day Carter walked up the Street of the Pillars to the turquoise temple and with the High-Priest. Though Nath-Horthath is chiefly worshipped in Celephais, all the Great Ones are mentioned in diurnal prayers ... Having thanked the orchid-crowned High-Priest, Carter left the temple and sought the bazaar of the sheep-butchers ...
>
> (*Dream-Quest,* pp 146-7)

In the tarot trump The Emperor, which on the Tree of Life connects Chokmah with Tiphereth (or Celephais with Dylath-Leen, my previous article suggested), the throne is decorated with rams' heads.

Maya Deren tells of a pilgrimage to sacrifice to Agwe, the God of the Sea, a story which is poignant in both its lyrical, idyllic aspects and its gritty realism: 'the two exceptional objects which caught the eye were the sacrificial ram and the barque d'Agwe. The ram had been throughly bathed ... in water steeped with certain purifying herbs. What was extraordinary was his bright blue colour, the result of massive amounts of indigo...' (Deren 1953 p 119) The *barque d'Agwe* was an altar on a raft, also painted blue, to be heaped with goodies and sunk over *Zile*, the *ile* or island beneath the waves.

As they reached the site in a sailing-boat, 'two women were almost simultaneously possessed by Agwe ... in an embrace of mutual consolation ... they wept. It is said that the gods of the Sky Pantheon all weep. Some say it is because they first came from the waters below the earth and are still, in a sense, wet. Others say that the rains which fall are the tears of the gods ...' (Deren 1953, p 129). Although a sea-god, Deren counts Agwe as one of the Sky Pantheon, which is appropriate for the symbolism of Chokmah, both in general and with regard to *The Dream-Quest*. Agwe may be seen as a generally benevolent deity of sea and sky (in the sense of weather), linked with the goddess Erzulie: his consort is La Sirene, her marine aspect.

The orisha Inle was also the lover of a siren, the avatar of the goddess Yemaya. Inle may be compared to Agwe: although the patron of fresh waters, his attributes include the trident (like Agwe), fishing hooks and nets, and the caduceus; such Neptunian attributes also occur with Nodens, as shown by Lovecraft in *The Strange High House in the Mist* (1926):

> ... there floated into that room from the deep all the dreams and memories of earth's sunken Mighty Ones ... Trident-bearing Neptune was there, and sportive tritons and fantastic nereids, and upon dolphin's backs was balanced a vast crenulate shell wherein rode the gay and awful form of primal Nodens, Lord of the Great Abyss.

Lovecraft's description is based on some of the finds at Lydney, including a mosaic floor, now lost but fortunately recorded by an artist in 1805, depicting an interlinked design of long-necked water monsters, together with dolphins and fish. Plus wings and minus faces, the water monsters may resemble the night-gaunts, who, it is stated in *The Dream-Quest*, serve Nodens as Lord of the Great Abyss: one wonders whether this could be the origin of the night-gaunts, combined with the ticklish abductors of Lovecraft's childhood dreams? On a bronze plaque appears an image assumed to be that of Nodens, riding in a chariot drawn by four horses over the waves, apparently crowned with solar rays and carrying a whip:

> On each side floats in the air a winged genius, clearly typifying the Winds ... Each end of the composition is filled up with a reclining Triton; the one brandishing two paddles of the very shape still employed by those that navigate the primitive British bark, the corracle; the other, an anchor, and his proper attribute, the shell-trumpet ... (Bathurst, 1879 p 40)

On two bronze fragments are traces of a design with Tritons holding anchors and conch-shell trumpets, and an angler hooking a salmon. In view of this constellation of marine imagery, it is not surprising that a fragmentary inscription from Chesterholm reads DEO NO/NEPTU, equating Nodens with Neptune. Neptune, of course, is often attributed to Chokmah by modern occultists (e.g. Grant 1972, opp p 212).

Nodens / Aforgomon

On the other hand, Nodens can be identified with other deities, including Mars: this identification comes as no surprise to a visitor to Lydney, bearing in mind the nature of the site: a hill of red rock, containing iron mines - red and iron both being characteristics of Mars. The equation of Nodens with Mars is evidenced by ancient inscriptions beginning *Deo Marti Nodonti* ('To the God Mars / Nodons'). Images of dogs and/or wolves were found at Lydney, and both these animals were attributes of Mars. There is also a dedication to Silvanus, the old Roman god of woods and trees, flocks and fields – who was in origin a form of Mars. Nodens was identified with 'Mars the healer rather than Mars the warrior' (Ross 1974, p 230).

In *The Dream-Quest,* Carter was abducted by a night-gaunt (ruled by Nodens) while still in the environs of Mount Ngranek in Oriab, which I identified with Geburah in my previous article, where a number of symbols linked to Geburah / Mars were noted in the area of Oriab: fire, the colour red, the sword; and the same constellation of attributes are applicable to the loa Ogoun and orisha Ogun. Ogoun / Ogun derives from the Yoruba god of iron and war Ogun, identical to the god Gu of the Fon and Ewe peoples, who may all be compared with Mars.

> The idea of force, conflict and power is almost inevitably linked to fire and heat. Ogoun is a deity of fire, and red is the colour sacred to him ... Power resides, too, in the sabre or machete which is sacred to Ogoun (Deren 1953, pp 132-3).

Nodens may thus be identified to some extent with both Geburah and Chokmah, and it is perhaps appropriate that he is Lord of the Great Abyss that lies between the two. It has been pointed out that 'These various attributes are in complete accord with those of the Otherworld-god of the Celts', and that deities such as Nodens cannot be departmentalised or pigeon-holed (O'Rahilly 1946, pp 469-70, 527; see also 320-1, etc.). Lovecraft's attention would have been drawn to Nodens by Arthur Machen's *The Great God Pan* (1894), who cites a fictional inscription based on a real one. Inscriptions found at Lydney confirm that the god's name was Nodens, Nodons or Nudens, and nineteenth-century Celtic scholars took *Deus Nodens* to be a Latinised form of a Celtic original *Deus Noddyns* - 'God of the Abyss', or 'God of the Deeps': hence Machen's 'god of the Great Deep or Abyss'. Lovecraft clearly follows this tradition in *The Dream-Quest of Unknown Kadath,* in which

Nodens is introduced as 'the potent and archaic [god] of unhinted deeps', and as 'hoary and immemorial Nodens, Lord of the Great Abyss'.

Apart from the possible attribution of Nodens, Geburah, the Sephira of strength or severity associated with Mars, is one to which no entity of Lovecraft's can be assigned. However, Aforgomon, Clark Ashton Smith's 'dreadful omnipotent time-god' in *The Chain of Aforgomon* (1935), seems to fill the bill: those who displease this 'dark divinity' are bound by his priests in iron chains on the brink of an abyss - which sounds like the crater of a volcano - from which 'a bolt of strange fire would leap upward, striking the many-coiled chain about him and heating it instantly to the whiteness of candescent iron'. Iron, chain, fire, and volcano are attributes of Mars, Ogun and / or Geburah, not to mention the severity of this punishment.

Iod

The Sephira of Chesed is linked to Jupiter in traditional symbolism, and in Santeria Chango is the Jupiter-like sky-god who wields the thunder-bolt., stemming from the original Yoruba Chango or Shango, who is said to have been a human king who was deified and identified with the thunder-god. His main attribute is a double-axe, a symbol of the thunderbolt. 'The cedar tree belongs to Chango' (Wippler 1992b, p 99) - it is also a symbol of Chesed, and was mentioned by Lovecraft in his description of Thran, equivalent to Chesed in *The Dream-Quest of Unknown Kadath*.

Which Mythos entity can be placed at this nexus? Lovecraft himself did not provide one, but the position seems to be filled by those avatars of

Jove or Jupiter chronicled by Henry Kuttner, one of the original Lovecraft circle, in his legend of Iod, the Hunter of Souls:

> Man had worshiped Iod in older days, under other names. He was one of the oldest gods, and he had come to Earth, the tale went, in pre-human eons when the old gods soared between the stars ... The Greeks know him as Trophonios; the Etruscans made nameless sacrifices diurnally to Vediovis, the Dweller beyond Phlegethon, the Riverof Flame. (Kuttner 1939, *The Hunt*)

Iod was thus under other names an older, elder god ... but who were these obscure Classical deities? Trophonios turns up in the Classical reference books as a mortal who was punished for a crime by being swallowed up by the earth. The site later became a celebrated underground oracle, where Trophonios was honoured as a god, Zeus Trophonios, with the sacrifice of a ram and other rites:

> The oracle was situated in a subterranean chamber, into which ... the inquirers descended, to receive, under circumstances of a mysterious nature, a variety of revelations ... The descent into the cave, and the sights which there met the eye, were so awe-inspiring, that the popular belief was that no one who visited the cave ever smiled again.
>
> (Seyffert 1906, sub Trophonios)

Vediovis or Veiovis (that is, Ve Jovis) was an old Italian god in ancient Rome, who was at one time identified with the young Zeus or Jove. The grove around his temple was a sanctuary for runaway criminals.

Rather than 'nameless sacrifices made diurnally', in Roman times a she-goat was sacrificed annually on March 7 in memory of Amalthea, the she-goat who suckled the young Zeus. At a later date he was identified with Dis Pater or Pluto, the ruler of the world below. (Seyffert 1906, sub Vediovis; cf Ovid, *Fasti*, III. 429-448). 'He was essentially associated with the Underworld, and seems to have presided originally over swamps and volcanic movements' (Grimal 1986, sub Vediovis).

The Ghouls

Speaking of the Underworld, it is represented in *The Dream-Quest* by the Peaks of Throk and the Vale of Pnoth below. In my previous article I related this site, described in *The Dream-Quest* as 'the haunted disc of sunless and eternal depths', to the occulted sephira of Daath in the Abyss. In Haitian Voudoun the family of loas known as the Ghedes, and their close relatives the Barons (including *Baron Cemetiere, Baron Samedi, Baron la Croix* and *Baron Criminel*), are appropriate for this site: Baron is the master of the cemetery and the guardian of ancestral knowledge, while Ghede is the spirit of the dead. Maya Deren's description of Ghede, given below, aptly summarises what we know of the world of the ghouls, whence they could easily reach the graveyards of the Earth above:

> If Legba was the sun ... Ghede is the master of that abyss into which the sun descends. If Legba was time, then Ghede is that eternal figure in black, posted at the timeless cross-roads at which all men and even the sun one day arrive. The cross upon the tomb is his symbol ... The cosmic abyss is both womb and tomb. In a sense, Ghede is Legba who has crossed

the cosmic threshold to the underworld ... If Legba was once Lord of Life, Ghede is now Lord of Resurrection, and the difference between them is Death, which is Ghede. It is the knowledge of death that has transfigured Legba ... As Death, he [Ghede] is the keeper of the cemetery ...

> (Deren 1953, pp 102-3)

Even his most common manifestation recalls Lovecraft's ghouls, not known for their table manners:

Ghede poses most frequently as a poor wandering beggar, famished of course, but content with the crudest of food, which he consumes ravenously ... As Criminelle, a Petro manifestation, he sinks his teeth into his own arm, and the friends who would protect the man possessed by Criminelle from this voraciousness must work hard and frantically to unclamp the jaws before the flesh is torn. (Deren 1953, pp 104-8))

The orisha Oya is the Guardian of the Cemetery and Goddess of Death in Yoruba mythology. She is connected with the secret society of the Egungun, associated with the cult of the ancestral dead: 'Egungun means 'bone' or 'skeleton', as the members impersonate the dead ... Sometimes they are called up ... from a covered well, thus appearing to come from the underground city of the dead ... They speak in guttural voices, supposedly in imitation of a sacred monkey' (Parrinder 1949, pp 143-4). A monkey is sacred to the cult, recalling the analogy between Lovecraft's dog-like ghouls and the dog-headed sacred baboons of ancient Egypt.

Discussion

As Alfred Metraux wrote in *Voodoo in Haiti* (1959, p 365), 'Voodoo is a paganism of the West. We discover it with joy or horror, according to our temperament or our background'. It is just possible, perhaps, that Lovecraft may indeed have discovered Voodoo, and that, due to his temperament and background, he reacted to it with horror; after all, his fiction is now normally classified as "horror". If not, the theology and pantheons of Voodoo and Santeria nevertheless provide a fascinating parallel for the Mythos, and shed an interesting light upon it.

This comparison with other mythologies which, like Lovecraft's, have grown from Old World seeds in the soil of the New World is, I believe, a fruitful and illuminating one. Robert M. Price made a similar comparison in his scholarly spoof, *A Critical Commentary on the Necronomicon*: referring to the cult of the Old Ones as though it were real, he wrote that 'The situation was analogous to that prevailing in most West African mythologies, where a primordial god has retreated far into the sky. The day-to-day business of religion is handled by a number of lesser godlings and spirits who receive sacrifice and answer prayers. So here: ... for now one may venerate the sea-monster Cthulhu, the messenger Nyarlathotep, and the universal gate Yog-Sothoth'. (Price 1996, p 278)

As Lovecraft made clear in *The Call of Cthulhu*, such African-American mystery religions are to be found in the New Orleans area (which he later visited in 1932), but it is quite possible that he had come across them in his sojourn in New York in 1924-5, then as now a multi-cultural port city with many sailors and immigrants from the Caribbean; or even perhaps his home town of Providence, Rhode Island, which enjoyed 'an ancient waterfront swarming with foreign mongrels', as he kindly put it. In other words, there may well have been clandestine Voodoo or Santeria cults and obscure *botanicas* in New York and elsewhere during the 1920s; and, if so, it is conceivable that Lovecraft came across them on his long walks around New York, sometimes looking for work, sometimes nocturnal; or perhaps heard of them at those social gatherings about whose multi-ethnic nature he notoriously complained to his wife. One wonders whether it was not perhaps Lovecraft himself who was 'jostled by a nautical-looking Negro' during a nocturnal ramble in search of 'a supposed voodoo meeting'.

Even if Lovecraft did not experience Vodou or Santeria at first hand - and that we shall probably never know - he may have received second-hand accounts from others. Haiti itself was occupied by the U.S.Marines (with accompanying civilians such as medical staff) from 1915 to 1934, so it is possible that Lovecraft obtained accounts of Vodou ceremonies and mythology - no doubt often prejudiced and exaggerated - from servicemen, civilian personnel or other visitors. William Seabrook, for example, published his book *The Magic Island* in 1929, too late to be a source for Lovecraft, but indicative of the exploration and revelation of Vodou, sometimes sympathetic if somewhat sensational, which was possible at the time. As Lovecraft so patronisingly and yet so aptly put it, referring to the Cthulhu cult: 'It savoured of the wildest dreams of mythmaker and theosophist, and disclosed an astonishing degree of cosmic imagination among such half-castes and pariahs as might be least expected to possess it'.

Books such as Mabel Steedman's *Unknown to the World: Haiti* (1939), while obviously too late for Lovecraft, display an understanding of

Vodou deriving from a background in occultism such as I have postulated for Lovecraft. Her bibliography includes occultists such as Crowley, Fortune, Hartmann, Levi, Mathers, Spence, and Ouspensky among others, in addition to other authors who might seem more relevant, and she occasionally makes intriguing remarks such as this: 'Readers who have studied the Hebrew Qabalah cannot fail to have noticed in how many ways Haitian Voudou approximates to the Qabalah'). She stresses that 'The Voudouists ... recognise that all things are controlled by natural forces. They personify these forces, which then become a pantheon of gods and goddesses ... known as the "LOIS". *A Voudou god or goddess, then, is a personified intelligent Force*. This fact is *most* important'. (Steedman, 1939 pp, 220, 159, 197 – her emphasis).

Her analysis closely resembles that of Geoffrey Gorer, a contemporary traveller in West Africa:

> At the head of every negro theological system I came across is a GOD who created all things .... This God created a number of forces which I have called FETISHES; these forces are part of God and are as it were the canalisation of a section of his power. God can be worshipped only through these forces, which bear in negro eschatology much the same relation to the godhead that saints and the BVM do for Catholics.'
> (Gorer 1945, pp 113-4)

(Many of these "fetishes" have of course been syncretised with Roman Catholic saints in Vodou and Santeria). It also recalls the analogy made by Robert M. Price between the Mythos and West African religion, cited above: 'The day-to-day business of religion is handled by a number of lesser godlings and spirits who receive sacrifice and answer prayers' (Price 1996, p 278).

As the quotations from *The Call of Cthulhu* above suggest, and as his letters and some poems abundantly make clear, Lovecraft was a racist not atypical of his time. Houellebecq suggests that, due to the proximity to other ethnic groups, the passive racist attitudes typical of one of his background became active during and after his stay in New York: 'it was in New York that his racist opinions turned into a full-fledged racist neurosis' (Houellebecq, 1991 trans. 2005, p 105).

It could be argued that as such he would be unlikely to investigate and benefit from African-American mystery religions such as Vodoun or Santeria. On the other hand, racism has hardly ever prevented, and in fact has often been perceived to legitimate, the plundering of indigenous and colonial peoples; in this case, a cultural appropriation, akin to the contemporary "appreciation" of West African sculpture by modernist artists.

As we have seen, there are parallels between the Mythos and Voodoo, which the Tree of Life of the Cabbala , as a chart of aspects of the divine / demonic, enables us to see more clearly.

Some of these parallels are surprisingly close, such as Legba / Ellegua and Yog-Sothoth; some may be explained as fairly inevitable similarities between pantheons, such as Shub Niggurath the Venus-like nature-goddess and Nyarlathotep the Mercury-like trickster; others are more tenuous. Some so tenuous, in fact, that I have omitted them from this discussion, due to the amount of explanation required - hence the omission of some Sephiroth and some Mythos entities. Nevertheless, the interesting question is why such parallels should exist between literary, fictional creations – which one might expect to have a fairly random collection of attributes – and the 'real' entities of a living religion. The answers to that question could include the following:

- the influence of one upon the other, i.e. of Voodoo upon the Mythos;
- the possibility that humankind 'naturally' envisages aspects of the divine in certain ways: a gate-keeper, a goddess whose sacred metal is copper, a messenger, an undersea god, and so on, some of which can be mapped upon the Tree of Life;
- the possibility that West African religion derives ultimately from the same (Middle-Eastern?) roots as the Cabala;
- the possibility that this tradition consciously or subconsciously influences modern writers.

Or at least, some writers: one may perhaps draw a distinction between Lovecraft and his circle, and other, later authors – one thinks of Ramsay Campbell or Brian Lumley - some of whose creations tend to appear in their fiction as reified avatars of greater materiality, that is to say as somewhat absurd, quasi-biological creatures, with 'a fairly random collection of attributes'. The fact that Lovecraft in particular and his contemporary circle in general were different suggests that some sort of tradition was exercising an influence upon them.

References

Bathurst, Rev.W.H., 1879, *Roman Antiquities at Lydney Park, Gloucestershire*, Longmans, London.

Brown, Karen McCarthy, 1991, *Mama Lola, A Vodou Priestess in Brooklyn*, University of California Press.

Campbell, Ramsay, 1994, *The Moon Lens*, in Price ed. *The Shub-Niggurath Cycle*, Chaosium.

Carter, Lin, 1996, *The Necronomicon: the Dee Translation*, in Robert Price (Ed) *The Necronomicon*, Chaosium.

Carter, Lin, 1997 [1980] 'The Thing in the Pit', in Robert Price (Ed), *The Xothic Legend Cycle: The Complete Mythos Fiction of Lin Carter*, Chaosium.

Denning, M. & O.Phillips, 1988, *The Sword and the Serpent*, Llewellyn, St.Paul, MN.

Deren, Maya, 1953, *Divine Horsemen / The Voodoo Gods*, Thames & Hudson, London.

Desmangles, L., 1992, *The Faces of the Gods: Vodou and Roman Catholicism in Haiti*, University of North Carolina Press, Chapel Hill, NC.

Farrow, S. 1926, *Faith, Fancies and Fetich, or Yoruba Paganism*

Geall, David, 2005, 'A half-choked meep of cosmic fear': Is there esoteric symbolism in H.P.Lovecraft's *The Dream-Quest of Unknown Kadath?*', *Journal for the Academic Study of Magic*, 3.

Gleason, Judith, 1987, *Oya: In Praise of an African Goddess*, Shambhala.

Gonzalez-Wippler, Migene, 1987, *A Kabbalah for the Modern World*, Llewellyn, St.Paul, Minnesota.

Gonzalez-Wippler, Migene, 1992a, *Powers of the Orishas*, Original Publications, New York.

Gonzalez-Wippler, Migene, 1992b, *Santeria: African Magic in Latin America*.

Gorer, Geoffrey, 1935, *Africa Dance*.

Grant, Kenneth, 1972, *The Magical Revival*, Muller, London.

Grant, Kenneth, 1975, *Cults of the Shadow*, Muller, London.

Grant, Kenneth, 1992, *Hecate's Fountain*, Skoob, London.

Grimal, Pierre, trans.1986, *The Dictionary of Classical Mythology*, Blackwell, Oxford.

Haskins, Jim, 1978, *Voodoo & Hoodoo*, Original Publications, Plainview, NY.

Herskovits, M.J. and F.S.Herskovits, 1958, *Dahomean Narrative, A Cross-Cultural Analysis*,: North-Western University Press, Evanston, Illinois.

Houellebecq, Michel, 2005 [1991], *H.P.Lovecraft: Against the World, Against Life*, Believer Books, San Francisco.

Johnson, Samuel, 1921, *History of the Yorubas*, Lagos

Kuttner, Henry, 1995 [1939], 'The Hunt', in Robert Price (Ed.), *The Book of Iod*, Chaosium 1995 [Trophonius is misprinted as 'Torphonius' in this volume]

Lovecraft, H.P., 1920, *Celephais, The Cats of Ulthar, Nyarlathotep*

Lovecraft, H.P. 1989, *The Horror in the Museum and Other Revisions*, Sauk City: Arkham House

Lovecraft, H.P., 1990 [1926], *The Call of Cthulhu*, Dell, New York.

Lovecraft, H.P., 1994 [1930], *The Whisperer in Darkness*, Chaosium.

Lovecraft, H.P., 1995 [1926], *The Dream-Quest of Unknown Kadath*, Arkham House/Del Rey.

Lovecraft, H.P. and August Derleth, 1945, *The Lurker at the Threshold*.

Martinie, Louis and Sallie Ann Glassman, 1992, *New Orleans Voodoo Tarot*, Destiny Books, Rochester, VT.

Metraux, Alfred, 1959, *Voodoo in Haiti*, Deutsch, London.

Muller, K. and U.Ritz-Muller, 2000, *Soul of Africa*, Konemann.

O'Rahilly, T.F., 1946, *Early Irish History & Mythology*, Dublin.

Parrinder, Geoffrey, 1949, *West African Religion*, Epworth, London.

Price, Robert M., 1996 [1988], '*A Critical Commentary on the* Necronomicon', in Robert M. Price (Ed.), *The Necronomicon*, Chaosium, Oakland, CA.

Ross, Anne, 1974 [1967], *Pagan Celtic Britain*, Sphere Cardinal, London.

Seabrook, W.B., 1936, *The Magic Island*, Harrap, London.

Seyffert, Oskar, trans.1906, *A Dictionary of Classical Antiquities*, Swan Sonnenschein, London.

Smith, Clark Ashton, 1974 [1935], *The Chain of Aforgomon* (in *Out of Space & Time*, Granada Panther.

Steedman, Mabel, 1939, *Unknown to the World: Haiti*, Hurst & Blackett, London.

Thompson, Robert Farris, 1984, *Flash of the Spirit: African and Afro-American Art and Philosophy*, Vintage, New York.

Tolkien, J.R.R., 1932, *The Name 'Nodens'*, Appendix 1 of *Report of the Excavation ¼ in Lydney Park, Gloucestershire*, by R. & T.Wheeler, Society of Antiquaries of London, Report IX

The Journey of The Lion King and the Collective Unconscious

Melinda Marsh

The Disney film "The Lion King" (*The Lion King* 1994) contains many references to a shamanistic journey similar to the story told by the Major Arcana. "The Lion King" is a tale which follows a young lion club, Simba, from his birth through his childhood as a young prince, his exile after his father's death, his return as an adult to take back the throne from his evil Uncle, and finally it ends how it begins, with the birth of King Simba's cub and the completion of the circle. The Major Arcana tells a similar story, that of a young man going through his rites of passage and overcoming obstacles in order to reach enlightenment. The Major Arcana and the Lion King are not the only stories which are similar. Many cultures share the same stories, even though they have never encountered each other's works. Identical ideas occurring thousands of miles and hundreds of years apart lends support to Carl Jung's Theory of Collective Unconscious. Ideals about primitive shamanism and the journey of the hero may have been picked up consciously or unconsciously, and spread to a mainstream audience. This idea can be put to the test by watching the "Lion King" and comparing Simba's spiritual journey, created in 1994 America, to the journey of the Fool in the tarot's Major Arcana, which was created significantly earlier in Eurasia.

Mythological stories have been around for as long as humanity, having been passed orally from generation to generation. Often very similar stories will be produced in two or more different cultures at the same time, and the only explanation for this, other than coincidence or one culture influencing another, is the presence of an intangible connection between the cultures. As Joseph Campbell once said, "the symbols of mythology are not manufactured; they cannot be ordered, invented, or suppressed. They are spontaneous productions of the psyche." Thus it is well within reason that two or more cultures could spontaneously produce an identical story at similar times, and it makes it very likely that several cultures spread out over an extended period of time could come up with the same ideas (Campbell 1949, p 4). This phenomenon, called the "collective unconscious," is probably why the story of *The Lion King* and the Major Arcana are so similar.

The *Collective Unconscious* is a theory developed by psychologist Carl Jung, which suggests that ancient memories come easily to the consciousness of living humans. The majority of these former recollections are recalled "unconsciously and spontaneously in the form of dreams" and visions (Jung and von Franz 1964, p. 4). These visions appear in an experience which has been likened to falling asleep. However, in this experience one is not asleep and one's awareness is temporarily reconnected with other "sleeping" minds, allowing the transference of thoughts. Such an overlap of minds would allow ideas from different cultures and from different times to communicate through pure thought, effectively removing the language barrier, and making it difficult to identify when and from where an idea came. These ideas can remain in the unconscious for a considerable length of time before they resurface, or they can be passed on to another mind where the idea would come to fruition. In this way, ideas can be passed from one time period to another, where they will wait for an expression of creativity or divination that enables them to emerge.

When these ideas do emerge, they often take the form of symbolic images, which Jung refers to as archetypes (Jung and von Franz 1964). These basic archetypes are familiar in any story across cultures. From the prodigal son to the evil old witch to the carefree lovers, all of these are characters found across cultures. Even cultures who have been isolated for hundreds or even thousands of years often have similar stories. For example, stories similar to the lost continent of Atlantis have been found not only in Europe, but also isolated groups in South America. While some have taken this as evidence that Atlantis is real, others have called it coincidence that both cultures came up with a similar story independently. Until we find evidence that cultural dissemination occurred, we cannot assume contact between both cultures.

The idea of the collective unconscious poses the possibility of having access to the knowledge of the universe through constant meditation or enlightenment. With this knowledge, a person

> "can achieve his highest goal: the full realization of the potential of his individual Self... 'Symbols of transcendence' are the symbols that represent man's striving to attain this goal. They provide the means by which the content of the

unconscious can enter the conscious mind, and they also are themselves an active expression of those contents"
(Jung and von Franz 1964, pp 146-7).

A fitting representatives of Jung's "symbols of transcendence" are tarot cards, which have been used for several hundred years as a way of accessing the unconscious (Franklin 1998).

These cards have been popularized by movies depicting their use in fortunetelling by Eastern European women, usually of Gypsy/Romani origin. The tarot deck is made up of two sections: the Minor Arcana and the Major Arcana. The Minor Arcana is very similar to modern playing cards, though with an additional court card in each suit. The suits are also slightly different and are traditionally Coins, Cups, Swords, and Wands. The Major Arcana contains 22 cards, numbered from zero to 21, and tells the story of the Fool's journey of enlightenment.

Ideally, when giving a tarot reading, the reader must be open to connecting with the querent (questioner) as well as others who might have information. One of the many things that the Tarot can tell is how someone is progressing on his spiritual journey, by reading the Fool's Journey in the cards (Franklin 1998). The Fool and the rest of the cards in the Major Arcana each either represent a character archetype or a situation that needs to occur before one is able to spiritually become an adult.

The fool (card 0) journeys through the other 21 cards of the Major Arcana in order to reach enlightenment. Such a journey is recorded time and time again in fairytales, though the stories are reconstructed and updated to reflect changing times and values. Fairy tales are so similar despite their cultural settings because they all come from the same source, the collective unconscious. In any collection of Hans Christian Andersen (1974), there are multiple tales of transformation and enlightenment. *The Ugly Duckling*, for instance, is a basic example of a physical enlightenment: the beautifying of the outside instead of the inside. In the tale of the Ugly Duckling, the duckling starts off being very ugly, and after many hostile encounters, he believes that he is not only ugly but also unwanted and unworthy. He has to gather *Strength* in order to leave his sorry situation, and before long, he finds friends who do not care about his appearance and are willing to accept him for what he is. However, hunters arrive in a blaze of gunfire and kill his friends. His next stop takes him to a crooked old house, which is quite literally a *Falling Tower*, where several egotistical characters live. They make for unpleasant company and so duckling decides to leave, and after several months of seclusion, he goes through his first winter and turns into the most attractive swan of all. If he had not undergone this physical transformation he would have remained an ugly duckling, nevertheless through his period in seclusion, he realizes that it is much better to be beautiful in his new home with the other very attractive swans than to live alone.

Another of Hans Christian Andersen's tales, *The Snow Queen*, also tells a story of journey and transformation. This seven-part story tells of a young boy and a young girl who were best friends. One day, the boy is hit by a devil's mirror and can see nothing but faults in everything. He started to insult the young girl and ran off to play with the boys who were hitching rides on farmers' wagons. The young boy hitched a ride like his friends were, but instead of hitching a ride with a farmer, he hitched a ride with someone who brought him hundreds of miles away to the Snow Queen's Palace. The Snow Queen kissed him and while he originally believed himself to be in paradise, he was effectively kept as a prisoner.

The young girl is the real hero of the story. When her playmate disappeared, she was told he died in the river. When she went to the river to ask the river if it had taken her friend, the river sent her on a journey. During her journey, she experienced a number of obstacles such as being enchanted by a witch, being given incorrect information, and being held hostage by a group of robbers. Eventually, she continues on her quest. She finds the young boy and gives him a kiss, breaking the spell keeping him there. When they come back home, they find they are no longer the children they left as. They spent their teenage years in seclusion and are now young adults.

Inchelina (aka *Thumbelina*), a young girl only an inch tall has her own obstacles which she must overcome in order to be happy. When she was a young girl, she was kidnapped from her house by a toad who believed her to be very pretty. Indeed she was the most beautiful creatures in the land. When Inchelina awakens far from her home and held captive, she learns she is to be married to the toad's son. She is horrified by this as the toad is very ugly. She eventually escapes her imprisonment through the help of a butterfly, but she then gets captured by a May bug who also wants to marry her. This does not last long as the May bug becomes convinced Inchelina is ugly, so he releases her.

Suffering from low self-esteem and believing herself ugly, she wanders through the forest alone until winter when she is helped by a field mouse who offers her a place to stay for the winter. The field mouse tries to marry Inchelina off to the mole because he is wealthy and Inchelina would be lucky to get any husband due to her looks. If Inchelina marries the mole, she will never again go outside which gives her tremendous happiness. During this winter, Inchelina finds a nearly dead bird and nurses it back to health and then releases him. She does not see him again until right before the wedding, the bird rescues her and brings her to a flowerbed near his nest as he thinks she will be able to call a flower home. She chooses a flower where a very handsome young king about her height lives. They fall in love and get married, allowing Inchelina to become the queen of the angels who live in the flower bed. While this is not a story of enlightenment, it does show a few of the difficulties of the teenage years. She was only a child when she was first kidnapped and after a year or so of trials and seclusion from other humans, she finds herself a young adult and back with a handsome man just like her.

The difference between these stories and the Journey of the Fool is that the Fool's journey is more spiritual than physical, as is Simba's in *The Lion King*. As Bettelheim (1976, pp 25, 7) points out "fairy tales' concern is not useful information about the external world, but the inner processes taking place in an individual…. The unconscious [is] a powerful determinant of behavior."

Perhaps when the time is right, it is natural to hide yourself away until your transformation is complete, after which you can come home in triumph as a full adult. In the Lion King, Simba leaves home as the equivalent of a child. After spending his entire adolescence in exile, he returns as a fully adult lion. His "return and reintegration with society... is the justification of the long retreat" (Campbell 1949, p 36). Simba returns to discover that he has become his father, and now he is the rightful ruler of his people. The changes he goes through were are not out there waiting to be collected, but instead they are were right inside him waiting for him to realize them. Simba's journey is about coming to that realization, just like the Fool.

Simba's journey is not only the start of the story, but also it is the start of his life; the meta-narrative beginning of a beginning. Simba's birth and progression down the path of life is the ultimate meaning of the first card of the tarot, *The Fool,* which symbolizes innocence and inexperience on the path that is pursued. The spiritual journey of the Fool, or the Green Man as it is known in some decks such as *the Sacred Circle Tarot,* is a quest for enlightenment and represents "powerful forces... breaking down the old order so that a new one might emerge" (Franklin 1998, p 44). This describes the relationship of a king to his successor: when one dies the "old way" dies with him, and the next king designs his own form of justice.

Simba's father, Mufasa, plays the role of the second card which is called variously *The Magician, The Juggler,* or *The High Priest.* This card is the teacher, friend and father figure to the Fool, because he is the first person the Fool comes across on his journey. It can be summed up in the phrase "the inner guide... who is always present" (Franklin, 1998, p 48). In one scene, Mufasa saves Simba from hyenas and gives him a stern talking to, but Mufasa is never truly annoyed at Simba, because it is hard for a father (or teacher) to stay upset at a son (or student). Mufasa then promises that he will guide Simba for as long as he lives, and when he is gone, the "great kings of the past" will continue to be his guides. Mufasa's untimely demise a few scenes later makes Simba doubt his father's words, though Mufasa lives on as a part of Simba's subconscious.

The *High Priestess* is another card that is present in *The Lion King*, providing not only the influence of subconscious, but also the influence of a strong female. Traditionally, the *Priestess* represents listening to the subconscious' advice as well as an increase in intuitive powers. With the lack of an external force to guide behavior, such as a parent, one's standards of behavior have to be set internally, and they are usually built without conscious recognition. In the movie, Simba's increased intuitive powers provide an excuse for him to act on Mufasa's spiritual guidance. This card also indicates a female presence who will play a significant role as a friend or a lover (Franklin 1998). In the Lion King, that female would be Nala, the love interest in the story, who plays a key role in Simba's return home. If Nala had not found Simba and told him of the destruction of their home by his evil uncle, Simba would have been less inclined to return home.

The two cards *Lady/Empress* and *Lord/Emperor* share enough in common to be considered together. *The Lady* represents a successful phase in life, when one recognizes powers outside of one's self-guiding actions. In the film, an equivalent harmonious time for Simba was the several years he lived with his friends, Timon and Pumbaa, in a sort of paradise. The *Lord/Emperor* represents the re-evaluation of moral codes as well as taking a stand as "a leader against a powerful individual" (Franklin 1998, p 62). During his harmonious period, Simba reassess his philosophy on life when he is introduced to the phrase "Hakuna Mata" (or "no worries"), and although he is not yet brave enough to face his now very powerful

Uncle Scar, the implication is he will eventually be able to fulfill his destiny and become king.

Rafiki is the spiritual character in the story, so it is most appropriate that he is seen as the equivalent of *Hierophant* or *"Druid,"* as the *Druid* also acts as a balancing force. Rafiki is the one who realizes Simba is still alive, but needs help to come back to the now destroyed Pridelands. Rafiki convinces Simba to face the past from which he has been hiding from for years. Rafiki quite literally knocks some sense into Simba. Although the past can still be painful, the important thing is to learn from it. Simba has been living in paradise for too long and he needs to be reminded of his pain. He realizes then that he has to take a new path in order to keep his life in balance. Further, he needs to face his fears about his father's death and what his family will say about his return.

As Simba's story continues, we need to reshuffle the Major Arcana somewhat as the following three cards would normally come after the *Druid*. In the movie, their influence is felt from the reintroduction of Nala until the return home. These cards are *The Lovers* — who not only represent the blossoming love affair between the two young lions, but also indicate that the Fool needs to take responsibility for his own actions (Franklin 1998) — and *The Chariot* and *Warrior/Justice* cards, which indicate the need to face one's fears, and a future success over a formidable opponent. At this point in the story, Simba has been running from his past and his destiny for far too long and now he must face his responsibilities. However, he is scared of going back home to his family as he remembers the psychological pain he felt from his father's death. Fortunately, Rafiki helps him overcome his reluctance, and leads him on his spiritual journey so that he can discover what he must do.

The *Shaman* card is different from the *Druid* card in that the Druid is a balancing force and can represent another person, whereas the Shaman marks the return to the primitive and represents the seeker (Franklin 1998). As Simba follows Rafiki through the forest until he practically reaches the point of exhaustion, he prepares himself for what he is about to encounter. At Rafiki's urging, he looks harder at the reflection in the lake in order to concentrate his mind so it can open up to the subtle realms. The conclusion of Simba's vision shows Mufasa, or the subconscious in the form of Mufasa, once again trying to give him advice. This time Simba listens and returns home.

The lessons taught in the Tarot by the cards, *Wheel of Life* and *Web*, go unheeded by villain of the story, Scar, who ravages the land to the point of permanent ruin. The Wheel represents the passing of time and the gradual swing from bountiful to barren, such as occurs during the winter months, whereas *The Web* teaches the same lessons as the Lion King's "Circle of Life" song; one of the lines in the reprised Elton John version (1994) states, "you should never take more than you give." On the contrary, Scar abuses the land by over-hunting the herds to the extent that they flee the region and the Pridelands become barren.

Simba made a premiere *Sacrifice* when he returned to the Pridelands. He gave up the beautiful residence of his teenage years for a barren land and the responsibilities of kingship. The challenge for the throne between Scar and Simba can also be considered as a sacrifice as only one of them can win and ascend the throne legitimately. Fortunately, Simba wins, and Scar is banished. Put simply, Scar loses his home because he was too greedy.

With the banishment of Scar, Simba takes on his father's role and *The Death* card reflects this change. Taken at face value, it can be said this card predicts Mufasa's downfall, but the more accepted meaning is transformation, such as the gradual transformation of Simba into Mufasa. This was foreshadowed by Simba's vision at the lake when his reflection slowly turns into Mufasa. Ascension to the throne ensures that the son becomes more like the father, and illustrates that a child always turns into his parents.

Next in the Tarot is *The Underworld* card, which is the unexpressed dark side of the Fool, and the *Falling Tower*, the sign that a flaw is going to bring about a collapse. These represent the eternal battle between good and evil. If one does not face evil it will cause destruction. In *The Lion King* the dark side is represented by the evil Scar. Scar is the evil to Mufasa and Simba's good, and both Mufasa and Simba must face Scar in a battle for dominance. When Mufasa is trying to climb up the cliff, he asks Scar to help, instead he is rewarded by being thrown into the gorge and killed. Later in the movie, Simba finds himself in the same position sliding down the cliff and attempts to get Scar to help. When Scar reveals that he killed Mufasa this way, Simba regains his strength, climbs up the cliff, and pushes Scar to the ground. Hence Scar's reign is brought down, first by the failure of the hyenas to follow earlier orders to kill Simba instead of letting him escape, and by Scar's own arrogant assumption that he could fill the role of the king, Scar leaves the Pridelands in exile and establishes his own pride.

Simba's coronation is the ultimate rite of passage, or in Major Arcana terms, *Initiation*. Simba, the son, becomes his father, while Mufasa, the father, takes his place in the other world as one of the great kings of the past. *The Star* in *The Lion King* is represented the knowledge of the ages and provides a glimmer of hope that shines when all is looking very bleak indeed. The Star could also represent "the great kings of the past," which was how Mufasa explained the stars in the sky. Simba could also represent hope, because with his return the healing rains come for the first time. The Tarot *Moon* tells the seeker that he "can't live in the past" and must adapt to a new role (Franklin 1998, p 129). Similarly, Simba left the Pridelands as an inexperienced child and he returns as an adult to take the throne from a ruthless tyrant.

The Sun is important in Tarot because it represents spiritual development in leaps and bounds, as well as the physical sun that makes the plants grow (Franklin 1998, p 133). In the movie, the presentation of the royal lion cubs to the sun reinforces the connection of royalty to the sun. In many other cultures, such as the Ancient Egyptians and the Aztecs, the king is considered to be the handpicked descendent of the sun god, and it is he alone who can make the sun rise every morning. The sun's disappearance during the reign of Scar represented more than gloominess and death; it also signified the take-over by one not qualified to do the morning rituals. When Simba returns as rightful heir and triumphs over evil, the sun also returns, and even during the healing rains it continues to shine.

The rains promise the *Rebirth* of the plants and a return of the herds, exalting Simba to greatness though his leadership during a crisis and his ability to successfully rebuild the Pridelands. The movie then jumps forward to show that after years of hard work, the new Pridelands have become a reality. The last card in the Major Arcana is *The World Tree* representing the successful end of the Fool's journey and the beginning of a new one. Hence, *The Lion King* ends as it starts, with the presentation of a new baby, this time a daughter. We can speculate that hers will be a similar story, though in the sequel, her role will be to reunite the two prides (*The Lion King II: Simba's Pride* 1998).

So we see that *The Lion King* represents the spiritual journey that we undertake as Fools and end as Trees, with the realization that there is no true end to our quest. Mufasa's guidance did not die with his body; it became imbedded in his son's subconscious. Simba's journey took him to a faraway paradise place where he learnt much of what he needed to know. Like an extended out-of-body experience, it enables him to return from the "dead" and to go home more enlightened as to the best way to deal with Scar, even though it means facing his own fears. Simba's decision to come back is the right one and he provides great hope for his former pride. His triumph over the evil Scar restores balance to the cycle of life, and the plants start to grow and the herds come back to graze.

While no one is sure of the exact origins of *The Lion King* story nor the inspiration behind it, it is readily understood by all peoples whose cultures have similar stories. Disney representatives have never officially revealed the inspiration for *The Lion King*, whether it is from a Japanese fairy tale or from Shakespeare's Hamlet. The ability to communicate with all peoples by reworking their traditional stories, or knowing which stories to choose, is what makes Disney so popular (Dorfman and Mattelart 1975).

The characters represented in *The Lion King* are well-known across cultures. Simba is the "guilty" child who goes away under the guise of being dead and comes back as an adult when his family needs him the most, even though he is terrified of what they will think about his absence. Sarabi, one of the few mothers still present at the end of a Disney film, is strong and regal; even when Scar is threatening her she shows no fear. Mufasa is the good man with a heart of gold and without a mean bone in his body, who is hurt undeservedly by those closest and dearest to him. Scar is the calculating individual who is always ambitious for more power, and the hyenas are his ever-ready accomplices. Nala is the eternal tomboy, always able to triumph over the boys even as an adult, and that is how Simba later recognizes her as an old friend. Although perhaps a little insane, Rafiki is the wizard, medicine man, healer, spiritual leader, diviner, and priest. He is an absolute necessity to have on your side because of his ability to provide moral support for the people. Zazu is the faithful lieutenant, following every order to the letter, even though he might be tricked or used as a teaching tool by Mufasa. The keepers of paradise are Timon, the smart trickster, who is constantly taking credit for work he so carefully avoids, and Pumbaa, who is a little on the slow side yet has a good soul even when he is being insulted about his flatulence problem.

In conclusion, journeys to enlightenment occur repeatedly in the fairy tales of almost all cultures. These journeys have so many similar characteristics across different cultures and different times that the only explanation for them is what Carl Jung has called Collective Unconsciousness. Collective Unconsciousness occurs when ancient memories from the past, or from other cultures, come into the consciousness of living humans through dreams and visions. Tarot cards provide a way to access this deep unconsciousness, and through their symbols provide a commentary of a person's journey to enlightenment by pointing out where on the spiritual path that person is. Tarot cards indicate to the reader what inner changes, spiritual transformations, seclusions, and returns have taken place. Disney's *The Lion King* meshes very well with tarot's Major Arcana in that it has similar characters and similar occurrences. On one level, the Lion King is all other fairy stories; on another it is none of them. All fairy stories end, but journeys of enlightenment will continue for as long as life exists.

References

Andersen, H. C. and Haugaard, E. C., 1974, *A Treasury of Hans Christian Andersen*, Barnes and Noble, New York.

Bettelheim, B., 1976, *The Uses of Enchantment: the Meaning and Importance of Fairy Tales*, Alfred A. Knopf, Inc., New York.

Campbell, J., 1949, *The hero with a thousand faces*, Pantheon Books, New York.

Dorfman, A. and Mattelart, A., 1975, *How to read Donald Duck : imperialist ideology in the Disney comic*, International General, New York.

Franklin, A., 1998, *The sacred circle tarot : a Celtic pagan journey*, Llewellyn, St. Paul, Minn.

John, E. and Rice, T., 1994, *Circle of Life* In *The Lion King: Original Motion Picture Soundtrack*, Label: Disney.

Jung, C. G. and von Franz, M.-L., 1964, *Man and his symbols*, Doubleday, Garden City, N.Y.

The Lion King, 1994, Feature Film, Walt Disney Pictures.

The Lion King II: Simba's Pride ,1998, Video Recording (VHS), Walt Disney Pictures.

"The Third Time's the Charm": Mythic Operative Magic in the Merseburger Zaubersprüche[1]

Michael Moynihan

On the 3rd of February, 1842, the industrious German philologist Jacob Grimm spoke before the Akademie der Wissenschaften in Berlin, and was nearly beside himself. The "recently made and so surprising of a discovery" (Grimm 1965, p 1)[2] which he would relate to his audience that day consisted of the partial contents of a single sheet of medieval parchment, namely two short charms with poetic features.[3] These two texts, written down in an Old High German dialect and likely dating from the first half of the tenth century, have come to be known as the *Merseburger Zaubersprüche*, or "Merseburg Charms." Grimm's lecture was soon published as an article, 'On Two Poems Discovered from the Time of German Heathendom,' the title of which reflects his belief that the poems emanated from the pre-Christian Germanic world.[4]

Today nearly a millennium has passed since the original transcription of the Merseburg charms, but this has done little to diminish their inherent power. These sparse texts seem as volatile to the imaginations of modern people as they undoubtedly were for those who once actively employed them in times of need. They have been a source of enduring fascination and speculation for scholars of many disciplines, ranging from anthropology to philology, linguistics, semiotics, and beyond. The resulting body of secondary literature on the charms is immense: Wolfgang Beck's authoritative 2003 study, *Die Merseburger Zaubersprüche*, contains the most complete bibliography to date, and this spans 49 pages. As Beck details (2003, pp XV-XXXII), since their discovery the charms have also served as a source of inspiration for writers, poets, musicians, and even propagandists. And like the scholarly literature, the creative productions in the cultural sphere continue apace: two recent works appearing in the time since Beck's study was published are poet Frank Geerk's 2003 collection *Von Wunden und Wundern: Handbuch der Zaubersprüche*, and the recording of the First Merseburg Charm on the CD *Die letzten Goten* by the Halle-an-der-Saale romanticist music group Barditus.

The existence of the charms was first discovered, quite unexpectedly, a year prior to Jacob Grimm's lecture by Dr. Georg Waitz, who was working in the Merseburg cathedral library. Waitz immediately realized the importance of the find and arranged for the manuscript to be sent to Grimm for inspection. Grimm (quoted in Beck 2003, p XIII) would later write to another colleague how "childishly gleeful" he was about the revelation of these artifacts of older Germanic culture.[5] He (1965, p 3) described the material as "amid Christian and pious phrases, twelve

Old High German lines" which in fact comprised "two independent, alliterating poems of openly heathen content," and immediately set to work trying to unravel its often puzzling linguistic and semantic content.[6]

The following discussion aims to introduce scholars of magic who may only have a limited knowledge of the Merseburg Charms to the texts themselves, and to summarize some of the key issues that have been debated over the past century and a half. The focus will be upon the content of the charms, but ultimately I will argue that some of the interpretational problems regarding the mythological references in the charms—which bedeviled Grimm and subsequent scholars, and continue to invite speculation up to the present day—are of less importance if the charms are viewed as examples of operative Germanic analogical magic.

The magic we are dealing with here comes in the form of formulaic incantations that would have been employed by the practitioner to effect an outcome in mundane reality otherwise unachievable by any direct, physical means on the practitioner's part at that particular moment. Given their form as verbal charms that were spoken or sung, it not surprising that semiotic theories of magic as a communicatory act (e.g., as detailed in Grambo 1975, Nöth 1977, and Flowers 1984) are an appealing lens of interpretation. But it is not my intention to exclusively apply a particular theory of magic to the Merseburg Charms. The aim is rather to look at them from various perspectives—structural, poetic, and mythic—to see what they are composed of and what deeper connotations they may have had within the cultural matrix that produced them, and which therefore combined to endow the charms with their potency.[7]

The First Charm

Although the main part of the following discussion will focus on the second charm, the longer of the two, a brief look at the first charm would be useful. Grimm was certainly correct that the two charms are independent from one another, but it will hopefully become clear that they share much in common, even if this may not be evident on the surface. A normalized version of the original text given by Beck (2003, p 1) is as follows:

> *Eiris sazun idisi, sazun heraduoder.*
>
> *Suma hapt heptidun, suma heri lezidun,*
>
> *Suma clubodun umbi cuonio uuidi*
>
> *Insprinc haptbandun, inuar uigandun!*

The most thorough summary of opinions regarding the linguistic and semantic content of the charm can be found in Beck's study (2003, pp 1-89). My translation below generally follows his reading and subsequent arguments:

> *Once upon a time sat [divine] women, they sat here and there*
>
> *Some restrained a prisoner, some hemmed in armies*
>
> *Some cleaved all around the sharp restraints.*
>
> *Break free of the bonds! Escape from the [enemy] battlers!*

The charm is generally interpreted as a type of "binding-and-loosening" spell, specifically intended for use in a context of warfare. The primary purpose appears to be loosening the bonds of captured prisoners of war. Gustav Ehrismann (quoted in Murdoch 1988, p 364) has elaborated on its utilization: "The charm was uttered either by the prisoner himself, provided that he knew it, or from a distance by members of his tribe, in this case probably magically adept women."[8]

Structurally the charm is relatively simple and can be divided into two parts. The first three lines function as a short mythic narrative, or *historiola*. This type of charm has a long history and appears in many cultural contexts. As Edina Bozóky (1992, p 84) notes, it is a "clearly defined subcategory of oral magical ritual" characterized by "a short story or anecdote—a microstory—preceding the actual magical formula, conjuration, or exorcism, and setting the stage for the actual ritual." For his general theory of magic, Marcel Mauss (quoted in Bozóky 1992, p 88) categorized a charm like this as a "mythic incantation" that "consists in describing an operation similar to that which one wishes to produce. This description takes the form of a story or an epic recital, and its actors are heroic or divine. One assimilates the present situation to the situation described as a prototype, with this reasoning: if a god, hero, or saint has been able to do something, often something very difficult, in a certain circumstance, can he not do the same thing in the present situation, which is analogous?"

The opening three lines of the First Merseburg Charm could be interpreted on a mundane level, but when considered from a philological perspective there are mythic overtones which become apparent. The word *idisi*, used to describe the active figures in the story, is glossed as "women," the plural of the strong feminine noun *itis* (cognate with Old Saxon *idis* "woman, wife" and Old English *ides* "woman"). The same word appears in Christian Old High German texts by Otfrid, and appears to have special connotations—for example in line 6 of his *Missus est*

Gabrihel angelus (7. I, 5; entire text in Braune 1962, pp 103-105) in the phrase *itis frono* "divine/lordly woman" referring to the Virgin Mary, whom the angel Gabriel flies to visit in a glorious, seemingly otherworldly palace. It is probably cognate to Old Norse *dís,* a term used for certain female deities, and may describe a valkyrie-type figure. The latter connotation would be especially apt if the charm does, in fact, describe battlefield scenarios. Grimm's conclusion (1965, p 6) regarding the *idisi* was: "they are wise women, valkyries who decide battles," and the majority of subsequent commentators follow this general line of thought.[9] The second part of the charm is the final line, a magical command in the imperative.[10]

Numerically, the most magically important value in the charm is indicated with the three types of tasks being undertaken by the divine women. Three is a prominent and recurrent element in a vast number of the Germanic charms and certainly had indigenous significance in Germanic cosmology, myth, and magical practices well before the arrival of Christianity. Specific associations between a magical rite and the number three can, for example, be seen in an early account of the Germanic tribes, when Tacitus describes (in *Germania*, Ch. 10, circa first century C.E.) their method of divining by casting down slips of wood with certain symbols on them, of which three are then picked up and interpreted.

In terms of the semantic content, there is an intriguing dynamic within the charm between acts of binding and "hemming in," and acts of untying or severing restraints and "setting free." This type of oppositional polarity is a discernible feature in many Germanic charms, and may have functioned as kind of intensifier that increased the power, and hence the efficacy, of the magical working. The folklorist and anthropologist Stephen C. Wehmeyer (2006) has recently analyzed a number of Old English charms with regard to this component, which he terms the "Oppositional Aesthetic Dyad." Wehmeyer (p 4) refers to this Dyad as "a central, pervasive, and characteristic element," and part of the "grammar" of archaic Germanic magic. The Old English charms bear many structural similarities to the Old High German and Old Saxon charms, and should undoubtedly be seen as two closely related branches of Germanic magical practice.[11]

Mythically there are parallels that connect this charm and its function to the god Wodan/Óðinn. These include his role as a preeminent battle god and his relations to the valkyries who bring the dead warriors to Valhalla. Most noteworthy, however, is the resonance with stanza 149 of the Eddic *Hávamál*, in which Óðinn brags of a charm he has at his disposal:

> *A fourth I know, if men shall fasten*
>
> *Bonds on my bended legs;*
>
> *So great is the charm that forth I may go,*
>
> *The fetters spring from my feet,*
>
> *Broken the bonds from my hands.*
>
> (translation: Bellows 1923, p 64)[12]

The Eddic charm's aim of loosening restraints imposed by an enemy bears an uncanny similarity with one possible interpretation of the First Merseburg Charm, especially if an alternate reading is accepted (cf. Beck 2003, pp 65-68) in which *cuonio uuidi* is taken to specifically mean "knee-binding withies," referring to a method by which prisoners of war were restrained in ancient Germanic warfare.

The Second Charm

The second and most famous of the Merseburg charms shares some significant structural similarities with the first, but its intentions are wholly different. A normalized version of the text, following Beck (2003, 90) is:

> *Phol ende Uuodan uuorun zi holza.*
>
> *Du uuart demo balderes uolon sin uuoz birenkit.*
>
> *Thu biguol en Sinhtgunt, sunna era suister,*
>
> *thu biguol en Friia, Uolla era suister,*
>
> *thu biguol en Uuodan, so he uuola conda:*
>
> *Sose benrenki, sose bluotrenki,*
>
> *sose lidirenki:*
>
> *Ben zi bena, bluot zi bluoda,*
>
> *lid zi geliden, sose gelimida sin!*

Translation:

> *Phol and Wodan fared to the holt.*
>
> *There the foot of Balder's* [or: *of the lord's*] *horse became wrenched out of joint.*
>
> *Then Sinhtgunt sang magic charms over it, Sunna her sister,*
>
> *Then Friia sang magic charms over it, Folla her sister,*

> *Then Wodan sang magic charms over it, as he well knew how:*
>
> *Be it bone-wrench, be it blood-wrench, be it limb-wrench:*
>
> *Bone to bone, blood to blood, limb to limb—be glued together again!*

From a philological standpoint, the text has a number of problematic elements that resist simple—or convincingly conclusive—solutions. The result of this has been what Jan de Vries already in 1957 (II, p 172) called a "tangle of opinions."[13] The same could of course be said of the First Merseburg Charm, although the number of conflicting interpretations for it is somewhat less dizzying in size and scope. In his recent comprehensive study of the charms, Wolfgang Beck has carefully waded through and analyzed the validity of various opinions; his readings of the texts are the product of these linguistic and grammatical assessments.[14]

Although there have been innumerable ideas advanced concerning linguistic and metrical aspects of the charm, the most heated and divergent opinions relate to possible explanations for the words in the poem which appear to be proper names of divinities.[15] This is particularly the case with *Phol* and *balderes* in the first two lines, but also with *Sinhtgunt* in the third line. Often the arguments for a specific religio-mythological identification (or lack of one) for a particular name/word will take into account both linguistic and metrical/alliterative considerations.[16] Deciphering exactly to whom the names refer is undoubtedly the aspect of the charm that has been most written about, yet we are no closer to clear answers now than Jacob Grimm was in 1841 when he (1965, p 17) wistfully hoped that future scholarship "will bring us to more decisive information."[17]

The most perplexing enigma lies with the very first word of the charm, *Phol*, which Grimm (1965, p 11) called an "unheard of name."[18] This word, or name, is transcribed *P^{h}ol* in the original manuscript. Cyril Edwards (2002, p 97) relates: "As a journey to Merseburg confirmed, the superscript *h* is written in the same hand as the rest of the text of the charms, suggesting an afterthought on the part of the same scribe. The inference is that what the scribe found before him was in some way problematic; conceivably, the first letter of his exemplar was no ordinary P."

Grimm tried to use geographical place-name evidence to prove that a god bearing this name existed in Germanic-speaking areas of the continent and England, but more concrete evidence for this supposition has never been found. Over the years *Phol* has also been equated with various known Germanic male deities such as Balder, Freyr/Frô (with *Phol* being etymologically cognate to Greek *phallus*), or Thor. The latter equation of *Phol* = Thor, put forth by Edwards (2002), is argued with interesting and even plausible justifications, but ultimately hinges on the unprovable assumptions that *Phol* was incorrectly copied by a scribe who should have written "Thor," and that the charm originated from a Scandinavian source.

The mysterious *Phol* has also been posited as Vol, an equally unknown male divine counterpart to the *Uolla* mentioned later in the poem. Most all of these theories rely heavily on comparative linguistic evidence, often from far afield, and none are especially convincing. Other past theories, now considered unlikely, have asserted that *Phol* refers to the apostle Paul, or is an abbreviated form of Apollo.

A much different, and more prosaic, solution was advanced in separate articles by Helmut Rosenfeld (1973, pp 1-12) and Kenneth Northcott (1959, pp 45-50), following from ideas in earlier commentaries by Preusler (1922) and Steller (1930). Both Rosenfeld and Northcott read *Phol* as *Fol* (or *Vol*—the letter *f* was alternately written as *v* or *u* in Old High German manuscripts), arguing that the P^h was intended to represent a voiceless labio-dental fricative (with the superscript 'h' an attempt to clarify the phonology). In order to explain the disparity between *Fol* and what we would expect to see—i.e., *folo,* the nominative form of the same weak masculine noun that appears properly declined as dative singular *folon* (written *uolon*) in the second line—Northcott (1959, p 47) further speculates that the charm must have been transcribed from an oral recitation, and an elision took place with the initial vowel of the following word, *ente*. Northcott then remarks (p 47), "Unfortunately there is no way of substantiating this [elision] theory since there is no other place in the charm where elision could have taken place." Alternate justifications for explaining *Phol* as Wodan's horse appear in Rosenfeld (1973, pp 5-10). Rosenfeld cites Preusler and Steller in his discussion, but seems to have been unaware of Northcott's article. He would have sympathized with the gist of the latter's reading of the charm, if not his specific arguments.

Karl Helm took fundamental issue with the *Phol* = "Wodan's foal" reading on the grounds that it would be disrespectful of Wodan if his horse were mentioned first, taking precedence before the god. Rosenfeld approaches this in various ways. His (1973, p 10) common-sense reply is that because the purpose of the charm is horse magic, or "*Fohlenzauber,*" the subject of the magical action would be addressed first, and that in these circumstances the entity mentioned second still carries more weight, according to the *"Gesetz des Achtergewichtes"* (Law of the Importance of Final Position, or "Weight of the Stern"), the tendency in folklore where something mentioned last bears more importance than what is mentioned prior to it (see Olrik 1965). He also points out an episode in the Old Icelandic *Heidreks saga* in which Odin refers to himself together with his horse Sleipnir as one being. As a further and possibly more speculative justification Rosenfeld (pp 11-12) brings up the more recent German poetic formula *Roß und Reiter*, which, although not attested in Old High German, may have deeper Indo-European roots since similar expressions exist in Latin and Avestan. It might be noted that English, too, has an identical longstanding expression "horse and rider" (rather than "rider and horse").

There are a number of other considerations that might be used to argue against the interpretation of *Phol* as the "foal" of Wodan. A foal is a young horse, often a colt, and not an animal that is old enough to be ridden. Achim Masser (1972, p 23) has asserted "Now Germanic gods were not, however, in the habit of riding on a foal!" and this is true.[19] But the text of the charm does not specify that anyone in fact rode upon the foal, only that its foot was injured. We could, therefore, be dealing with an otherwise unattested myth that simply describes Wodan and his foal (which could be a young Sleipnir, or some other horse) traveling together to the woods. The verb used is Old High German *faran*, "to go, travel, fare" rather than *rîtan*, "to ride," which would imply riding on horseback.

The next highly debated word in the text is *balderes*. This is clearly a genitive form, but still confounding any clear answer is the question:

whose foal?[20] Since Sophus Bugge first proposed the idea at the close of the nineteenth century, many have sensibly argued that *balderes* may well refer back to *Phol* or Wodan. In either case it would have to be an alternate name (or *heiti*, to use the Old Norse term) for the god—presuming that these are god names!—or it could either be a general appellative ("the lord's") or comparative adjectival noun ("the bolder one's"). As an appellative, this would be the only extant use of the word this way in Old High German, although there are examples of similar usage of a cognate in Old Norse.[21] The adjective *bald*, meaning "bold, brave, strong, (etc.)" appears in various Old High German texts. The idea of *balderes* as a comparative adjectival noun seems to rarely be considered, although it is unclear why it would be any less reasonable than many of the other conjectures. I can only suspect the reluctance to consider this idea may be due to the lack of a preceding definite article—and, if the text were emended to include one, this might induce metrical complications.

Another proposition with a long history is that *balderes* is a proper name, and refers to a god Balder, presumably similar to the Norse Baldr. This would then be the only overt evidence for a continental Balder cult; it would also seem to indicate an otherwise lost myth which is unknown in the Scandinavian sources. Attractive as this notion has been to many scholars going back to Grimm, Anatoly Liberman (2004, p 28) is probably right when he states: "the Second Merseburg Charm admits of too many interpretations, and *balder* does not look like a name in it." This last point has often been argued for metrical reasons especially: as a proper name, it could not be in an unstressed position.[22]

In examining these alternate theories, one begins to see that equally convincing arguments can be made for many of them; each is syntactically valid. Yet if one part is switched with another, the entire narrative of the charm must change—and be justified—accordingly. For example, if *Phol* = Balder then we can envision him going to the woods together with Wodan; but if we assume Balder to be an independent figure from *Phol* or Wodan, then the story has a quite different sense of the latter two gods riding to the rescue, to the place where Balder's horse wrenched his foot.

The task of unraveling the charm only becomes more complicated when the female figures arrive in the next stage of the narrative. Lines three and four refer to two pairs of names: *Sinhtgunt—Sunna*, and *Friia—Uolla*. They are ordered as pairs of sisters, and the latter two can be identified with some confidence as known goddesses.[23] The first name is undoubtedly the most obscure. While it would be satisfying to determine it as a name for the moon, with the sun (*Sunna*) her sister, this is problematic since the moon is considered male in all Germanic languages (as is the Norse Máni, a quasi-divine personification of the moon). Even in English, for example, where the Romance-language notion of the lunar feminine has deeply influenced our conception of it, we still refer to "the man in the moon." Various possible explanations for the name have been put forth, ranging from Grimm's "heavenly constellation" (1965, p 18), Schröder's "the nightly walking one" (1953, pp 161-3), or, if the spelling is emended to *Sinthgunt*, a valkyrie name: "the one moving into battle" (proposed by Hugo Gering, referred to in Simek 1993, p 285). Schröder argues that his proposed "nightly walking one" was originally a male moon-god, but the gender of the word became confused in the tradition over time.

The remaining three names are much less difficult to identify, at least by drawing parallels to known Norse deities. *Sunna* seems to be self-evident; she is either a personification or a deified form of the sun, possibly comparable to the position of Sól in Norse mythology. It is worth noting in this context that the sun also plays a semi-divine and functional role in a number of Old English charms. *Frîia* refers to Frea or Frîja, who has other continental attestations in weekday names (for Friday) and in Paulus Diaconus's *History of the Langobards* where she is mentioned as the wife of Wodan. She thus neatly corresponds to the Norse goddess Frigg—one of the few instances in the charms where a clear-cut solution is evident. *Uolla* in turn probably has a correspondence with the Norse Fulla, "hand-maiden" (but not sister) to Frigg.

In the end we have a collection of names, some with clear reference points in light of Germanic myth, and others which will—barring the unlikely discovery of a heretofore-lost text that could give better clues to their background—remain forever shrouded in mythic darkness. Given the obscurity of those in the latter category, it is not surprising that scholars over the years have tried to unravel their mystery by finding possible connections to Old Norse, Indo-European, or even Christian mythic paradigms and iconography. Part of our frustration in not being able to comfortably situate these names in their indigenous framework relates to a corresponding lack of knowledge about the entire framework in question. While we continue to gain new insights (at this point, mainly from archeology) into older Germanic culture, we are dealing with an oral culture—one that was overtaken and subsumed by an external written culture. The primary agenda of this external culture was to eradicate or, at the very least, completely overwrite the religio-cultic practices of the Germanic tribal populations in terms of a new spiritual mythology and ideology. There was no conscientious attempt to preserve a record of the previous belief systems. References that do occur in internal Church documents and correspondence were typically made for the instructional benefit of missionaries, in order to help them most effectively deal with undermining native beliefs and customs. Their success in reaching these goals is attested by the paucity of sources regarding continental Germanic divinities.

Another factor which should always be kept in mind when pondering these mysterious names is that Germanic religion was not codified, and significant differences must have existed depending on geographical location and local history. As Rudolf Simek (in Murdoch and Read 2004, p 74) notes, "It would ... be more appropriate to refer to the Germanic *religions* of the first millennium which had certain unifying traits, rather than to a single religion. ... It should also be stressed that pre-Christian Germanic religion cannot be viewed without reference to its contemporary setting: it should be seen in terms of its historical, geographical, and social background."

The Form and Functionality of the Charm

The issue of determining exactly "who's who" in the first four lines of the charm diminishes in some of its importance if we shift focus over to the historical circumstances, usage, structural form, and functional characteristics of the text as an example of operative analogical magic. We do not know why or in what exact circumstances the Second

Merseburg Charm was written down, and this has offered an interesting opportunity for speculation. Susan Fuller (1980, p 168) fascinatingly situates it, together with the first charm on the same page, in a very specific context involving a "frightened" monastic scribe in southern Saxon terrritory between 924-28 C.E. who "may have had the Charms dictated to him. They ... functioned as defense measures against the Magyar onslaughts." Earlier (p 167) she notes: "The content of the Charms reflects two of the most dominant concerns of the time ... namely, the dread of being captured by the Magyars and the awareness of the urgent need to use horses in warfare." Edwards (2002, p 91) does not outline quite as specific a scenario, but claims, "The only possible motive for preserving the charms, in the face of the official hostility of the Church [against any form of pagan magic], was that they were held to work." Regarding the charm's usage, however there can be little doubt: it is clearly a pragmatic incantation for the healing of an injured horse or, to reiterate Hellmut Rosenfeld's term, an example of *Fohlenzauber*. As such, it falls thematically into a large subgroup among the Germanic charms, as quickly becomes apparent when surveying the original texts.[24]

Despite exhibiting a distinctly different aim from the First Merseburg Charm, some common structural features are in evidence. The Second Merseburg Charm can be similarly divided into two sections: the first part, a five-line narrative generally called the "epic portion" of the text, is distinct from the second part, the actual magical conjuration. However, it would be more accurate to call the opening segment a "mythic" rather than "epic" introduction, for the names and interactions it describes are part of a world beyond that of the merely human. It is best viewed as a *historiola,* and as such is a vital ingredient for the overall magical efficacy of the charm.[25]

In order to cause an action to occur which is outside the realm of everyday occurrence, the magician must invoke—or at least mentally evoke—the realm in which such things are possible, and indeed where they are already reported to have occurred. Wodan's act (like the actions of the divine women in the first charm) occurred at some point in the past, but as a mythic deed it is eternally contemporary and "true" as long as the larger mythic superstructure to which it belongs is believed in and adhered to. In this sense it is continually recurring outside mundane time, *in illo tempore*; it becomes revalidated every time it is properly recited or contemplated in a sympathetic way. If a particular magical act was performed by Wodan in the parallel divine world, it is hoped that by communicating and enacting the correct procedure—a special combination of words and performance style—the same effect can be achieved here. A communicative magical working can thus take place: the natural world will respond similarly to the magician's invocation just as the divine world did to Wodan's act of enchanting (*bigalan*). In effect, what may really occur is a process described by Bozóky (1992, p 85) as the "true transposition of the mediation from the actual to the mythic level" in which "both the present and the hoped-for states are integrated into the myth; there is no distinction between the actual and the supernatural realms. Thus present time is projected into mythic time, and the magical action that is imagined to bring about the patient's cure is presented as if it were a deed already accomplished in past time." It should also be acknowledged that for a practitioner of magic in the ancient Germanic world—indeed for the average member of tribal society—the dividing line between the mythic and mundane realms may have been far less concrete to begin with, than it is for us today. Regarding the related disconnection between the natural and supernatural realms, Winfried Nöth (1977, p 63) is correct in asserting: "the problem of a distinction between natural and supernatural effects presents itself only from the detached point of view of modern observers."

While the opening *historiola* is a crucial part of the charm for structural reasons, only the gist of the story is essential from a functional standpoint. As David Frankfurter (in Meyer and Mirecki 1995, p 463) has noted in his analysis of various *historiolae* from Egypt, Babylonia, and the Classical world, these sometimes do not have specific mythological antecedents, and that "it is to the credit of historians of religions that the *historiola* has been unpacked as a functional aspect of ritual and not just derivative mythology."

Whether or not the event described in the *historiola* had a specific mythological antecedent may be secondary to the importance of the general mythic foundation that underlies it. Discussing Christian narrative healing incantations that begin with *historiolae* (a number of which share a similar form with the Second Merseburg Charm, or are even variant versions of it) Bozóky (1992, p 85) remarks that "Probably most of these little stories were extemporized to fit the needs of the therapeutic magic worker, though some of them obviously take their inspiration from the legends of Christ and the saints." There is no reason why a similar extemporization process could not have taken place at earlier stages concerning pre-Christian mythic figures.

With this in mind, let us assume—following the arguments of Rosenfeld and Northcott—that the horse belonged to Wodan himself. While the specific anecdotal narrative would still be one for which we know of no antecedent (and quite possibly the contemporary utilizers of the charm also knew of no other stories regarding this particular incident), it would conceivably have amplified the basic, mythic force of the charm due to Wodan's deep-seated connection to horses. Assuming Wodan shares key characteristics with the cognate Norse Óðinn, one of his attributes would be a special personal horse (in Norse tradition, the eight-legged Sleipnir). There is a rich mythological and folkloric tradition surrounding this relationship, and even into the modern era folk beliefs lingered in northern European countries about Wotan/Wodan or Óðinn as the mounted leader of the Wild Hunt, a raucous, ghostly host that rides the night sky during certain seasons (often Yuletide).[26] Evidence that this relationship was already well established in early Germanic culture can be seen in the corpus of metal bracteates that date to the middle of the first millennium C.E. In Rudolf Simek's words (in Murdoch and Read 2004, p 81), these portray a "dominant figure of a particular type, always shown in conjunction with a horse, ... successfully identified as the god Wodan/Odin, in his function as the divine healer." Simek and others, following the extensive work of Karl Hauck on the subject, have pointed out how a number of the bracteate images seem to depict the god-figure in proximity to a horse with injured feet, and could therefore symbolically correspond to the Second Merseburg Charm.[27]

Structurally, certain features of the mythic anecdote coincide as well with other narrative healing charms from the European Middle Ages. As Bozóky (1992, p 90) notes: "The action of the *historiolae* refers mainly to places that have an intermediate position in space. It is the idea of a transition that is dominant, as if to underline the mediating process that brings about the transition from illness to healing. As places of *passage*, one finds in the Latin formulae locations such as 'before the gate' of the town; 'on the bridge', 'on the threshold', and most obviously, 'on the road', mentioned explicitly or not, but essential in the incantations with an *encounter* motif." In the Merseburg charm we similarly find Phol and Wodan traveling to the woods, where an encounter takes place with a number of other gods. The journey to the woods implies the crossing of threshold between the settled world and that of the unknown wilderness. For the ancient Germanic peoples, the forest had connotations as a realm inhabited by creatures and humans who were literally "beyond the pale," and the liminal space in between this realm and that of settled existence, embodied in the hedgerow which divided the two, was also one associated with powers of witchcraft and magic. This is evident from various Germanic terms for witches that relate to hedges (e.g., Old High German *Hagazussa*, literally "hedge woman") or the ability to ride between the settled realm and the unsettled—and unsettling—woods (e.g., Middle High German *Zunrite* or Old Norse *Túnriða,* both meaning "fence rider").[28]

On a more abstract level, the magical purpose behind the charm concerns the restoration of a sacred order. With the occurrence of the horse's injury, it is not just the foot that was wrenched out of sync with itself. Much else was also affected by this mishap. The natural order, and its equations such as the "horse and rider," cannot operate smoothly until the situation is remedied and returned to wholeness. It is worth recalling in this regard that "whole" and "health" ("healing," etc.) have an identical linguistic root in the Germanic languages. To the ancient

Germanic mind, the word field associated with the etymon *haila-* carried connotations of health, holiness, wholeness, strength, and personal power in both a physical and spiritual sense.[29] The health of a horse was crucial to its rider, and in the uneven, unfamiliar terrain of the uncleared woods, with hidden rocks, holes, streams and creeks, and so on, there existed an ever-present risk for injury. An injured horse would be a serious setback—and we all know what fate usually portends for a permanently lame horse. By charming the horse's wrenched foot to realign itself and rejoin where it has separated, Wodan—along with the magician who repeats his feat in the human world—is restoring the physical and spiritual well-being of the animal, and by extension its proper healthy and symbiotic relationship to its master.[30] This coincides with T. Todorov's remark (quoted in Bozóky 1992, p 89) on how formulae in folklore can "affirm the possibility of a relationship between events belonging to quite different categories, to permit putting the universe in order."

The number three is a frequent component in Germanic verbal charms. We have already seen its presence in the First Merseburg Charm with the three groups of divine women, each performing a different task. It is the activity of the third group, loosening and freeing—as opposed to binding and hemming in—that becomes the aim of the overall conjuration. A similar "dynamic of three" is at work in the second charm: two failed attempts at magically healing the horse's foot take place before Wodan achieves the desired magical goal. Working energetically in a way that might be akin to aforementioned "Oppositional Aesthetic Dyad," the prior attempts cause a mythic build-up of negative polarized tension which Wodan's act positively reverses, finally altering reality. We can thus observe how an old saying might literally apply to both examples from Merseburg: *"the third time's the charm."* As Northcott (1959, p 49) remarks on the second charm, "Much of the magical property attached to the number three resides in this cumulative effect as much as in any formulaic significance. There is enough evidence from the Christian charms to support this view, where the paternoster has to be repeated three times." In this context Northcott (p 49) also quotes Helmut de Boor: "Germanic medieval lyric poetry created for itself a language and form of urgency. Its primary method is the use of repetition with emphasis ... of the last part of the magical triplicity."[31] De Boor was making a general observation, but its specific relevance to the Merseburg Charms should be obvious. Identical principles are also described in Axel Olrik's 'Epic Laws of Folk Narrative' when he (1965, pp 136-37) remarks: *"Achtergewicht* [Importance of Final Position] combined with the Law of Three is the principle characteristic of folk narrative—it is an epic law." Indeed, many of Olrik's "laws" of the *"Sagenwelt"* (legendary realm) inhabited by myth and folkore, find resonance in the Merseburg Charms.

There are further discernible tripartite elements in the second charm. As Carol Lynn Miller (1963, p 37) notes, "The text is frequently divided into three strophes. The first strophe tells of the accident, the second of the attempts to heal, and the third is the actual formula." The "threefoldness" of the charm is reinforced by the number of pairs of beings (*Phol* [Wodan's horse]—*Wodan*; *Sinhtgunt*—*Sunna*; *Friia*—*Uolla*), along with the types of affliction (*benrenki, bluotrenki, lidirenki*) and corresponding magical commands for reconnective healing. It may also be a deliberate structural feature that the charm breaks down easily into 9 lines, or 3 x 3.[32]

Three and nine are both numbers very much connected to the god Óðinn, and especially to his facility with verbal magic. Stanzas 139-40 of the Eddic *Hávamál* famously describe, from a first-person perspective, Óðinn's nine-night ritual of self-sacrifice by which he gains his magical insight into the runes. He then boasts of the eighteen (2 x 9) charms that he knows. These include the aforementioned loosening charm, but the very first of the series (st. 146: 4-7) is concerned with restorative healing:

> *The first is called help, and help it can bring thee*
> *In sorrow and pain and sickness.*
>
> (translation: Bellows 1923, p 63)[33]

Beyond its magical uses—or maybe as part of their origin—the number three is even genetically important to Óðinn. He has two brothers, Vili and Vé, and together they form a triumvirate of the first gods. Their names semantically relate to "inspiration" (Óðinn, cf. Old Norse *oðr*), "will" (Vili), and "holiness" (Vé). One of Óðinn's many bynames is Þriði (literally "the third one"), who is mentioned elsewhere as part of another divine triad. Óðinn is able to operate in all the three realms of existence: Ásgard, Miðgard, and Hel. These geographical divisions—which Bill Griffiths (2003) has evocatively called "The Up World," "The Around World," and "The Dead World"—are just one example of numerous tripartite elements within wider Norse/Germanic cosmology and myth. Dumézilian tripartite analyses have highlighted manifold other correspondences.[34]

An intriguing symbolic link from the eighth century comes in the form of the "knot of the slain" (Old Norse *valknutr*), a figure made up of three interlocking triangles (3 x 3). This sign is visible on several of the picture stones from Gotland, Sweden and seems to have cultic associations with the god Óðinn. In nearly all of its appearances where other iconography is also present, it is found in close proximity to a horse. On the Tängelgårda I stone from Lärbro, for example, it appears twice amid the striding legs of a warrior's—or god's—steed.

Of the gods who try to heal the horse's injured leg in the Second Merseburg Charm, only Wodan's incantatory magic was powerful enough to succeed. The term describing the magical technique used by the gods, and excelled at by Wodan, is *bigalan* (i.e., *bi* + *galan*), a class-VI verb used here in the preterite third person. This verb appears nowhere else in Old High German literature, although other words with the same root do. The meaning of the main verb *galan* is "to sing," derived from proto-Germanic **galanan*, which has reflexes in Old Norse *gala* "to crow (like a raven)" and Old English *galan* "to sing." (A modern English cognate, now rendered innocuous in implications, can be found in the verb "to yell.") Old High German *galan* has, however, quite distinct connotations compared with a more general verb, *singan* "to sing." This becomes clear when cognate words deriving from the same proto-Germanic root as *galan* are considered. Schützeichel (1981), for example, has entries for Old High German *kalster* "Zauberei" (magic), *galsterara* "Zauberin" (sorceress), and *calstrare* "Zauberer" (sorcerer), all of which originally appear in the writings of Notker. Cognates deriving from the substantive proto-Germanic **galdran* are also revealing, such as Old Norse *galdr* "song, witchcraft" and Old English *gealdor* "incantation, charm."[35]

We can now see why this particular word appears in the Second Merseburg Charm: it is a technical term for a specific type of verbal magic, somehow sung or chanted. As Jolly (1996, p 99) remarks concerning the employment of similar Old English charms: "Words were channels of power; chanting or singing words added a special element of rhythm and controlled tone that gave even more power to the words." To the ancient Germanic mind, the act of *(bi)galan* was indeed so powerful that it could directly affect the state of an object, for the phrase in the charm *thu biguol en Uuodan* literally means "then Wodan charmed it," with the verb acting transitively. He was not singing *to* the horse's foot, he was singing the horse's foot into a new "encharmed" state that set it immediately on the path to recovery. Speaking of similar Old English charms, Stephen Glosecki (1989, p 109) comments that the Anglo-Saxons "placed genuine effective power in the human voice, especially the poetic voice; the same might be said for the early Germanic tradition at large." In his semiotic analysis of Old English charms, Nöth (1977, p 66) observes that "the magic act, as it is formulated in the charm, is believed to achieve a direct transformation of the objects."[36]

When we consider the semantic fields of the two Latin-based terms that we have just seen as translations for *gealdor*, it becomes apparent that these connections between singing/chanting, magic, and poetry must go further back in the past to a place where the languages and cultural conceptions of Germanic and Romance branches share common Indo-European ground. The word "incantation" derives from Latin *incantatus* "incantation, spell," which is related to the verb *(in)cantare* "to sing; to sing of; to harp on; *(of birds)* to crow." Another definition given for *cantare* is "to predict," which would also appear to indicate a magico-divinatory connotation. "Charm," on the other hand, derives from Latin *carmen*, with meanings that include "song; poem; incantation; oracular utterance; ritual formula." (All preceding definitions from Traupman 1995)

In the latter Latin term, *carmen,* a relationship between poetry, singing, and magic is evident. This is likewise true of the **galanan*-derived words when we consider their connection to Wodan/Óðinn, who refers to himself in Old Icelandic tradition as *galdrsfaðir* "father of *galdr*." He is also the patron of skaldic poets and poetry, but most importantly he brought about mankind's access to the sacred mead of poetic inspiration in the first place. Godfrid Storms (1948, p 33) remarks: "the power of magic came to be ascribed to the incantatory formula, and ... the knowledge of charms was specially attributed to the gods, who as spirits could only apply words. The Germanic peoples believed that charms originated from Woden..." He also notes (p 32) that "the word *song* has come to denote the magical practice in all the Indo-European languages and in a great many outside this group." He assumes that words related to singing took on the connotation in response to the prevalence of this particular magical technique, but in the case of the **galanan*-derived terminology, the semantic connotations may have been inherent to the original word. Regarding the wider Indo-European context for incantatory speech, similarities between the Second Merseburg Charm and a section (IV, 12) of the *Atharva Veda* were noticed in 1864 by Adalbart Kuhn (1894, pp 58-63) and may point to a provenance in the deepest Indo-European antiquity for the closing magical formula of the charm.[37]

Whether or not there is a direct correspondence with a Vedic charm that dates to 1,000 years earlier, the *Merseburger Zaubersprüche* in the forms in which we have them could well have arisen as early as the middle of the first millennium C.E. Even if they were conceived by one or two magically adept individuals in specific locations, they clearly reflected deep and central concerns of the wider Germanic culture. This is not only apparent from the well-attested range of later variants of the second charm in the Germanic linguistic realm (and beyond), but can be inferred from the content and structure of both charms.[38] These qualities reveal them each to be intrinsically connected to the central Germanic god Wodan/Óðinn. Their potency is not related to the mere invocation of divine names, but rather stems from an operative form of analogical, restorative enchantment. This reflects the god's connections to battle, binding and loosening, horses, and the number three—but above all it represents the incantatory use of a specific form of poetic magic. The charms themselves contain verbal formulas of this type, but these are most efficacious in their context as the culmination of the mythic *historiolae*, and dynamic polarizations of energy, which precede them. With the inevitable post-conversion decay of the older Germanic tradition, the traditional secrets of their proper generation and utilization returned to that magical place whence they had originated: the mythic world of Wodan/Óðinn.

Notes

1   For their thoughtful suggestions with regard to this paper I would like to thank Professor James E. Cathey, whose teaching of Old High German inspired a deeper interest in the subject at hand; Stephen E. Flowers, Ph.D.; and Stephen C. Wehmeyer, Ph.D. Any errors of fact or judgment that may remain are solely my responsibility.

2   *"jüngst gemachter so überraschender fund"*.

3   There is a third text on the page, a Christian prayer in Latin. For the text and a discussion of the original manuscript, see Beck 2003, pp 216-51.

4   Original title: 'Über zwei entdeckte Gedichte aus der Zeit des deutschen Heidenthums'.

5   *"kindisch gefreut"*.

6   *"mitten unter kirchlichen und frommen sätzen zwölf altdeutsche zeilen ... zwei unter sich unzusammenhängend, alliterierende gedichte, offen heidnischen inhalts"*.

7   For two historical overviews that help to situate the Merseburg Charms in the context of magical practices in early medieval Europe, see Richard Kieckhefer (1990, especially pp 44-45), and Valerie Flint (1991, especially pp 325-36). Eugene D. Dukes (1996) specifically examines the attitudes and policies of the Church toward magical and pagan practices in ancient and early medieval Europe. See, in particular, Ch. VII: 'The German World and Magic,' pp 187-224. Focusing more specifically on northern Germanic conceptions of magic is Raudvere 2002.

8   *"Gesprochen wurde der Segen entweder vom Gefangenen selbst, sofern er ihn wusste, oder auch von Angehörigen seines Volkes, also wohl von zauberkündigen Frauen von der Ferne aus."*

9   *"es sind weise frauen, schlachtentscheidende walküren"*.

10 Some dissenting commentators have preferred to interpret the charm in a completely different, usually medical, context (e.g., Schirokauer 1954, pp 353-364; Murdoch 1988, pp 364-68). For the various views regarding magical content and use and application of the charm, see Beck 2003, pp 350-64.

11 Nearly every study of the Old English corpus of charms also discusses the Merseburg texts. The classic study in English of the subject is Storms 1948; see in particular Ch. V. For recent interpretations of the Old English charms, see Jolly 1996; Griffiths 2003; and Pollington 2003.

12 Original Old Norse:

Þat kann ec it fiórða, ef mér fyrðar bera

bönd at boglimom:

svá ec gel, at ec ganga má,

sprettr mér af fótom fioturr,

enn af höndom hapt. (Neckel 1983, p 42)

Due to font limitations, in any Old Norse quotes I have rendered the "o with hook" as "ö." This stanza appears as number 150 in Bellows.

13 *"Wirrwarr der Meinungen".*

14 The linguistic arguments are detailed in the section 'Das Wortmaterial' in Beck 2003, pp 90-207; grammatical issues are discussed on pp 208-213.

15 Regarding the identification of proper names (or, alternately, the designation of some of them as substantives which are not personal names), summaries of the primary arguments can be found in de Vries 1957, pp 171-73; Bostock 2001, pp 29-36; Schaffner 1999, pp 162-81, paying particular attention to Old Norse parallels and comparative linguistics; and, most thoroughly, in Beck 2003, pp 90-207.

16 An overview of the metrical considerations and arguments can be found in Beck 2003, pp 276-86. An example of an extended analysis of mythical and metrical considerations, largely in the light of Old Norse poetry, can be found in Baesecke 1966, pp 418-36. Baesecke calls the poem the "Pholspruch."

17 *"wird uns ... entscheidender aufschlüsse bringen".*

18 *"unerhörter name".*

19 *"Nun pflegten jedoch germanische Götter nicht auf einem Füllen zu reiten!"*

20 The various arguments appear in Beck 2003, pp 136-53.

21 For a detailed study of the term and its usage, see Green 1965, pp 3-18. The famous article arguing against such an interpretation for *balderes* is Hans Kuhn's 'Es gibt kein *balder* "Herr"' (1951). Kuhn's position has been challenged by many subsequent scholars.

22 For arguments in favor of the Balder interpretation from an Old Norse scholar, see Schröder 1953, pp 161-83.

23 For the various interpretations, see Beck 2003, pp 163-86, and also the entries in Simek 1993.

24 For what still appears to be the best collection of these texts, with detailed analysis based on a concise survey of scholarly opinions, and a

thorough bibliography to its time of publication, see Miller 1963. Her discussion of the Second Merseburg Charm, labeled 'Charm for a Horse's Leg,' appears on pp 31-43. Gerhard Eis's 1964 anthology of articles, *Altdeutsche Zaubersprüche*, also illustrates how many of these relate to horse injuries and afflictions, although none of his essays focuses on the Second Merseburg Charm per se. Regarding classification, see also Bacon 1952.

25 For a discussion of the use of the *historiola* in various types of archaic magic, see David Frankfurter, 'Narrating Power: The Theory and Practice of the Magical *Historiola* in Ritual Spells' in Meyer and Mirecki 1995, pp 457-76. The Merseburg Charms are also discussed as examples of *historiolae* in Schumacher 2000 (pp 207-211 in particular). On the genre of *historiolae* in medieval narrative healing incantations, see Bozóky 1992.

26 For a recent far-reaching investigation into the linguistic and historical Indo-European roots of this mythos, see Kershaw 2000. Regarding Wodan/Óðinn as "rider god" see in particular Ch. 3, *'Der Schimmelreiter'* (pp 20-40).

27 The possible connections between the bracteates and the charm are discussed in detail in Beck 2003, pp 265-75; the relevant motifs are also illustrated in figs. 2-15.

28 For a brief discussion of these conceptions see Wolf Dieter-Storl's chapter 'The Old Woman in the Hedgerow' in Müller-Ebeling et al. 2003, pp 29-40. For a thorough study of Germanic conceptions of witches and witchcraft see Morris 1991.

29 On the notion of Germanic "restoration magic" see 'Magic Formulae and Magic Words' in McKinnell et al. 2004, p 85; and Flowers 1986, p 348.

30 On the importance of the horse generally and the religious beliefs specifically centered on the horse in Indo-European cultures, of which the Germanic is one branch, see the entry for 'Horse' in *The Encyclopedia of Indo-European Culture* (1997, pp 274-79).

31 *"Die germanische Spruchdichtung hatte sich eine Sprache und Form der Eindringlichkeit geschaffen. Ihr Hauptmittel ist Wiederholung mit Heraushebung ... des letzten Gliedes der magischen Dreizahl."*

32 Achim Masser (1972) has argued that the original, now lost, archetypal charm would have been fully based on metrical groups of three, and suggests emendations that would create a hypothetical version with these qualities.

33 *hiálp heitir eitt, enn þat þér hiálpa mun*

við sócom oc sorgom oc sútom gorvöllom (Neckel 1983, p 41)

34 In addition to Dumézil's comparative studies, see the work of those he has influenced such as Jan de Vries, Jaan Puhvel, Edgar Polomé, and others.

35 For semantic discussions of this word field in relation to continental and other Germanic traditions, see Storms 1948, pp 1-6, 113-14 and *passim*; Raudvere 2002, pp 91-93 and *passim*; Flowers 2005, pp 6-11 and *passim*.

36 For a useful introduction to a semiotic definition of magic, primarily focusing on Germanic (Scandinavian) sources, see Grambo 1975. A semiotic interpretation of older Germanic magical traditions and runic inscriptions is Flowers 1984.

37 For an English translation of the Vedic text, see Griffith 1968, pp 146-47. The Vedic charm also refers to the use of plants in the context of the ritual. For a recent assessment of Germanic magic from an ethnobotanical perspective, see Christian Rätsch, *Der Heilige Hain: Germanische Zauberpflanzen, heilige Bäume und schamanische Rituale*. Aarau: AT Verlag, 2005. In regard to the Indo-European magical tradition, see also Ch. 59, 'The Poet as Healer' in Calvert Watkins 1999, pp 540-44.

38 For a survey of these analogues with both Christian and pagan settings, in various lands ranging from Scotland to Finland and Estonia, see Kuhn 1894, pp 49-57, Ebermann 1903, pp 1-24, and Krohn 1901 and 1905.

References

Bacon, Isaac, 1952, 'Versuch einer Klassifizierung Altdeutscher Zaubersprüche und Segen' *Modern Language Notes*, Johns Hopkins Press, Baltimore, 67, 4, 224-32.

Baesecke, Georg, 1966, *Kleinere Schriften zur althochdeutschen Sprache und Literatur*, Francke, Bern.

Barditus, *Die letzten Goten*, 2005, NoltEx Records, Halle an der Saale.

Beck, Wolfgang, 2003, *Die Merseburger Zaubersprüche*, Reichert, Wiesbaden.

Bellows, Henry Adams, trans., 1923, *The Poetic Edda*, American-Scandinavian Foundation, New York.

Bostock, J. Knight, 2001, *A Handbook on Old High German Literature*, second edition, revised by K. C. King and D. R. McLintock, Oxford University Press, Oxford.

Bozóky, Edina, 1992, 'Mythic Mediation in Healing Incantations,' in *Health, Disease and Healing in Medieval Culture*, edited by Sheila Campbell et al., St. Martin's, New York.

Braune, Wilhelm, *Althochdeutsches Lesebuch*, revised by Ernst A. Ebbinghaus, 14th ed., Niemeyer, Tübingen, 1962.

Dukes, Eugene D., 1996, *Magic and Witchcraft in the Dark Ages*, University Press of America, Lanham, Maryland.

Eis, Gerhard, 1964, *Altdeutsche Zaubersprüche*, de Gruyter, Berlin.

Flint, Valerie, 1991, *The Rise of Magic in Early Medieval Europe*, Princeton University Press, Princeton.

Geerk, Frank, 2003, *Von Wunden und Wundern: Handbuch der Zaubersprüche*, von Loeper Literaturverlag, Karlsruhe.

Glosecki, Stephen O., 1989, *Shamanism and Old English Poetry*, Garland, New York.

Grambo, Ronald, (1975), 'Models of Magic: Some Preliminary Considerations', *Norveg*, Oslo, 18, 77-109.

Green, D. H., 1965, *The Carolingian Lord: Semantic Studies on Old High German Balder—Frô—Truhtin—Hêrro*, Cambridge University Press, Cambridge.

Griffith, Raph T. H., 1968, *The Hymns of the Atharvaveda*, vol. 1, Chowkhamba Sanskrit Series, Varanasi.

Griffiths, Bill, 2003, *Aspects of Anglo-Saxon Magic*, rev. ed., Anglo-Saxon Books, Hockwold-cum-Wilton.

Grimm, Jacob, 1965, *Kleinere Schriften*, vol. 2, Georg Olms, Hildesheim.

Edwards, Cyril, 2002, *The Beginnings of German Literature: Comparative and Interdisciplinary Approaches to Old High German*, Camden House, Rochester, N.Y.

The Encyclopedia of Indo-European Culture, 1997, Fitzroy Dearborn, Chicago.

Flowers, Stephen Edred, 1984, *Runes and Magic: Magical Formulaic Elements in the Elder Tradition*, Ph.D. University of Texas at Austin.

————, ed. and trans., 2005, *The Galdrabók: An Icelandic Book of Magic*, second, revised edition, Rûna-Raven, Smithville, Texas.

Fuller, Susan D., (1980), 'Pagan Charms in Tenth-Century Saxony? The Function of the Merseburg Charms', *Monatshefte*, University of Wisconsin, Madison, vol. 72, no. 2, 162-70.

Jolly, Karen Louise, 1996, *Popular Religion in Late Saxon England: Elf Charms in Context*, University of North Carolina Press, Chapel Hill.

Kershaw, Kris, 2000, *The One-eyed God: Odin and the (Indo-)Germanic Männerbünd*, Journal of Indo-European Studies Monograph No. 36, Institute for the Study of Man, Washington, D.C.

Kieckhefer, Richard, 1990, *Magic in the Middle Ages*, Cambridge University Press, Cambridge.

Krohn, Kaarle, (1901), 'Wo und wann entstanden die finnischen zauberlieder?', *Finnisch-Ugrische Forschungen*, Finno-Ugrian Society, Helsinki, vol. 1, Heft 3, 147-81.

————, (1905), 'Lemminkäinens tod < Christi > Balders tod', *Finnisch-Ugrische Forschungen*, Finno-Ugrian Society, Helsinki, vol. 5, Heft 1-3, 83-138.

Kuhn, Hans, 1951, 'Es gibt kein *balder* "Herr",' in *Erbe der Vergangenheit. Germanistische Beiträge. Festgabe für Karl Helm zum 80. Geburtstag 19. Mai 1951*, Niemeyer, Tübingen, 37-45.

Liberman, Anatoly, (2004), 'Some Controversial Aspects of the Myth of Balder', *Alvíssmál*, Freie Universität Berlin, Berlin, 11, 17-54.

Masser, Achim, (1972), 'Zum zweiten Merseburger Zauberspruch', *Beiträge zur Geschichte der deutschen Sprache und Literatur*, Niemeyer, Tübingen, 94, 19-25.

McKinnell, John, Rudolf Simek and Klaus Düwel, 2004, *Runes, Magic and Religion. A Sourcebook*, Fassbaender, Vienna.

Miller, Carol Lynn, 1963, *The Old High German and Old Saxon Charms: Text, Commentary and Critical Bibliography*, Ph.D. Washington University.

Morris, Katherine, 1991, *Sorceress or Witch?: The Image of Gender in Medieval Iceland and Northern Europe*, University Press of America, Lanham, Maryland.

Müller-Ebeling, Claudia, et al., 2003, *Witchcraft Medicine: Healing Arts, Shamanic Practices, and Forbidden Plants*, trans. Annabel Lee, Inner Traditions, Rochester, Vermont.

Murdoch, Brian, (1988), 'But Did They Work? Interpreting the Old High German *Merseburg Charms* in Their Medieval Context', *Neuphilologische Mitteilungen*, Helsinki, 89, 358-69.

—————, 1989, '*Peri Hieres Nousou:* Approaches to the Old High German Medical Charms' in *mit regalu bituungan. Neue Arbeiten zur althochdeutschen Poesie und Sprache*, eds. John L. Flood and David Yeandle, Kümmerle, Göppingen, 142-59.

Murdoch, Brian, and Malcolm Read, 2004, *Early Germanic Literature and Culture*, Camden House History of German Literature, vol. 1, Camden House, Rochester, N.Y.

Neckel, Gustav, ed., 1983. *Edda: Die Lieder des Codex Regius nebst verwandten Denkmälern I: Text*, rev. Hans Kuhn, 5th ed., Winter, Heidelberg.

Nöth, Winfried, (1977), 'Semiotics of the Old English Charm', *Semiotica*, Mouton, the Hague, 19: 1/2.

Olrik, Axel, 1965, 'Epic Laws of Folk Narrative', trans. Jeanne P. Steager, in *The Study of Folklore*, ed. Alan Dundes, Prentice Hall, Englewood Cliffs, N.J., 129-141.

Orel, Vladimir, 2003, *A Handbook of Germanic Etymology*, Brill, Leiden.

Pollington, Stephen, 2003, *Leechcraft: Early English Charms, Plantlore and Healing*, Anglo-Saxon Books, Hockwold-cum-Wilton.

Preusler, Walther, 1922, 'Zum zweiten Merseburger Spruch', in *Beiträge zur Deutschkunde. Festschrift Theodor Siebs zum sechsigsten Geburtstag dargebracht von seinen Schülern*, ed. by Walther Steller, Emden, 35-49.

Raudvere, Catherine, 2002, 'Trólldomr in Early Medieval Scandinavia' in *Witchcraft and Magic in Europe: The Middle Ages*, eds. Bengt Ankarloo and Stuart Clark, University of Pennsylvania Press, Philadelphia.

Rosenfeld, Hellmut, (1973), 'Phol end wuodan vuorun zi holza: Baldermythe oder Fohlenzauber?', *Beiträge zur Geschichte der deutschen Sprache und Literatur*, Niemeyer, Tübingen, 95, 1-12.

Schaffner, Stefan, (1999), 'Die Götternamen des Zweiten Merseburger Zauberspruches', *Die Sprache*, A. Sexl, Vienna, 41/2, 153-205.

Schröder, Franz Rolf, (1953), 'Balder und der zweite Merseburger Spruch', *Germanisch-Romanische Monatsschrift*, Winter, Heidelberg, 34, 161-83.

Schumacher, Meinolf, 2000, 'Geschichtenerzählzauber: Die *Merseburger Zaubersprüche* und die Funktion der historiola im magischem Ritual' in *Erzählte Welt—Welt des Erzählens. Festschrift für Dietrich Weber*, Cologne, 201-215.

Schützeichel, R., 1981, *Althochdeutsches Wörterbuch*, Niemeyer, Tübingen.

Simek, Rudolf, 1993, *Dictionary of Northern Mythology*, Brewer, Cambridge.

Steller, Walther, (1930), 'Phol ende Wodan', *Zeitschrift für Volkskunde*, Waxmann, Münster, 40, 61-71.

Storms, G., 1948, *Anglo-Saxon Magic*, Martinus Nijhoff, The Hague.

Tacitus, Cornelius, 1914, *The History, Germany, Agricola, and Dialogue on Orators*, vol. 2 of *The Works of Tacitus*, Bell and Sons, London.

Traupman, John C., 1995, *The New College Latin & English Dictionary*, rev. ed., Bantam, New York.

Vries, Jan de, 1957, *Altgermanische Religionsgeschichte*, 2 vols., de Gruyter, Berlin.

Watkins, Calvert, 1999, *How to Kill a Dragon*, Oxford University Press, New York.

Wehmeyer, Stephen C., (2006), 'Elf-Quern and Elf-Shot: The Sensuous Language of Healing and Harming in Germanic Ritual Practice', *Symbel: A Journal of Early Germanic Studies*, Woodharrow Institute, Smithville, Texas, vol. 1, 3-25.

The Old Irish Impotence Spell: The *Dam Díli*, Fergus, Fertility, and the Mythic Backround of an Irish Incantation

Phillip A. Bernhardt-House

The scholarship devoted to medieval magic is gaining in volume, but certain aspects of this, including the magical texts of medieval Ireland, have yet to be incorporated into the wider inquiries of this academic pursuit. Even within the field of Medieval Irish and Celtic Studies, the various spells, charms and incantations found scattered in the marginalia of manuscripts have not been the focus of much attention. While this will soon be changing, with forthcoming studies by Jacqueline Borsje and larger edition of the magical texts by John Carey, the lack of attention which these texts have received in general is lamentable. Notable among the recent studies are those by John Carey (2000; 2004, p 19-21). Carey notes that the lack of attention to these texts, considering the great debates between "nativist" and "anti-nativist" interpretations of medieval Irish literature,[1] is quite surprising, since these texts appeal directly to pagan supernatural powers for their efficacy, therefore implying continuing belief in them (2000, p 98-99). The syncretism of these texts, which often invoke God, Jesus, the Holy Spirit, and saints or angels along with Irish mythological figures like the smith-god Goibniu or the divine physician Dian Cécht, may strike some readers as unusual and perhaps even shocking. This may not be as surprising as one might think, considering that an appeal to as many powers as were known to the spell-writing magician concerned has been a feature of magical texts since late antiquity, with many examples in the *Greek Magical Papyri* invoking, for example, Apollo and Zeus along with Michael, Gabriel, and Adonai (Betz 1986, p 11). Whether or not a particular medieval author believed the mythic history of the narratives he wrote, or whether or not a spell-writer/caster had a literal belief in the powers invoked in his incantations, the narrative references found in spells can be illuminated by and in turn illuminate aspects of the narratives, and can elucidate how all of these may have functioned in a pre-Christian cosmology and its reflexes in ritual.

For the purposes of the present discussion, I wish to revisit the spell dealt with briefly by Carey (2004, p 19-21), which is a charm for causing (or possibly curing) impotence. This spell was first published in 1952 by Richard Irvine Best (p 32), and while a full translation of the rubrics after the spell detailing its possible uses was given then (which include staunching blood-flow, delaying birth, and for defense in battle), the actual text was not fully translated.[2] Carey's translation and edited text is given here:

> *Fo-rriug do lúth,*
>
> *fo-rriug do láth,*
>
> *fo-rriug do nert,*

fo-rriug do thrâcht,

fo-rrig ben drúth

dam tuli i n-âth.

I bind your vigour,

I bind your passion,

I bind your strength,

I bind your force.

A wanton woman binds

a 'stag of flood' in a ford. (2004, p 19)

Carey suggests that the spell was from the Old Irish period (sixth-ninth century CE), and points out that the details given in the final two lines point toward a connection with the death-tale of the Ulster Cycle figure Fergus mac Roich (p 20-21). Before examining the details of this death-tale, it would, first, be useful to investigate how the *dam díli* (in the spell above as *dam tuli*) is portrayed in other Irish narratives, and second, to explore the manner in which Fergus is depicted in the Ulster Cycle stories as a paragon of male fertility.

The term *dam díli* or *dam dílenn*,[3] which translates as either "stag" or "ox of flood," is found as the name of a creature in many locations within Irish mythic literature. One such occurrence is found in the *Triads of Ireland* §236, the Three Wonders of Glen Dallan in Glencar, Sligo, where it is related that the Dam Díli's father came from a lake (the same from which the second monster of the triad also originated) and engendered it on the cow of a nearby landholder (Meyer 1906a, p 30-31). Later Scottish and Manx folklore seems to indicate that calves engendered in this manner—in effect, any calf begotten in which the bull who did so was not known or seen—were often looked upon with disfavour (Maier 1999, p 6-7), but the medieval Irish sources do not seem to imply this. The various collections of place-name lore, known as *dindshenchas*, also connect the *dam díli* to specific locations in Ireland, but here they are reinterpreted as oxen belonging to a woman called Díl. In the account of the naming of Mag mBreg, the metrical *dindshenchas* (Gwynn 1903-1935, Vol. 4, p 190-193), as well as the prose versions from Rennes (Stokes 1895, p 62-63) and the Bodleian (Stokes 1892, p 470-471), narrate that Díl is the daughter of Lugmannair from the land of the men of Falga (Isle of Man), and a certain calf was born at the same time as she was; she took this calf with her when she eloped with Tulchainde to Ireland, and the calf's name was Brega. It was driven to the plain called Mag mBolgaide, and loved the plain so much that thereafter it became known as Mag mBreg. The metrical *dindshenchas* (Gwynn 1903-1935, Vol. 3, p 198-199, 204-205) and the prose version from Rennes (Stokes 1894, p 435-437) also connect this same Díl to two other oxen, called Fe and Men, who died on the plain which was thereafter named Mag Femen. While these collections of place-name lore were made in the twelfth century (though often showing linguistic evidence of being in existence much earlier), older texts attest to this latter tradition of Mag Femen as well. *Sanas Cormaic*, a glossary compiled *circa* the late ninth-early tenth century, as well as a Middle Irish (tenth-twelfth century CE) text called by its editor *Tuath Dé Miscellany*, contains the same information about the oxen Fe and Men giving their names to the plain (Meyer 1994, p 49 §603; Carey 1992, 28, 30-31), and the further details that the two were the "kings of oxen."

The reinterpretation of the genitive *díli/dílenn* as the personal name Díl continued in two twelfth-century sources. A character called Cáilte Ua Daim Derg Dílinn ("C. descendant of the Red Ox of Flood") is named amongst the heroes of Finn mac Cumhaill's warrior band (Meyer 1910, p 50-51 §22). In the eulogy of Cú Chulainn for Fer Diad in the *Book of Leinster* version of *Táin Bó Cúailnge*, Fer Diad is said to have slain a warrior called Dam Dílend (O'Rahilly 1967, p 97, 233). Another lament for a warrior from the early-thirteenth century text *Acallam na Senórach* (Stokes 1900, p 24) compares the cries of the stag of Druim nDá Leis for the doe of Druim Silenn (who are the paired *dam dílenn*) to the waves of the sea which lament the slain warrior Cáel.[4]

A final instance of the term *dam dílenn*, from a seventeenth-century manuscript within the singly-attested copy of the tale *Cath Findchorad*, is difficult to interpret in context. It praises the Donn Cúailnge, one of the two great bulls that is the object of the cattle-raid in *Táin Bó Cúailnge*, as "*Moamh damh nDilenn*" (Dobbs 1923, p 402), which is either "the greatest ox of flood" or "the greatest ox of Díl." As the Donn Cúailnge is nowhere else said to be owned by Díl or related to any offspring of the oxen of Díl, the meaning "ox of flood" seems to make more sense. The two bulls of the *Táin Bó Cúailnge* could equally be described as "oxen of flood," as both of them were engendered mysteriously via the "conception through swallowing" motif that occurs frequently in Irish narrative. The bulls were originally two opposed swineherds, who changed forms throughout many years and continued to fight one another until they each became maggots in different streams and were swallowed by different cows, to be reborn as the great bulls (Stokes 1894, p 464-467); and one of their forms before their final incarnations as maggots and then bulls was as two stags (Windisch 1891). The bulls are superlatively fertile, of gigantic size, and Donn Cúailnge is said to be able to bull fifty heifers at a time, which if they did not give birth the following day would burst and die (O'Rahilly 1967, p 36, 174). In the final battle between the two bulls, the Donn Cúailnge is victorious and strews the body-parts of his adversary, the Finnbennach Aí, across the landscape, and in the first recension of the *Táin*, at one stage he plunges into the lake near Crúachu (the capital of the territory of Queen Medb, from which the Finnbennach originated) and emerges with the few remaining pieces of the adversary bull on his horns before depositing them in various locales where he stops to drink (O'Rahilly 1976, p 124, 237; Stokes 1892, p 493-494).

It is no coincidence that Fergus mac Roich, the heroic figure whose death-tale echoes the lines relating to the *dam díli* in the Old Irish impotence spell, is one of the major figures in the Ulster Cycle of medieval Irish literature, of which the *Táin Bó Cúailnge* is the centerpiece. Fergus' first name seems to mean "manly," and his matronymic derives from a female figure whose name seems to mean "great mare," *Ro-ech* (Ní Chatháin 1991, p 128-129). He was a former king of Ulster, but was deposed from the kingship by Conchobor mac Nessa, and later went into exile and sought refuge with the Ulstermen's enemies in Connacht under Queen Medb (Ó hUiginn 1993). The early Middle Irish tract *Scéla Conchobair maic Nessa* relates that Fergus was of an immense size in many physiognomic dimensions, including genitally: "*Secht n-artim na luirg. Bolg meich ina thistu* (Seven fists [forty-two inches] in his penis. A bushel-bag in his scrotum" (Stokes 1910, p 26-27 §13). In the same text, it states that seven women were needed to satisfy him every night, unless he was with Flidais, while in the longer recension of *Táin Bó Flidais*, it instead says that Medb was able to provide for his needs (Dobbs 1916, p 136, 142). This Flidais is said in some texts to be a member of the Tuatha Dé, one of the supernatural races of Ireland (Carey 1992, p 28, 30), and she also appears in genealogies (O'Brien 1976, p 362) in which she was said to have had a son who could milk does, and that her cows were does (Carey 1992, p 35). In the long recension of *Táin Bó Flidais*, it is related that she had a hornless cow that could give milk sufficient for the consumption of three hundred men (MacKinnon 1904-1908, 2, p 310-311). This Flidais is also invoked in part of an Irish spell from the *Leabhar Breacc* manuscript: "*Trëële treibeoil: / fuil chon, / fuil hilchon, / fuil fletha Flithais* (A threefold charm from a threefold mouth: / blood of a hound, / blood of many hounds, / blood of the feast of Flidais)[5]....*Ad-muiniur teora ingena Flithais* (I invoke the three daughters of Flidais)" (Carey 2000, p 116).[6] Fergus' warrior-prowess, with implications for his fertility, is compromised in the course of the *Táin Bó Cúailnge* when Ailill, the husband of Medb, arranges for Fergus' sword Caladbolg (which was of superlative size as well) to be stolen (O'Rahilly 1967, p 68, 208; 1976, p 32-33, 154-155), and he is belittled throughout the tale for this loss, until it is restored to him during the final battle and he flattens three hill-tops with it (Sayers 1985; O'Rahilly 1967, p 131-132, 267-268; 1976, p 121-123, 233-235). In recent times, the phallic stone located at Tara has been referred to as *Bod Fhearghusa*, "Fergus' Penis" (Carey 1999, p 165), thus indicating that his associations with fertility have been carried through until the modern period.

Now we may be able to examine the death-tale of Fergus with an understanding of the full implications found in it. A late-tenth century poem by Cinaed Úa hArtacáin on the deaths of various heroes relates Fergus' death in brief: "Fergus was smitten one morning early by Lugaid's spear in Findloch: that is the tale from which is the 'Sole keen Jealousy of Ailill'"[7] (Stokes 1902, p 308-309 §21). It is noteworthy that this same lake, Findloch, is said to be where the Finnbennach Aí met his death in the Bodleian *dindshenchas* account (Stokes 1892, p 493-494). In the death-tale *Aided Fergusa maic Róich*, the details are elaborated: Fergus is demonstrating his prowess while swimming in the lake, and Medb is overcome with desire for him, goes to him, and wraps herself around him as he swims. Ailill then says to his brother Lugaid Dalléces ("L. the Blind Poet"), "*Is álaind a ndogní an dam, a Lugaid, ┐ an eilit isin loch* (It is beautiful, Lugaid, what the stag and the doe are doing in the lough)" (Meyer 1906, p 32-33; Carey 2004, p 21). Lugaid, whose aim was infallible, then offers to kill the stag and the doe, and Ailill points him toward the cavorting couple; he casts a spear, and wounds Fergus mortally.[8] Ailill then beats a hasty retreat in his chariot, but Fergus removes the spear from his body and casts at him, which causes the death of a greyhound under the wheels of the chariot (Meyer 1906, p 34-35). Fergus and Medb are here cast in the role of the "stag of flood" and his doe, as likewise Fergus' lover Flidais is portrayed as a doe; Fergus' death is likewise located in the same place that another great "ox of flood" was killed. The paragon of fertility, cut down in the midst of sexual play with one of the most promiscuous female figures in Irish tradition, is an apt metaphor for the impotence that is invoked in the Old Irish spell: even as the most fertile and phallic figure in Irish mythology is vulnerable to death and defeat (in effect, anti-fertility), so those same powers are invoked to bring about impotence, lack of strength in adversarial warriors, and a cessation of blood-flow and birth at the spell-caster's pleasure.

The various elements discussed thus far have comparanda in other Indo-European cultures. Maier's 1999 study, while it never mentions the *dam díli*, discusses various water-bulls in Scots and Manx tradition, and compares them (as well as German and Near Eastern examples) to Greek traditions involving the mating of Dionysos in bull-form with the Athenian *basílinna* during the Anthesteria festival (p 14).[9] Norse parallels to Fergus' death are obvious in the case of the death of Baldr via the machinations of Loki and the blind Hoðr's (who was Baldr's brother) mistletoe-javelin cast (Carey 2004, p 21 note 34). However, further Norse parallels to points of Fergus' adventures and his associations are present in the character of Freyr. According to Adam of Bremen, Freyr was depicted with phallic priapic representations at his shrine in Uppsala (Simek 1993, p 92, 93 s.v. Freyr, Fricco). However, Freyr's animal attribute tends to be a boar, rather than a bull or a stag; though a further animal may connect the two figures: the horse. Recall that Fergus' matronymic connects him to horses,[10] and his brother Sualtaim was said to be one of the three horsemen of Ireland who first rode *"ar srian aeneich* (on the rein of a single horse)" rather than in chariots (Ní Chatháin 1991, p 127; Van Hamel 1933, p 116), which he does in *Táin Bó Cúailnge* on his son Cú Chulainn's legendary horse, the Liath Macha, to warn the Ulstermen of the advancing armies of Medb (O'Rahilly 1967, p 111, 246). Tacitus reports in his *Germania* that the Naharvali worshipped the dioscuri under the name Alcis (Mattingly and Handford 1970, p 137; Simek 1993, p 7 s.v. Alcis). Dioscuric pairs in Indo-European mythology often have horse associations (Puhvel 1970; Ward 1970), and it has been commonly thought that the Anglo-Saxon leaders Hengist and Horsa (whose names connect them to horses) were probably the Germanic reflex of such divine twin types; Ward further suggests that often one of the pair of twins is associated with fertility and perhaps cattle, while the other is more associated with horses and warrior-activities. It seems at least possible that a reflex of the Norse dioscuri/Alcis might be the brother-and-sister pair amongst the Vanir, Freyr and Freyja. Freyr is connected with horses in several of the early sagas (Simek 1993, p 157-158 s.v. horse), and horse sacrifices occurred at the shrine at Uppsala.[11] One of the suggested etymologies for "Alcis" is through a Germanic word *alsces*, meaning "elk" (Simek 1993, p 7 s.v. Alcis), and while it has been suggested that the elk association might be a further indication of horse connections, there may be another possibility in relation to Freyr and Freyja. Two of the four harts which are said to feed on the Yggdrasil tree are called Dáin and Dvalin (Hollander 1962, p 60; Young 1954, p 45), the names of which are shared with dwarves who in later eddic lays are said to have made special objects for Freyja (Simek 1993, p 55-56, 67), and the harts are also said to have rivers flowing from them (Davidson 1988, p 170-171). Freyr was known to have loaned his horse and his sword (again, as with Fergus, with phallic connotations) to his youthful servant Skírnir in his errand to woo Gerðr (Hollander 1962, p 67, 98-99), and the loss of this sword is said to be the cause of Freyr's death at Ragnarok (Young 1954, p 88). In a curious detail given in Snorri Sturluson's *Gylfaginning*, it is said that because of the loss of his sword, Freyr was forced to fight the giant Beli with a hart's horn (Young 1954, p 62). The loss of a sword and resulting loss of fertility and defeat in battle, and an association with both horses and "stags of flood" in the form of the harts of Yggdrasil and the replacement weapon for the sword, seems to point toward a variety of similarities between Freyr and Fergus.

While these Indo-European parallels are highly suggestive, they do not present us with a one-to-one correspondence and matching significance. However, there is one further comparison with Indian material which might prove especially fruitful. Before proceeding to examine the Indian parallels, though, it is to be noted that water-bulls or water-stages have been the focus of much of the present discussion, but there is a further aquatic animal which is noteworthy here: namely water-horses. The majority of traditions relating to these animals in the Insular Celtic world come from later folklore (Mackillop 1998, p 66 s.v. cabal-ushtey, 83 s.v. ceffyl dwfr, 164 s.v. each uisce, 254 s.v. glashtin, 281 s.v. kelpie), but Mackillop also notes that these often malevolent creatures are not to be confused with the horses of Cú Chulainn, which were said to originate from and to have returned to lakes.[12] In the tale *Fled Bricrenn*, Cú Chulainn reports that he had gained the Liath Macha from the Linn Léith ("Grey Pool") at Slíab Fúait, and had stealthfully mounted it and rode the length and breadth of Ireland upon it for an entire day to tame it, and likewise had obtained the Dub Sainglenn from Loch Duib Sainglenn (Koch and Carey 2003, p 85). When Cú Chulainn was about to die, his killer Lugaid cast a spear at him and hit the Liath Macha, who then retreated into Linn Leith (but later re-emerged to defend the hero's body and attack his killers), and when the final fateful spear struck Cú Chulainn, the Dub Sainglenn left him and retreated to its lake, which seethed when he entered it (Koch and Carey 2003, p 139-140).[13] We recall that this same Liath Macha was ridden by Fergus' brother/Cú Chulainn's father Sualtaim mac Roich in the *Táin*.

It has long been suggested that the account of the kingship inauguration ritual given in Giraldus Cambrensis' *Topographia Hiberniae* and the Indian kingship ritual called the *aœvamedha* bear striking similarities, and perhaps originate in a similar Indo-European matrix (Puhvel 1987, p 269-276). The account of Giraldus relates that kings of the Cenél Conaill were inaugurated through a ritual at a tribal assembly in which, first, the prospective king copulates with a white mare, which is then killed and cut up, and boiled in a vat which the king also bathes in, and then he drinks some of the broth directly by mouth (O'Meara 1948-1950, p 168; 1982, p 109-110). Further, Medb's name has an etymology linking her with the name of the *aœvamedha* ritual, with connections suggesting a common root meaning "intoxication," and echoed in the Arvernian name Epomeduos, the latter suggesting both a personal name meaning "horse-intoxication" and a ritual name involving those two elements (Puhvel 1970, p 167). The Indian ritual consisted of a chaste fireside vigil between the prospective king and his favorite wife, followed by the selection of a prize stallion that was sprinkled with water in a pool, and as this occurred a dog was killed and thrown under it. The stallion then roamed free for a year with a hundred aged or gelded horses and four-hundred accompanying youths of all castes; at the end of this time, a three-day ritual occurred, in which the king drove the prize stallion and three other horses in a chariot, the stallion was anointed in various ways, and was smothered to death, followed by a mock copulation between the queen and the stallion, and culminating with the stallion being further butchered and other sacrifices occurring (Puhvel 1987, p

270-271). The major difficulty in the Irish and Indian ritual comparisons has always been that it is stallion and queen in India, whereas it is king and mare in Ireland, but Puhvel explains this by saying that the typical Indo-European theriomorphic hierogamy was clearly represented by the king and mare pattern, with the Mediterranean variants involving queen and beast (usually a bull), and the Indian example being a compromise of sorts with queen and stallion (Puhvel 1987, p 275-276).

While what I am about to suggest lacks the convenience of a single ritual attestation for comparison, I believe there is enough evidence to support the notion that a more direct common descent can be shown between the Indian *aśvamedha* ritual and the Irish narratives surrounding Fergus and his death. If Fergus is understood as, in some senses, a horse (though he is called a *dam* specifically in the text), who wandered in exile from Ulster, and the queen Medb (whose name derives from roots related to the *aśvamedha*) copulates (or at least has erotic play) with him in his death-tale, he is then "sacrificed" by order of the queen's husband and rightful consort Ailill in a manner similar to the Indian ritual. That the events take place in a lake connects them to the Indian ritual's initial phases in which the stallion is sprinkled in a pool, and the death of the dog in Fergus' death-tale as it runs beneath the chariot also matches the detail in the Indian ritual. Flidais, who seems to encompass the ambiguity of *dam* (as either "ox" or "stag") in feminine form with her cow and doe associations, is also connected to Fergus as a consort. In the long recension of *Táin Bó Flidais*, there is an incident in which a great ferocious hound and fifty attendant hounds attack Fergus in his chariot, which he eventually kills (MacKinnon 1905-1908, 4, 114-119, 216-217). Perhaps these are the hounds referred to in the spell invoking Flidais and her daughters, which was used to prevent wounds, inflammation of wounds, and rabies (Carey 2000, p 116-117), in the same way that Fergus was not harmed by the vicious attacks of these hounds. Both of these incidents with hounds seem to echo the Indian ritual, which implies that the stallion is victorious over the hound by its trampling upon it. A further similarity between the Fergus material and the *aśvamedha* is that a blessing is whispered into the ear of the stallion in the preparatory ceremonies, so that favour accrues to the priests, kings, cows, oxen, horses, women, chariot fighters, youths, and other blessings in the natural and cultivated environment.[14] In *Táin Bó Flidais*, Fergus' generosity is praised in analogously socially-comprehensive terms: "it is he that gives three thousand steeds, three thousand chariots, three thousand swords, three thousand variously coloured suits, three thousand shields, three thousand gilt helmets, three thousand sharp long spears and three thousand many-hued mantles to the three thousand kings, rulers, champions, soldiers, warriors and heroes of the race of Rudhraige that are about him: and it is he that gives the stipend none ever gave before to the wives of the mercenaries, fighting men, kings' sons and rulers of the race of Rudhraige that are with him, namely, three thousand *íorna* of red gold to ornament their dresses and for other adornment" (Dobbs 1916, p 136, 142). There are further similarities between the various stag-connected figures and horses which could be outlined,[15] but the basic picture which emerges in these relations between mythological figures of fertility and their aquatic theriomorphic counterparts—whether stag, bull, or stallion—is quite clear.

It seems that the mythic narrative from which the Old Irish impotence spell derives its symbolic power is not only concerned with fertility, but also with rightful kingship and its rituals. The two concepts are connected intimately in Irish cosmology, with the fruits of good and just rulership and the proper relationship between king and the representatives of sovereignty and the supernatural being reflected in agricultural plentitude and harmony with nature, as stated in ideal terms in the gnomic text *Audacht Morainn* (Koch and Carey 2003, p 188-193). The situation of the Indo-European sacred marriage and the matching symbolic animals and genders for differing cultures is not quite as simple or formulaic as that outlined by Puhvel when these further pieces of evidence are taken into account. Fergus unites in himself the bull, the stag, and the horse, and whether he is the king in right relation to the feminine sovereignty or the male representative of sovereignty with which the queen intercedes is a matter for individual interpretation. The impotence spell and the narratives related to it suggest that the regulation of male fertility as well as queenly conduct were just as important as (and within) the sacred marriage to the sovereignty goddess itself.[16] Magic and ritual practices designed to ensure fertility or bring it about have always had appeal for humans, but in the present case, we have seen that the opposite of fertility—whether it be the death of a character, stopping the flow of blood to prevent injury, or even the "clinical" creation of erectile dysfunction—can be just as important for the regulated cosmos and equally appealing for humans in ways beyond their possible uses for the cursing of others.[17]

Notes

1 In brief, the "nativist" position emphasized that a great amount of authentic pre-Christian belief and mythological content has been preserved in the Irish literature written since the mid-sixth century, whereas the "anti-nativist" position preferred to find analogues to the

incidents in Irish narrative amongst classical (especially Latin) literature and biblical analogues which were known to the Irish *literati*. The polarization of these two "schools" of thought is generally no longer acknowledged by many modern scholars, since a more moderate position, taking into account the biblical- and classical-educated background of the Irish authors as well as their interest in their pre-Christian heritage, seems both closer to the reality of the situation as well as a more fertile ground for argument and explication of evidence.

2   Interestingly, another Celtic spell, the *defixio* found at Chamalières, seems to have been intended to cure failing eyesight, rheumatism, and decreased potency (Meid 1994, p 38-40; Koch and Carey 2003, p 2-3).

3   It is to be noted that in Old and Middle Irish, "nn" and "nd" were indistinguishable, and so some forms given in the examples to follow fluctuate between these two options. Further, unstressed "i" and "e" in final syllables also fluctuate.

4   For further references to *dam dili* as a warrior epithet, see Carey 1992, p 31; Carey 2004, p 20 note 32.

5   Eleanor Hull, basing her text on that of Lady Wilde, mistakenly gives "The blood of one dog, the blood of many dogs, the blood of the hound of Fleithas" (1910, p 438).

6   In a late narrative I have yet been unable to locate, Fergus was said to have mistrusted Flidais, and he drowned her in a river flowing from Carrowmore Loch (Mackillop 1998, p 238 s.v. Flidais). Generally, she is said to have died for unspecified reasons on the strand known as Tráig Baili (e.g. Best and Bergin 1929, p 57), or, in the later recension of *Táin Bó Flidais*, she disappears with her wondrous cow at Loch Letrech (MacKinnon 1904-1908, 4, p 218-219), thus having a "watery end" in all cases.

7   One of the requirements for the king/consort of Medb was that he be without jealousy, for she was said to have never had a lover without another waiting in the shadows (O'Rahilly 1967, p 2, 138).

8   Carey 2004, p 21 note 35 remarks that an incident in *Acallam na Senórach* might echo the death of Fergus, when a herd of deer that has run into the sea is killed by the mermaid-like woman Lí Ban (who was a human that drowned in the inundation of her father's kingdom) with a spear,

just after a poem is recited in which various famous waves on the seas around Ireland are enumerated (Stokes 1900, p 91-92). The constellation of watery women, floods, deer, and spears here is indeed worthy of further consideration.

9   The Ulster Cycle character Furbaide Fer Benn, the nephew of Medb via one of her sisters and the Ulster king Conchobor mac Nessa, was born via caesarian section and was said to have had horns, and his relationship to Dionysos is a subject that I have treated briefly (Bernhardt-House, forthcoming), and will return to again in more detail in a future study. He will also feature again in note 16 below.

10 Bruford 1989, p 129-139, makes an interesting but ultimately reductionistic argument for the identity of Fergus and Ailill as the two children born to the territorial/horse-goddess Macha, the birth of which gave the name Emain Macha ("Twins of Macha") to the ancient capital of the province of Ulster. The names of the twins in one version of the story were Fír ("truth") and Fial ("modesty"), the former male and the latter female. Horse-connections and dioscurism will be discussed presently.

11 Though in other accounts, oxen are specifically offered to Freyr as sacrifices (Davidson 1988, p 53, 138).

12 At the same time, the oldest tale concerning these horses states that they were both born at the same time as the first birth (of his two births and three conceptions) of Cú Chulainn (Van Hamel 1933, p 4-5).

13 The argument for dioscuric horse-connections seems especially apt to point out at this stage, where two supernatural horses were said to have originated from the horse-goddess Macha, who was said to have given birth to twins, as mentioned in notes 9 and 11 above. Sayers 1996, p 66-67, and Carey 2004, p 12, both discuss Greek parallels with names of rivers/water sources and the names of horses in the careers of Achilleus and Cú Chulainn, with the Liath Macha and Xanthus both lamenting or foretelling the death of their heroic counterparts.

14 There are also echoes of such a blessing in Italic materials, connected perhaps with the Roman October Equus sacrifice, also mentioned by Puhvel.

15 Including, but not limited to, the frequent occurrence of the name Eochaid, which is also horse-connected, as the father of many of these characters (e.g. Medb, Lí Ban). In the story of *Fingal Rónáin* the female character who would fulfill the role of the "sovereignty goddess" is never given a personal name, only the patronymic "daughter of Eochaid" (Koch and Carey 2003, p 274-282), and there is a crucial episode in which the "cows of Aífe" are mentioned in a poem that suggests possible sexual infidelities to the king Rónán, who then slays his son wrongfully for this suspicion.

16 I would note here that the bull-horned, Dionysos-like Furbaide Fer Benn is responsible for the death of his aunt Medb in vengeance for his mother, and that he strikes the fateful blow when she is seen bathing in a lake (V. Hull 1938).

17 For the generous funding which made this research possible, I would like to thank Merle Ann Leytze, Annabelle House, Dr. Bill Bethards and Debbie Bethards. I also acknowledge the indispensable research assistance of Lizabeth Johnson, David Kraetzer, Kicki Ingridsdotter and Sarah Bernhardt. All opinions and ideas expressed in this article, both valuable and in error, are the sole responsibility of the author.

References

Bernhardt-House, Phillip A., forthcoming, "'It's beginning to look a lot like Solstice'": *Snechta*, Solar Deities, and *Compert Con Culainn*', *Ulidia II: Proceedings of the Second International Conference on the Ulster Cycle of Tales*, ed. Ruairí Ó hUiginn.

Best, Richard Irvine, 1952, 'Some Irish Charms', *Ériu*, 16, 27-32.

Best, Richard Irvine and Osborn J. Bergin, 1929, *Lebor na hUidre: Book of the Dun Cow*, Royal Irish Academy, Dublin.

Betz, Hans Dieter, 1986, *The Greek Magical Papyri in Translation, Including the Demotic Spells, Second Edition, Volume One: Texts*, University of Chicago Press, Chicago and London.

Carey, John, 1992, 'A *Tuath Dé* Miscellany', *Bulletin of the Board of Celtic Studies*, 39, 24-45.

Carey, John, 1999, 'Varia I: *Ferp Cluche*', *Ériu*, 50, 165-168.

Carey, John, 2000, 'Téacsanna draíochta in Éirinn sa mheánaois luath', *Léachtaí Cholm Cille*, 30, 98-117.

Carey, John, 2004, 'The Encounter at the Ford: Warriors, Water, and Women', *Éigse*, 34, 10-24.

Davidson, Hilda R. Ellis, 1988, *Myths and Symbols in Pagan Europe: Early Scandinavian and Celtic Religions*, Syracuse University Press, Syracuse.

Dobbs, Margaret C., 1916, 'On *Táin Bó Flidais*', *Ériu*, 8, 133-149.

Dobbs, Margaret C., 1923, 'The Battle of Findchorad', *Zeitschrift für Celtische Philologie*, 14, 395-420.

Gwynn, Edward, 1903-1935, *The Metrical Dindshenchas*, Todd Lecture Series 8-12, 5 volumes, Royal Irish Academy, Dublin.

Hollander, Lee M., 1962, *The Poetic Edda*, University of Texas Press, Austin.

Hull, Eleanor, 1910, 'The Ancient Hymn-Charms of Ireland', *Folklore*, 21.4, 417-446.

Hull, Vernam, 1938, '*Aided Meidbe*: The Violent Death of Medb', *Speculum*, 13.1, 52-61.

Koch, John T. and John Carey, 2003, *The Celtic Heroic Age: Literary Sources for Ancient Celtic Europe & Early Ireland & Wales*, Celtic Studies Publications, Andover and Aberystwyth.

Mackillop, James, 1998, *The Oxford Dictionary of Celtic Mythology*, Oxford University Press, Oxford.

MacKinnon, Donald, 1904-1908, 'The Glenmasan Manuscript', *The Celtic Review*, 1, 208-229, 296-315; 2, 20-33, 100-121, 202-223, 300-315; 3, 10-25, 114-137, 198-215, 294-317; 4, 10-27, 104-121, 202-219.

Maier, Bernhard, 1999, 'Beasts from the Deep: The Water-Bull in Celtic, Germanic and Balto-Slavonic Traditions', *Zeitschrift für Celtische Philologie*, 51, 4-16.

Mattingly, Harold and S. A. Handford (trans.), 1970, *Tacitus: The Agricola and the Germania*, Penguin, London.

Meid, Wolfgang, 1994, *Gaulish Inscriptions: Their interpretation in the light of archaeological evidence and their value as a source of linguistic and sociological information*, Archaeolingua, Budapest.

Meyer, Kuno, 1906a, *The Triads of Ireland*, Todd Lecture Series 13, Royal Irish Academy, Dublin.

Meyer, Kuno, 1906b, *The Death-Tales of the Ulster Heroes*, Todd Lecture Series 14, Royal Irish Academy, Dublin.

Meyer, Kuno, 1910, *Fianaigecht: Being a Collection of Hitherto Inedited Irish Poems relating to Finn and His Fiana*, Todd Lecture Series 16, Royal Irish Academy, Dublin.

Meyer, Kuno, 1994, *Sanas Cormaic (Cormac's Glossary)*, Llanerch, Felinfach.

Ní Chatháin, Próinséas, 1991, 'Traces of the Cult of the Horse in Early Irish Sources', *Journal of Indo-European Studies*, 19, 123-131.

O'Brien, M. A., 1976, *Corpus Genealogiarum Hiberniae*, Dublin Institute for Advanced Studies, Dublin.

Ó hUiginn, Ruairí, 1993, 'Fergus, Russ and Rudraige: A Brief Biography of Fergus Mac Róich', *Emania*, 11, 31-40.

O'Meara, John J., 1948-1950, 'Giraldus Cambrensis in *Topographia Hiberniae*: Text of the First Recension', *Proceedings of the Royal Irish Academy*, 52C, 113-178.

O'Meara, John J. (trans.), 1982, *Gerald of Wales: The History and Topography of Ireland*, Penguin, London.

O'Rahilly, Cecile, 1967, *Táin Bó Cúalnge from the Book of Leinster*, Dublin Institute for Advanced Studies, Dublin.

O'Rahilly, Cecile, 1976, *Táin Bó Cúailnge Recension I*, Dublin Institute for Advanced Studies, Dublin.

Puhvel, Jaan, 1970, 'Aspects of Equine Functionality', *Myth and Law Among the Indo-European: Studies in Indo-European Comparative Mythology*, ed. Jaan Puhvel, University of California Press, Berkeley, Los Angeles and London, 159-172.

Puhvel, Jaan, 1987, *Comparative Mythology*, Johns Hopkins University Press, Baltimore and London.

Sayers, William, 1985, 'Fergus and the Cosmogonic Sword', *History of Religions*, 25, 30-56.

Sayers, William, 1996, 'Homeric Echoes in *Táin Bó Cúailnge*?', *Emania*, 14, 65-73.

Simek, Rudolf, 1993, *Dictionary of Northern Mythology*, trans. Angela Hall, D. S. Brewer, Cambridge.

Stokes, Whitley, 1892, 'The Bodleian Dinnshenchas', *Folklore*, 3.4, 467-516.

Stokes, Whitley, 1894, 'The Prose Tales in the Rennes Dindshenchas', *Revue Celtique*, 15, 272-336, 418-484.

Stokes, Whitley, 1895, 'The Prose Tales in the Rennes Dindshenchas', *Revue Celtique*, 16, 31-83, 135-167, 269-312.

Stokes, Whitley, 1900, *Acallamh na Senórach, Irische Texte 4.1*, S. Hirzel, Leipzig.

Stokes, Whitley, 1902, 'On the Deaths of some Irish Heroes', *Revue Celtique*, 23, 303-348.

Stokes, Whitley, 1910, 'Tidings of Conchobar son of Ness', *Ériu*, 4, 18-38.

Van Hamel, Anton G., 1933, *Compert Con Culainn and Other Stories*, Dublin Institute for Advanced Studies, Dublin.

Ward, Donald J., 1970, 'The Separate Functions of the Indo-European Divine Twins', Myth and Law Among the Indo-European: Studies in Indo-European *Comparative Mythology*, ed. Jaan Puhvel, University of California Press, Berkeley, Los Angeles and London, 193-202.

Windisch, Ernst, 1891, '*De Chophur in dá muccida*', *Irische Texte 3*, S. Hirzel, Leipzig, 235-247.

Young, Jean I. (trans.), 1954, *Snorri Sturluson, The Prose Edda: Tales from Norse Mythology*, Bowes and Bowes Publishers, Cambridge.

Reading the Turkish Coffee Cup and Beyond: The Case of North Cyprus

Gulnara Karimova

Coffee-cup fortune telling is a phenomenon that is especially common in Bulgaria, Greece, Egypt, Macedonia, Bosnia (Turkoglu 2000), Turkey and other countries. Coffee-cup reading is also practiced in North Cyprus where this process appears to be both a pastime performed by neighbors and friends and a business operated by professional fortune tellers. The multiform meanings of symbols have been expounded in numerous works including *A Dictionary of Symbols* written by J.E. Cirlot (1971),[1] *An Illustrated Encyclopedia of Traditional Symbols* by J.C. Cooper (1978) and *1000 Symbols* by Shepherd and Shepherd (2002). The history of Arabic and Turkish coffee has also been investigated by many researchers including A. S. Kaye (1986) and Turkoglu (2000). However, what I am always interested in, as a person who practices coffee-cup reading, is the magnetic relations between the symbols produced in the cup and the individual's psychological state. This paper is an attempt to illuminate this relationship between the symbols in a coffee cup and the individual whose cup is read. I venture to presume that fortune telling brings pleasure to many people because it is not only about their future but also reflects their emotional states. Through coffee-cup reading, the verbal expression of feelings and psychological conditions materialize in the presence of the person whose fortune is read in more vivid hues and are enriched with exciting details.

The focus of this paper is tasseography or tasseomancy (*kafemandeia* in Greek), the ancient art of reading tealeaves. The term is derived from the French word *tasse* (cup), which in turn is derived from the Arabic *tassa* (cup) (Melton (n.d) cited in *Tasseography*). The term tasseography was later applied to a divination or fortune telling method that interprets patterns in coffee grounds in the Middle Eastern tradition. This study however, pays particular attention to the Turkish tradition of reading a coffee cup. But before moving to the main principles of tasseography and interpretation of coffee cup symbols, I would like to shed a little light on the origin and history of the coffee itself and how it became a part of Turkish tradition.

A History of Coffee

What is now known as Turkish coffee was brought to Istanbul, according to one source, by the governor of Yemen (*Turkish Coffee*), and according to another source it was introduced by either two Syrians called Hukum and Sems in 1555 or by Ozdemir Pasha, Ottoman governor of Ethiopia during the reign Suleyman the Magnificent (1520 - 1566) (Turkoglu 2000). Later the beans of *Coffee Arabica* were introduced to Venice, London and Paris via the Ottomans and consequently, acquired its epithet *Turkish* (*Turkish Coffee*). John Crawford (1852) writes, "A Turkey merchant of London, of the name of Edwards, brought the first bag of coffee to England, and his Greek servant made the first dish of English coffee. This was in 1652, under the Commonwealth" (p 51).

The roots of the word 'coffee' can be traced back to the Arabic *qahwah*. The *Oxford English Dictionary* (1966, p 188) notes that the word coffee is "supposed to be ultimately from *Kaffa*, name of a part of Abyssinia, the native home of coffee plant" (cited in Kaye 1986, p 557). Certain Arabic lexicographers claim that the Arabic word *qahwah* is an old word for 'wine' (Crawford 1852, p 50). Sahar Huneidi (2004), a professional intuitive who gives spiritual psychic readings, teaches meditation and conducts workshops on the ancient art of tasseography, refers to the following historical detail, "The invigorating effects of this new 'wine of Islam' enraptured the Persians because real wine was strictly forbidden to Muslims, Turkish people claimed coffee to be an aphrodisiac and husbands kept their wives well supplied; if the husband refused, it was a legitimate cause for a wife to divorce!". In his article *The Etymology of "Coffee": The Dark Brew*, Alan S. Kaye (1986) says that, "the fact that the medieval Arab lexicographers thought *qahwah* meant 'wine' can certainly be attributed to the fact that 'wine' can be very dark (in colour) like 'coffee' (p. 557).

Whilst Turkish coffee does not appear in the list of healthy drinks and is often associated with the risk of heart diseases, blood pressure and stomach upsets (*Coffee Science Information Center*), there are other sources that claim that it might have some positive effects on health. Turkoglu (2000), for example, believes that it has a calming and relaxing quality. In her article *Traditional Turkish Coffee*, Turkoglu points out that, "There is 50 mg of caffeine per cup, and this is expelled immediately without accumulating in the body, so in this respect Turkish coffee cup is ideally proportioned. It also aids in digestion [...]". It is also claimed that Arabian women drank coffee in order to alleviate menstrual discomforts (Huneidi 2004).

Turkish coffee is not just a drink that gained popularity due to its relaxing, soothing and stabilizing quality, but it is also an integral part of Turkish culture. It is associated with a long history, established institutions (coffeehouses), rituals and the traditions of fortune telling.

Fortune Telling

The origins of coffee-cup readings are derived from the ancient Chinese art of tasseography. The principles of tasseography had been later adapted to coffee grounds by the Arabs, "who first discovered coffee beans around 600 AD and managed to keep coffee as a secret [sic], having a monopoly on cultivating and drinking coffee for several hundred years" (Huneidi 2004). Coffee became known in Western Europe and in the Americans only in XVII century.

Cup reading is not only practiced by professional readers but is very common among the general public and especially within the company of friends. Both the preparation of the coffee and reading the coffee cup has certain ceremonies and particular rules. The most wide spread method of coffee preparation is described in the article *Your Fortune in a Cup of Coffee*:

> Turkish coffee is prepared in tiny pots called *cezve*, which can be used to make two cups of coffee at each shot. For perfect coffee, first put two cups of water in the *cezve*, and then add two spoons of Turkish coffee. When the coffee starts to boil, a

thin layer of foam will appear on the surface of the liquid. Using a spoon, distribute this foam among the cups. Then boil the coffee in the *cezve* until it foams up again, and break it among the cups. This boiling action gives it its unique taste. Traditionally, each cup of coffee should be served along with a glass of water. Sugar may be added to taste into the *cezve* right before the cooking stage. One will be asked to specify the amount of sugar when ordering, sweet, *sekerli*, medium sweet, *orta sekerli*, and plain, *sade*.

After the coffee has been prepared, the individual should remember that the coffee be drunk from only one side of the cup. Sahar Huneidi (2004) suggests that whilst drinking Turkish coffee, the person should pose the question "What do I need to know about my present situation?" or "What will be the important changes in my life in the near future?" When the coffee is finished, the saucer is placed on top of the cup. After making a wish, the cup, held at chest-level, should be turned counter clock-wise a few times (usually three), and then turned upside down onto the saucer and left to cool. Sometimes a coin might be placed on the top of the cup to make it cool faster and to dispel bad omens (*Your Fortune in a Cup of Coffee*). At other times a little bit of water can be poured on the top of the cup as well. Turkish coffee is usually served with a glass of cold water so that one can better palate the taste of the coffee.

Sahar Huneidi gives some advice that should be taken into consideration whilst reading a coffee cup; she notes "symbols convey messages; focus on the message rather than the symbol. With practice, you will develop your own dictionary". What is important for a fortune teller is not the shapes molded by the coffee sediments but the feelings that they evoke.

Symbolism

What is the source of the symbols in the tradition of tasseography? Is there any common source from where the symbols of myth, ritual, mysticism, and religion have been derived? The symbolic meanings of images often have archetypal derivations. In their book *Myth, Rites, Symbols: A Mercea Eliade Reader*, Wendell C. Beane and William G. Doty (1975) write "[...] it is probable that the magico-religious complex of 'binding' corresponds closely to an archetype or constellation of archetypes" (p 100). Besides, there are also cultural and historical roots of symbols. Beane and Doty suppose that symbols are not spontaneous; "not all of them depend directly upon the ideal archetype; a great many of them are 'historical' in the sense that they result from the evolution or the imitation of previously existing form" (p 99).

As it was noted by Monica Wilson (1967), "Symbolism is always based on association, a feeling of likeness between things. The intrinsic quality of an object or relationship, or event, is expressed in terms of another object or action which it is felt to resemble" (p 160). These associations are basically determined by social and cultural particularities. However, certain associations may have common interpretations.

In Turkish coffee-cup fortune telling the interpretation of the fish symbol has very significant meanings. For most fortune tellers in Northern Cyprus the fish symbol stands for fate or fortune or, as they say in Turkish, 'kýsmet'. Sahar Huneidi however, suggests interpreting this symbol as a specific sum of money; the bigger the fish, the bigger the amount of money. The symbol of fish also plays an important role in the symbolic systems of meaning in other cultures as well.

Fish symbolism attained its pinnacle in the early Christianity. The fish was used as a symbol of Christ (Hooke 1961 p.537). In very early times in Mesopotamia the fish was perceived to be a symbol of life and rebirth (Hooke 1961, p 536). In the tomb paintings from Gambound the sacred oxyrhynchus fish replaces the usual Ka bird symbol, indicating the hope of immortality (*ibid*). In the Messianic age, on different seals, the fish depicted in different religious scenes represents female genitalia (p 536). Hooke (1961) also emphasizes the fertility quality of the fish symbol (*ibid*). In *An Illustrated Encyclopedia of Traditional Symbols,* J.C.Cooper (1999), refusing to limit symbols to specific definitions and meanings, claims that the fish presents "a point of departure for a voyage of exploration" (p 7).

In many instances the same symbol can have several different meanings within the same culture. Symbols can also have various ambiguous meanings. For example, in the religious rituals of the Lele cult the fish symbol stands for fertility and also for the spirit (Douglas 1967, p 240). Symbols acquire many definitions because of their "integrative function" (Anonymous Editorial, *Communication through Symbols* 2006).

In this paper I do not aim to provide the various possible interpretations of symbols because their meanings have already been thoroughly described.[2] I would however, like to underline the psychological and cultural aspects of coffee-cup fortune telling.

Beyond the Coffee Cup

For many people in North Cyprus coffee-cup reading is a very common, everyday procedure that is not wrapped in a shroud of mystery or magic. In order to find out what value Turkish Cypriots give to coffee-cup fortune telling, I addressed a few questions to Ipek Hallim, a non-professional fortune teller. She insisted that she was not a professional fortune teller and said that "Usually in North Cyprus we do not have a specific name for the person who reads a coffee cup; we just say that this person 'can read a cup'. We do however, have a name for the process of cup reading and we approach someone by asking them 'Falýma bakarmýsýn?' ('Would you read my fortune?')".

I asked Ipek Hallim how she learned to read coffee cups and she answered by saying, "I was introduced to it by my grandmother. I remember our neighbours gathering together to drink coffee in our house. They would turn their cups upside down and look at each others' fortune. I used to imitate them. My grandmother would read the cup by telling a story; she would say, 'I see a big snake' or 'I see a house with a dog near it' and then she would explain what these things meant. Much later, when I attended University, I became very interested in the meanings of symbols and began reading some additional material".

For some people, fortune telling is a psychological act which brings peace and relief from the stresses and strains of the everyday, "No wonder cup readers were referred to as 'soothsayers' in early 'coffee literature' in Europe" (Huneidi 2004). I asked Hallim what coffee-cup reading means to her. She replied, "It is a way we socialize, and a way to escape from stress. We talk about our feelings. If you say something nice to people it makes them happier and maybe even stronger.

Sometimes it is a way to open up a conversation. The things we are talking about are imaginary, thus, we feel free to talk about them openly […]. It is not a personal conversation […]. However, people like my grandmother perceived the process of coffee cup reading to be a very serious matter. Some professional fortune tellers follow certain rituals and rules and even have coffee cups especially intended for this purpose: these cups are thick and entirely white".

In the *Symbols of Transformation*, Jung (1956) states that, "The psychological mechanism that transforms energy is the symbol" (cited in *Communication Through Symbols* 2006). If this phrase was to be taken literally, one may assume that Turkish cup reading is not only the prediction of the future but also the interpretation of the present psychological state of a person whose energy has been transformed into certain symbols. Sahar Huneidi suggests drinking coffee whilst relaxing and "in a contemplative mode" in order to make an accurate reading. Thus, she draws a link between the emotional state of the person and the images formed in the cup. In these terms, coffee-cup symbols may be seen not as the reflection of the future but rather, as the expression of current psychic energy. Hallim however, added that the psychological condition of the coffee-cup reader is also important and that she usually does not read a cup if she is in a bad mood, under stress or concentrating on other work. Hallim says "for me, my mood is important. I get tired while reading a cup, because I give my energy away trying to figure out the meanings of symbols and relaying their stories". Maybe this is why Hallim likes it when the person for whom she reads a cup, participates in creating the story. She says "When I feel that the person listens carefully to me and writes the story along with

my story by finding similar situations in life, it encourages me". Thus, the meaning appears through the dialogical relations between the fortune teller and the one whose fortune is told. This is why not only should the psychological and emotional associations of the fortune teller be taken into account but that the associations of the person whose fortune is read should also be considered. The role of the fortune teller is to then connect these associations into certain compositions.

While Hallim was reading my coffee cup, she revealed the details of the interpretation of symbols, "The very bottom of the cup represents your heart. The end of the handle from the inside is your home. The symbols outside of the cup may represent people who are far from you, such as friends abroad". She commented that animals do not disclose the gender of the person whom they represent. Thus, a snake represents an enemy, but it is rather difficult to define whether it is female or male. Also, the meanings of the symbols change according to the color deposited in the cup: it may be white or black (constructed from the coffee ground or the background of the cup). The dark figures acquire negative meanings even if the symbol itself has a positive connotation. For example, a dog symbolizes a friend but the dark color of a dog represents a person who pretends to be your friend. After the interpretation of the coffee-cup is accomplished, the cup reader asks one to silently choose a number from 1 to 9 and to make a wish. Then, one should press the coffee grounds at the bottom of the cup with the index finger and leave a coffee covered finger print on the outside of the cup. If the cup reader manages to guess the number within three trials, the wish has a greater chance of coming true.

Most of the interviewees have ambiguous feelings towards the phenomenon of coffee cup reading. Many of them are waiting for some magical moment and anticipating for unusual events but at the same time, they do not believe in the predictions of a coffee cup reader. Many people want their coffee cup to be read because they are curious and fascinated. One of the male interviewees told, "People have some problems, and they are looking for ways to solve them. They need to be comforted. A fortune-teller eases their situation. It is a kind of the psychological treatment". One should note that tasseography is not the only divination method in North Cyprus. There are fortune-tellers (called 'falcý') who predict the past, present and future by, for example, using water ('su falý'), Islamic writings ('yýldýz falý') and hoarsebeans ('bakla

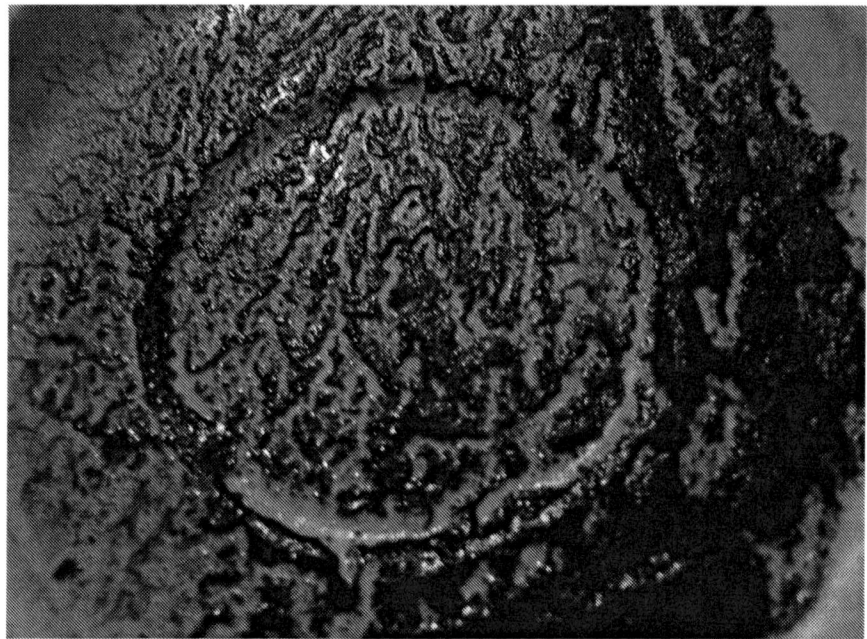

falý'). Some of the fortune-tellers are well known in North Cyprus by the accuracy of their predictions. Even the popular stars and famous politicians address to these fortune-tellers. In the words of the famous in North Cyprus soothsayer, who tells the fortune using water as a 'medium' ('araç'), "The deputies and other political leaders are coming to me to learn if their party has chance to win the elections. Those who did not follow my predictions in recent elections regretted". She adds that politicians are not the only customers, "Usually those, who have problems and cannot overcome them alone, refer to me. They need someone with whom they can share their secrets, worries and sorrows. They see me as a stranger whom they can trust those secrets. After releasing their sad experiences they, probably, feel peaceful". However, she does not only listen; she sees one's past, present and future through the water, and tell about their personality, situation, and future by looking just at the person's photo. The services of famous fortune-tellers are usually rather expensive. Maybe, this is one of the reasons, why the coffee-cup reading remains a popular type of divination. Another reason of its popularity maybe related to the aspect that much more people are able to read coffee-cup, while other methods, like 'broad beans' or 'water' fortune telling, are relatively rare ones.

Coffee-cup reading evokes contradictory emotions. For some people, tasseography is a way of communication and a means of psychological therapy. Some people go to fortune tellers not only to learn about their future but to also to learn about themselves. Sometimes the individual wants to be comforted, or to organize their desires and future plans and sometimes they want to become excited about the predicted events and to possess knowledge about their possible future. But mostly, the tradition of coffee-cup reading gives invaluable insights into a culture and reveals how myth and magic are incorporated into social life.

Notes
1   The *A Dictionary of Symbols* by J.E. Cirlot is used by S. Huneidi a professional intuitive in her coffee cup readings
2   I have attached a list of symbols and their common meanings in coffee cup reading traditions in The Appendix.

References:
Anonymous Editorial, 7-2-2006, [On-line], *Turkish Coffee*, http:/www.adiyamanli.org/Turkish_coffee.html

Anonymous Editorial, 7-2-2006, *Your Fortune in a Cup of Coffee*, [On-line], http://www.turkishculture.org

Beane, W. C. and Doty, W. G., 1975, *Myth, Rites, Symbols: A Mercea Eliade Reader*, Vol.1,

Harper and Row Publishers, USA

Cirlot, J.E., 1971, *A Dictionary of Symbols*, The Philosophical Library, New York.

Coffee Science Information Centre, 7-2-2006, [On-line], http://www.cosic.org/coffee-and-health/summary

Cooper, J.C., 1999, *An Illustrated Encyclopedia of Traditional Symbols*, Thames and Hudson Ltd., London.

Crawford J., 1852, 'History of Coffee', *Journal of the Statistical Society of London*, Vol. 15, 50-58.

Douglas M.,1967, *Animals in Lele Religious Thought*, in Middleton J. (ed), *Myth and Cosmos. Reading in Mythology and Symbolism*, The Natural History Press, USA.

Encyclopedia of Occultism & Parapsychology, 7-2-2006, [On-line], http://www.answers.com/topic/tasseography?method=22

Hooke S.H. (1961) 'Fish Symbolism', *Folklore Enterprises*, 535-538.

Huneidi S., (2004), retrieved 7-2-2006, [On-line] 'Prediction Turkish Cup Reading, Your Fortune in a Cup', *Prediction Magazine*, May 2004, 65,

http://www.psychicsahar.com/artman/publish/article_202.shtml

Kaye A. S., 1986, 'The Etymology of "Coffee": the Dark Brew Tasseography', *Journal of American Oriental Society*, Vol. 106, 557-558.

Turkoglu S., 2000, Retrieved 7-2-2006, [On-line] *Traditional Turkish Coffee*, http://www.maths.uwa.edu.au/~alice/pages/kahve.html

Union of International Associations, 28-2-2006, [On-line] *Communication through Symbols*, http://www.mythdreamssymbols.com/symbols.html

Wilson M. (1967) *Nyakyusa Ritual and Symbolism* in Middleton J. (ed), *Myth and Cosmos. Reading in Mythology and Symbolism*, The Natural History Press, USA.

Appendix

Here are some of the interpretations of coffee symbols proposed in the article *Turkish Coffee*:

Angel means that good news and happiness is approaching

Ant means that an activity will bear fruit

Candle means that another person will help you to succeed

Cat means that a quarrel will disrupt your life but only for a short time

Chain symbolizes a legal union, a marriage or business partnership

Chair represents an unforeseen guest

Circle connotes success. Circle with a dot near signifies a new addition to the family (baby)

Circle with lines nearby means that your efforts are being hindered

Devil or horns represents influential people and danger

Dog has a connotation of good, reliable friends, faithful partner

Eagle signifies great improvements in one's life

Egg represents wealth and success

Eye is a sign of envy and jealousy

Fish means that life will become richer, happier and more attractive

Fruit stands for prosperity in one's endeavors

Heart signifies love, faith and trust

Horse is a symbol of strength and independence

Key means that doors are opening for you

Knife stands for enemies and danger

Ring is a sign of marriage. A broken ring means that marriage is in trouble

Scissors stands for possibility of arguments at home

Spider stands for unexpected money

Sun symbolizes power and success

Sword means the vanquishing of enemies

Reviews

Linda C. Hults, 2005, *The Witch as Muse: Art, Gender and Power in Early Modern Europe*, University of Pennsylvannia Press, Pennsylvania. xiv + 345 pp, ISBN 0-8122-3869-9, Hardback £32.50.

Linda Hults is an American professor of the history of art, who has produced the first sustained study ever made of the image of the witch in early modern drawing and painting. It is not a general survey of the topic, but what she terms a 'deep reading' of the way in which certain artists engaged with it. None the less, the individuals and works whom she selects are the most famous of all those associated with the image, and span the period, and most of Western Europe: Albrecht Dürer and Hans Baldung Grien in early sixteenth-cenury Germany, Frans Francken and Jacques de Gheyn in the Spanish and Dutch Netherlands (respectively) in the early decades of the seventeenth century, Salvator Rosa in Italy during the middle decades, and Francisco Goya in Spain at the end of the eighteenth century. That just six artists can fill a substantial volume indicates how close and extensive her analyses of each are, and they are bonded by a cement of feminist critical theory.

What she tries to do, in each case, is explain what the pictures are about and to set the artist and his work in two overlapping contexts: that of artistic conventions in his time and place, and that of attitudes to witchcraft. By this essentially strong, simple and sensible strategy, she seeks to bring about a greater understanding of the people and products concerned, and of the way in which art can mirror contemporary anxieties and ambitions. The results are, naturally enough, different in each case. She represents Dürer's brief but influential foray into representing witches as a reflection of the deeply misogynistic connection between female sexuality and witchcraft made by the notorious, and recently-published, witch-hunting manual, the Malleus maleficarum. Baldung's more extensive portrayal of the image is related to his residence in the university city of Freiburg. There, it is argued, the powerful local community of academics, especially experts in jurisprudence, were presented by him with a challenging and titillating feminine world of irrationality, gullibility, bestial sexuality, malevolence and apostacy. This would reinforce their own masculine sense of reason and moderation. Francken is presented as articulating in art the presentation of witchcraft made by demonologists writing just before he worked, especially the great local one, Martín del Rio. In doing so he portrayed an anti-society of disorder, sacrilege and inversion, representing a serious threat to the godly states of Counter-Reformation Catholicism, and working especially through the curiosity and corruptibility of upper-class women. De Gheyn, by contrast, reflected the more sceptical and restrained Dutch attitudes, and presented witchcraft as primarily a delusion and fantasy of weak and mentally unstable women. Rosa, a radical and freethinker, experimented with pictures of witches as burlesque exercises in mingled comedy and horror, mocking human credulity. Goya took this approach a great deal further, using images of witchcraft to satirize the follies of humanity in general and the superstitions of contemporary Spanish society in particular. In doing so, Professor Hults argues, he at last decentred women from those images, making male and female figures equally implicated in them and suggesting that, as the human flaws that they exposed were so timeless and ubiquitous, there was nothing gendered about them.

This is a book written essentially for colleagues and students within the author's own discipline. It is rich in jargon, technicality and allusion to parallel academic work, and not an easy read for an outsider, although an intelligent and determined lay person should find it accessible. Its less tractable difficulty lies in the source material on which it depends. Works of art are rarely self-evident in the messages that they convey, and to be absolutely certain of the context and meaning of one we need to have both a firm statement of intention by the artist and an equally clear idea of the patron or audience for whom the picture was designed. In none of the cases considered here do such materials exist, and so the best that Professor Hults can do is to reconstruct apparent contexts and suggest likely linkages. There is no absolute proof that Dürer's most famous drawing associated with witchcraft is actually of witches at all, and none that he ever read the Malleus maleficarum. Baldung made well have worked for the jurists of Freiburg, but there is, again, no clinching evidence that he did so, and none of the audience for which his art was designed. The latter deficiency is also true of Francken and de Gheyn. Because de Gheyn worked in major Dutch cities, in which a debate over the reality of witchcraft was being conducted, it is reasonable to view him as a contributor to those debates, but it is not clear on which side we should position him. We know so little about him that it is not even clear if he was Protestant or Catholic, and therefore whether we should regard the elements of Catholic imagery in his paintings as satirical or sincere. Superficially, his portaits of witchcraft are very similar to those of Francken, whom we are invited to see as a serious proponent of witch-hunting as one aspect of an aggressive and reformed new Catholicism.

In Francken's case, certainly, time and place make such a reading plausible; but is it definite? The problem here is that, even within a single society and state at this period, attitudes to witchcraft were so complex and contested. When conjoined with our ignorance of the customers for whom the works of art were designed, it becomes deeply frustrating. It is not clear whether the relevant paintings and drawings of any of the first four artists considered here were designed as serious contributions to a belief in the danger from witchcraft, or a satire on that belief. We do not know whether their purchasers were deeply religious people who wished to display their acceptance of the reality of witchcraft, or libertines who rather enjoyed the scenes of bad behaviour in the pictures, and especially their erotic content which representations of witches (like scenes of classical mythology) licensed as few other subjects could. In the cases of Rosa and Goya we are on firmer ground, because we know something about the general attitudes of both artists to religion and magic, and in Goya's case we know a lot about one, at least, of the patrons who bought the works. None the less, our ignorance of Rosa's intended market leaves some doubt hanging over interpretation, and the fact that previous criticism has sometimes accused Goya of misogynism makes the argument that he uncouples women from witchcraft an interesting rather than a decisive one. It is to Professor Hults's credit that she is aware of these difficulties; but even she cannot overcome them.

One further consideration arises from this courageous and ambitious book, which runs against the grain of its own argument: it implicitly underlines that fact that witchcraft was not a common subject for artists, even in the most intense period of witch trials. This is really not surprising, because it did not commonly attract either scholarly or creative writers either, and indeed the trials themselves were relatively rare events. Witchcraft was, for most of the time, a side-issue for Europeans, even in the period in which some of them were most deeply concerned with it, and it was always one that provoked controversy, uncertainty and unease. That is certainly an issue which this book amply substantiates, and may be regarded as another of its services to scholarship.

Ronald Hutton

Kocku von Stuckrad, 2005, *Western Esotericism: A Brief History of Secret Knowledge*, Equinox Publishing, London. 167 pages, 1-8455-3034-9, Hardback £60, Paperback £17.99.

Western Esotericism is a short book of some 167 pages including notes and appendices, but this belies the book's ambition, breadth and lucidity. Perhaps it is a foolhardy task to try and capture the history of Western Esotericism in short a brief volume but the fact that von Stuckrad manages not only to do this accessibly but also to innovative on existing scholarship makes this essential reading for anyone with an interest in esotericism.

von Stuckrad begins with a first chapter that seeks to elucidate what he means by esotericism. Clearly he is influenced by the works of Antoine Faivre - who in the field cannot be in some way? – and like Katz's *The Occult Tradition* (also reviewed in this journal) he begins with an overview of Faivrean scholarship. Unlike Katz however he enters into a critical dialogue with Faivre and develops his own view of esotericism, one that looks to relationalism and the disjunctures present in esoteric discourses over time rather than the Faivrean model which seeks to minimise historical and cultural difference in looking for universal features of esoteric practices. It has to be said that von Stuckrad does not merely concentrate on difference – indeed he looks for common motifs or crystallisations between esoteric discourses such as *philosophia perennis* – but it is the grounding of his analysis in particular(istic) discourses rather than Faivrean 'patterns of thought' that is the real innovation here. In this sense von Stuckrad has set himself a much more difficult and ambitious task than Faivre. As von Stuckrad states of his methodology:

> One might ask: What is actually gained by such a concept of esotericism? … this analytical model enables us to demonstrate the complexity of European cultural history, without playing off religion against science, Christianity against paganism, or reason against superstition. In reality these large factors are inseparably related to each other and their relationship is the most interesting aspect of the history of esotericism in Europe. (p. 11)

After this opening methodological chapter von Stuckrad moves on to a chapter-by-chapter analysis of the history of Western Esotericism, each chapter examining a different type of discursive formation. It has to be said that there is little innovation in terms of content here. He moves breathlessly from the esotericism in the ancient world through to that in modernity, via the usual suspects of The Renaissance and The Enlightenment, but does so in an accessible and engaging manner which confirms not only that he is an accomplished communicator but he is also destined to challenge received wisdoms in the field.

von Stuckrad opens chapter 2 with discussions of Plato and the Pythagoreans before moving on to Stoicism. It has to be said that whilst these are necessarily brief discussions his economic style packs a lot of detail into a small face and so the essences of each esoteric school of thought are elucidated. He then moves on to discussions of Hermeticism and Gnosticism and the way that their discourses were shaped by cultural forces before their transmission to the early modern world.

Chapter 3 develops such transmissions via a brief historical explication of the Kabbalah, which is then linked to Chapter 4 on The Renaissance where von Stuckrad rightly charts the ways in which the discourses of the esotericisms of the ancient world were rethought and reshaped by the early moderns, especially via the works of Ficino and della Mirandola. The next chapter - in many ways the pivotal chapter of the book in the same way that the Renaissance functioned as a pivotal period in the development of modern esotericisms - develops the way in which the Christianity and Humanism of the period shaped more ancient *emanationist* philosophies for a nascent modernity. In particular he discusses the legacy of *magia naturalis*. He does this, in a sense predictably, through the major magical players of the period – Lazzarelli, Agrippa, Paracelsus, Reuchlin, Trithemius, Bruno and Postel among others. He then goes on to explicate the complicated relationship between esotericism, natural philosophy and The Scientific Revolution. At all times von Stuckrad is very conscious of trying to avoid dichotomised relationships between religion and magic on one hand, and science and magic on the other.

Chapter 6 looks at the relationship between esotericism and the Enlightenment. Rather than merely seeing esotericism as becoming subject to secularisation, von Stuckrad charts the discursive shifts that underpinned the esotericism of the period. He begins the chapter by contrasting the discourses of Swedenborg and Kant before going on to discuss Mesmer and how Mesmerism was pivotal in bringing esotericism out of the realm of superstition and into that of science. This shift is then charted via the rise of the natural as an object of study and spiritual sustenance which von Stuckrad visits in various ways through the works of Schelling, The Romantics, Darwin and Haeckel.

The next chapter looks at the esoteric underground embodied in the secret societies of the 17th to 19th Centuries. von Stuckrad begins with an exploration of the Rosicrucians, moves on to Freemasonry and forward to The Hermetic Order of the Golden Dawn and Aleister Crowley, again all in various ways influenced by *emanationist* philosophies.

Chapter 8 moves on to look at Theosophy and its legacies in esoteric Christianity through brief biographies of the 3 Bs – Blavatsky, Bailey and Besant. Throughout the chapter von Stuckrad dissects how the ambivalent nature of modernity, and Blavatsky's own personality, gave Theosophy, on the one hand, its schismatic quality, but, on the other, how it became a systematised form of knowledge that was ideal for modern consumption.

The final chapter which charts the relationship between esoteric thought and modernity develops these points further seeking to illuminate how modern ambivalence gives rise to simultaneous forms of disenchantment and re-enchantment. With disenchantment as a starting point von Stuckrad chronicles the ways in which modern man has searched for his soul. He begins with all too brief discussions of Jung, Eliade and Campbell and they way in which these understood in various ways the *soul* as a psychological landscape which could be shaped by techniques which involved hierophany and individuation and are, once more, rooted in emanationist thinking. He ends the chapter with brief discussions of The New Age, Channelling and the shifting boundaries of esotericism and science exemplified by the rise of Deep Ecology, Complexity and *New Age Science*. He ends the book with a discussion about how these, coupled with transpersonal psychology, are rooted in the same discursive *moments* which characterise esotericism. The project continues.

This book is at once wonderful and frustrating. I heartily recommend it to scholars and non-scholars alike, and certainly to students with or without knowledge of Western Esotericism. Whilst it innovates the Faivrean paradigm – and about time too – and von Stuckrad is a skilled writer and enthusiastic communicator, there are times when one wants more words to do justice to these complex relationships. von Stuckrad is certainly gifted with a economic style but sometimes one craves a longer work - akin to his colleague Hanegraaf's musings on The New Age, for example - which does not devote a mere page to The Golden Dawn or summarise the Transcendentalists in a couple of sentences. Alas, this is the nature of the beast – to be 'a brief history'. Despite its brevity, this book is to be commended for its breadth of ambition as much as its authoritative scholarship. Highly recommended.

Dave Green

Philip Ball, 2006, *The Devil's Doctor: Paracelsus and the World of Renaissance Magic and Science*, Farrar, Straus and Giroux, USA. 448pp, ISBN 0-374-22979-1, Hardback £20, Paperback £8.99.

Let us rescue great men from oblivion. In the Renaissance we find a band of individualists who made small but key contributions to human knowledge. Their scientific breakthroughs may have excited them less, however, than their passion for theology, the Black Arts, or other pastimes. Oftentimes, their discoveries were an afterthought, a distraction from a life spent chasing shadows.

Consider Philip Theophrastus Aureolus Bombast von Hohenheim (1493-1541), who is remembered today as "Paracelsus"—if he is remembered at all. The blurb for this biography describes him as "A contemporary of Luther, an enemy of the medical establishment, a scourge of the universities, an alchemist, an army surgeon, and a radical theologian (…) a charlatan, a windbag who filled his books with wild speculation and invented words."

Still others claim him as the father of modern medicine. Let us read Paracelsus's own language and decide for ourselves.

> "Who does not know that most contemporary doctors fail because they slavishly abide by the precepts of Avicenna, Galen and Hippocrates, as though these were Apollo's oracles from which it is not allowed to digress by a finger's breadth. If it pleases God, this way may lead to splendid titles, but does not make a true doctor. What a doctor needs is not eloquence or knowledge of language and of books, illustrious though they may be, but profound knowledge of Nature and her works." (Basle, June 5, 1527).

Paracelsus had nothing against books—he wrote prolifically—but his own output has aged less well. Where he excelled was in healing the sick. A student wrote: "He cured lepers, dropsicals, epileptics, syphilitics and gout patients, besides innumerable other diseases. The Galenic doctors could not do likewise and envied the honours he earned."

Paracelsus came of age in an era when the population lived in a state of filth, cross-contamination, and malnutrition. Even if Paracelsus had simply cured patients through good food, clean bandaging, the placebo effect coupled with a pleasant bedside manner, this was a breakthrough in its own right. But it was not the stuff of which immortal reputations were made.

And yet Philip Ball has immortalized his flawed subject, warts, buboes and all. He is no hero—and he may not be much of a scientist, let alone an anatomist. Paracelsus shares more than a few of the characteristics of the conmen he attacked. At times he seems worse than Galen himself.

As biographer, Ball cuts through clouds of Paracelsian rhetoric and sets out the myths and facts about the man together with an assessment of their probability. The Swiss physician is said to have successfully transmuted base metal into gold, but contemporary accounts must be taken with a large pinch of philosopher's stone ("the fact is that the distinction between transmutation and fakery was hazy even in the minds of those who attempted either one of them."). Not for the first time, the biographer outclasses his subject, for Ball unfailingly provides coherent explanations of the incoherent.

But before we go further and write Paracelsus off as just another practitioner of the occult, we must define "occult." Ball takes up the story, in another masterful example of his ability to clarify complex issues:

"That magic was an *occult* art leaves many scientists uncomfortable (…) Today, "occult" is equated with superstition, irrationality, charlatanism. But much of contemporary science is itself occult in the Renaissance sense, insofar as it is "hidden" from our senses—(…) As modern science emerged, it did not banish the concept of occult forces; rather, it accommodated those that seemed useful, such as magnetism and gravity, relegating others (…) to a ragbag of outmoded notions that, in retaining the label "occult," gradually rendered the word disreputable. But without this belief in the occult, science would have been stymied."

Paracelsus traveled far. By standing sufficiently apart from his fellows on key points, he brought down the curtain on the farce of medieval medicine. He shook to its foundations the caste system of university professors who would sooner pore over texts by Avicenna than touch a patient, bonesetters who cauterized open wounds with boiling oil, apothecaries who passed off topsoil as medicine to their customers and charged exorbitantly for the privilege. Ball again:

"Imagine it, after all: you are the seller of rare imported powders costing prodigious sums; no one has the means or the knowledge to check what they contain, and the people are desperate for them. What temptation there is, then, to mix in a little flour, a little brick dust or powdered marble, a few dried leaves from the local hedgerow. The jar that has sat on the shelves for the past three summers; who can tell that it is out of date? Who will know?"

When others cut corners, Paracelsus insisted on effort. In an era of doubletalk, he demanded accountability and regulation—and so do we. But even today, anyone who has lost a loved one afflicted from a "curable" cancer—fed soothing reassurances that the prognosis is "excellent"—to complications from traditional cancer therapy must ask themselves how far we have really come.

The author has painted on a triptych-sized canvas and relies on a kind of comparative history, sketching the lives of other quirky long-forgotten intellectuals who were near contemporaries of Paracelsus. Two in particular—Agricola and Agrippa—are a study in contrasts. A future US President (by name of Herbert Hoover) was to contrast Agricola's "sober logic and real research and observation" with Paracelsus's "egotistical ravings." Agippa was more of a wild card: "He had a magic glass, people said, that enabled him to see things distant in space and time"—what Forteans would call a *chronovisor*.

Ball seldom passes up an opportunity to make connections. I spotted just a couple of missing details; Paracelsus runs into the Knights Hospitaller on Rhodes in the Mediterranean during one of his better-documented escapades; today (and back then too) the Hospitallers were also known as healers.

Ultimately, identifying recurrent patterns in the lives of these scientific vagabonds *as a group* does a service to them all, for they were denied this kind of collective support in their lifetimes; and through repetition, the comparative approach impresses upon the reader the great challenges each man faced in turn. But if there are similarities in their behavior, is it because they were copycats? Or do men with with the same temperament, placed in the same predicament, react in predictably similar ways? Tacit or explicit recognition of debts of gratitude can occasionally be found. Whether this tipping of the hat is due to fundamental archetypes, or is a matter of conscious or unconscious emulation, is a topic for individual assessment in each case.

Catalan physician Arnald of Villanova a.k.a. Arnau de Villeneuve (1235-1311) was said to have "tried to create a man from a pumpkin stuffed with chemical drugs". Paracelsus made a similar boast (about creating a Frankenstein monster) centuries later. According to Spanish historian Marcelino Menéndez y Pelayo, Arnau was accused of bringing corpses back to life in a graveyard. Allegations of dabbling in forbidden knowledge swirl around Paracelsus: "another of Paracelsus's late-sixteenth-century editors, speaks of a [drug referred to as a] Laudanum Theophrasti [i.e., named after Paracelsus, which can cure every disease except leprosy and can even (…) *raise the dead.*"

Now, Paracelsus explicitly acknowledges de Villeneuve while saying that the Catalan's books "contain nothing of value" but are "all mere boasting, in which there is no philosophy, medicine, or astronomy"—unlike Paracelsus's own, of course.

To give an example pointing in a different direction, Paracelsus's Spanish contemporary, Michael Servetus (1509-53) likewise healed patients rather than speeding them on their way to the mortician. He made medical observations of vital importance—we beg for more—but he careened off down the blind alley of theological disputation, which claimed his life in the fires of Champel, Geneva. In his life on the run, Servetus adopted the name of his hometown Villanueva as one of his aliases, *Michel de Villeneuve.*

We would expect these Renaissance mavericks to land in hot water with the ecclesiastical authorities—and they do. We find, time and again, that they are separated from, estranged from—or even betrayed by—their own families. A common theme in Counter-Reformation propaganda (see Pelayo above) is that reformers somehow lay outside the normal bonds of family regeneration. Paracelsus was rumored to be a eunuch or a victim of congenital syphilis; Servetus had suffered an unspecified "rupture" which would have made normal marital relations impossible. What is the connection between their own personal medical handicaps and their lifelong, obsessive quest to heal? One further leitmotif; beyond the pale of acceptability and family, Reformers die in obscurity, or in shipwrecks, or at the stake, far from the succor of family, and by implication, the church and consecrated ground.

As for the doctors in Ball's study, their jobs intrinsically required some skill at self-preservation, an ability to lead double lives. Paracelsus was poor at this game; Servetus adept; Arnald best of all.

"It has been said that Arnald practiced two types of medicine, one wholly conventional, for the benefit of his learned colleagues and for presenting to royal clients, and the other more radical and experimental, used in Arnald's daily routine where the strictures of scholarship need not apply. Through this latter art he anticipates Paracelsus by directing alchemical knowledge toward medicine. He recounted how distillation separates human blood into its constituent elements, which have potent medicinal properties."

So, all of these physicians enjoyed occasional periods of calm employment on some wealthy person's staff, punctuated by uproar and narrow escapes. "There is something uncanny about the way turmoil follows in Paracelsus's footsteps," as Ball tells us. Then as now, if a warrant were out for your arrest on trumped-up charges—with a strong likelihood of execution to follow—it made sense to relocate far away. Starting a family is seldom practical under those conditions. This was a necessary trade off; for by virtue of spending so much time on the road, their fund of personal observation was immeasurably enriched.

They were courageous to a man. Never forget their working conditions for an instant. For once outside the safe confines of university libraries, they were faced with mortal danger at every step. As Ball describes, "By resolutely making his way to this endangered and perilous town, Paracelsus showed a degree of recklessness in which courage is hard to distinguish from obsession." These doctors walked into plague-infested communities to heal the sick, at perennial risk to themselves, and if all they really did was to bring relief to the suffering, then that deserves a mighty tribute all its own. Neil L. Inglis

David S. Katz, 2005, *The Occult Tradition: From The Renaissance to the Present Day*, Pimlico, London. 272pp, ISBN-10: 0712667865, Hardback £17.99, Paperback, £8.99.

Katz, an Israeli professor of History, ambitiously attempts to chart the twists and turns of Occultism over the course of the last 500 or so years; as Katz himself terms the book – 'the cartography of a secret esoteric body of knowledge that has had an indelible influence on Western culture' (p.10). As a taster of this history for those new to Occultism he succeeds with an engaging introduction, but, as we shall see, for those with an intermediate or advanced knowledge of the area this book fails to innovate or really say anything new.

Katz begins the book by affirming the credible intellectual roots of his books, disparaging those 'trashy books on the occult' which 'fill shelves of used bookshops everywhere' (p.9). An informative introduction which demonstrates the ambivalence which surrounds both the Occult tradition and its arch critics – notably Adorno – seems to suggest that there is a discernible singular Occult tradition which permeates and influences Western culture. Given the slim size of this volume it is unsurprising that Katz has to take short cuts rather than the scenic route on his intellectual journey, but that appears to be a big claim given the plurality of spiritualities and Occult philosophies given the Katz treatment.

Chapter 1 introduces a largely uncritical Faivrean analysis of the components of Renaissance Occultism. Katz's main departure from Faivrean orthodoxy concerns the term 'Esotericism' which Faivre uses as an umbrella term differentiates from the more specific Occultism of The Nineteenth Century. Katz, however, dismisses such a distinction, substituting 'The Occult Tradtion' for Faivre's 'Western Esoteric' one. He traces the magical roots of The Renaissance back to the usual *emanationist* suspects – Renaissance Neo-Platonism, back to Plato and thence to Proclus et al, before extremely brief treatments of Gnosticism and Hermeticism. Although truncated, Katz does manage a surprising amount of detail in his treatment of the Christianization of the Kabbalah. This also reveals Katz's own Judaic interests which pervade the book.

Chapter 2 centres on the relationship between the Occult and Enlightenment thought, as filtered through The Scientific Revolution, particularly the Natural Philosophy of Isaac Newton. Although not breaking new ground, Katz tells the rise of esoteric masonry in an engaging way beginning with Rosencreutz, borrowing heavily from Frances Yates, and ending with Newton and his incommensurability with Descartes and mechanistic philosophy.

Katz continues, in Chapter 3, by tracing the increasing rationalization of the Occult following the Enlightenment. He does this by paying particular attention to the way in which The Occult became organised and transmitted, especially through the bureaucratization of esoteric knowledge. He uses three main case studies to illustrate these processes: The development of Freemasonry, Swedenborgianism, and, more surprisingly, Mormonism. Again Katz skilfully and engagingly blends history with mythmaking and it is to his credit that he illuminates relationships between Occultism and Christianity throughout the book instead of sidestepping them in an age of Evangelism and accusations of ritual abuse.

In Chapter 4 Katz considers the relationships between Nature and The Occult with particular emphasis on how the Romantic sublime went on to influence The Occult Revival of the later Nineteenth Century. Given the later North American focus of this book it is perhaps surprising that Katz makes only brief mention of The Transcendentalists instead making more circuitous links between psychical research and many of the most important technological innovations of the era, such as Edison's phonograph. Katz ends the chapter by exploring other ways in which Occultism influenced Western culture, most notably its literature. Katz particularly charts how Romanticism was transformed into Gothic Horror, for example in the works of Henry James, Robert Louis Stevenson and Bram Stoker.

In the next chapter Katz goes on to explore how the ferment of interest in Spiritualism and psychical research in the mid to late Nineteenth Century influenced the rise of Western forms of psychological, and eventually psychoanalytic, theory. Here, another of 'The James Gang', this time William, is held up to be a pioneer of modern psychology and consciousness studies and, as such, an influence on Freud. Whilst Katz gives an accurate overview of the differences between Freud and the psychologists influenced by psychical research, what is surprising is that he singularly fails to make stronger links between psychoanalysis and the embryonic psychology of the Renaissance, with its rootedness in the *emanationalism*, Kabbalism, and Humanism of the time. Instead, for Katz, Freud's theories appear as more like a critical development of psychical research.

Chapter 6 concentrates on the influence of *The East* on The Occult Tradition, predictably making the links between Blavatsky, Theosophy and Nazi Occultism. Again, this makes for entertaining and thoughtful reading but these relationships have been much more developed by authors such as James Webb and Nicholas Goodrich-Clarke.

The final chapter, Chapter 7, charts the ways in which The Occult Tradition – subject to increasing rationalization and secularization since The Enlightenment – returned to its religious roots and character. Katz sees this as happening in two main ways – through The Occult's relationship to *Dispensationalist* Christian Fundamentalism and The New Age. Again, Fundamentalism seems a curious if thoughtful choice given the decentralized and individual nature of much Occultism. I am not sure that Katz convincingly demonstrates this relationship, instead being content to survey something of the mystical and revelatory character of North American Fundamentalism. The New Age functions as a more straightforward case study which, although well executed, owes a lot to the scholarship of Wouter Hanegraaf and which appears to ignore Paganisms altogether.

Katz concludes with a meditation concerning the messiness of The Academy's boundaries concerning religion, magic and The Occult. Katz, as for most of this book, offers much description and many questions, but little in the way of answers and this is a real deficit and makes it stand in stark contrast to von Stuckrad's much more economical and analytical *Western Esotericism: A Brief History of Secret Knowledge* (reviewed in this journal). To his credit, however, Katz is an engaging and gifted story-teller and the book is a worthwhile read for this aspect alone. The book appears to be written for an intelligent audience with little or no prior knowledge of The Occult Tradition, or, perhaps for a student audience. However, having said this, the works of Lachmann, for example, are more even accessible to a popular audience and the von Stuckrad book is a much superior academic text despite being significantly shorter. Given Katz's undoubted academic credentials it is perhaps surprising that he offers little in the way of intellectual innovation or gravitas here. He cannot match the depth or profundity of the works of James Webb or the analytical skill of much shorter texts covering much the same ground such as those by von Stuckrad or B.J. Gibbons. In sum, Katz's book is an accessibly diverting read with entertaining flourishes but broadens rather than deepens the literature on the subject.

Dave Green

Emma Wilby, 2005, *Cunning Folk and Familiar Spirits: Shamanic Visionary Traditions in Early Modern British Witchcraft and Magic*, Sussex Academic Press, Brighton. 317pp, ISBN-10: 1845190793, Hardback £47.50, Paperback £15.95.

Emma Wilby opens her book with 'a cunning woman's tale': Scotswoman Bessie Dunlop was tried for witchcraft in 1576 and the summary of the trial's lengthy proceedings (nine pages of Wilby's Preface) informs us that Bessie had an intimate and long-standing relationship with a 'ghost' named Tom Reid. Wilby argues that such accounts of human engagements with spirit familiars – 'encounter-narratives' – are consistent in witch-trials and confessions in the sixteenth and seventeenth centuries to the extent that this feature must be considered seriously as evidence for actual belief. This leads Wilby to argue that a veneer – albeit an all-pervading, official one – of Christianity overlay enduring traditions of pre-Christian 'shamanic' practice in Britain.

At first glance, such an argument is problematic: scholars post- Margaret Murray and Montague Summers have deconstructed witch-trial and confession evidence to establish that much data is unreliable, extracted under conditions of torture and riddled with witch-hunt propaganda discourse, derived from the 'learned' or 'elite' medieval theologians. The notion of an unbroken 'old religion' of witchcraft appears to be a fabrication, with apparent vestiges of folk-belief insufficient as evidence in themselves. Wilby's re-visiting of the evidence is certainly 'courageous' (as Hutton's rear-cover plaudit puts it). Her book is also refreshing in moving beyond metanarratives: she does not support the notion of an 'old religion' nor an enduring singular 'tradition', and she does not read the trial and confession sources uncritically. Rather, she approaches the sources with the interpretative framework of 'shamanism'.

This, of course, has its own problems: shamans are paradoxical to the extent that every definition offered can be challenged, and 'shamanism' as another '-ism' suggests something orderly which everyone would recognize, yet the diversity of shamans resists such generalisation (see Harvey & Wallis 2006). We continue, nonetheless, to call shamans 'shamans' and shamans continue to do what shamans do. So Wilby's approach to shamanism as a constructed term appropriate for assessing early modern accounts of cunning folk and witches, is intriguing – particularly with her contextualisation of shamanism within 'animism'.

Although animism is clearly important to Wilby's discussion (there are nineteen entries in the index and animism is first mentioned on p14) there is no explicit definition of the term until half way through the book (p128). I was also disappointed to find no sustained engagement with how animism (particularly in shamanistic contexts) is constituted, particularly in light of recent theorising. Revising Tylor's 'old animism' notion that animists mistakenly perceive inanimate objects as alive in some way and containing 'spirit(s)', recent scholarship engages with 'new animism' as a relational ontology wherein humans are understood as one 'people' amongst a diversity of 'other-than-human people' including tree people, cat people and stone people. Humans are not privileged in this worldview; indeed they depend on harmonious relations with non-humans. Shamans are often the agents who negotiate harmonious relations if a seal-person or other 'prey' has been offended. Ambivalence is crucial to understanding a pragmatic animist worldview where humans must of necessity do violence to other 'people', whether plant or pig, and other-than-human people do violence to us – to a panther or virus, human people are prey of sorts. By altering consciousness (or deploying adjusted styles of communication), shamans are able to engage with other-than-human people: shamans 'do' animism by brokering good relations between humans and non-humans.

Wilby's approach stands between old and new animism, her interest being the shamanic doing of animism by early modern witches and cunning folk in their engagements with helping spirits and/or demons. Wilby attends to the moral ambivalence raised by an animist ontology (if it existed) in early modern Britain (p224): there were cunning folk who tended to help (healing sickness, finding lost property) using familiar spirits, and there were witches who did harm (blighting crops, causing sickness) aided by demons. But there was much crossover: in pragmatic circumstances there was not a simple 'good/bad', 'black/white' distinction (p154-6), but a precarious greyness. It is somewhat confusing when Wilby distinguishes between maleficent witch and benevolent cunning person and their respective animal familiars and demon familiars (p58), marks ambiguity and permeability (e.g. p123), and then uses these terms interchangeably throughout. But this is a useful reminder that early modern ontology resists our modern wish to compartmentalise. While Davies (2003) suggests, then, that descriptions of fairy encounters are more corporeal than spiritual (Wilby note 28, p174), from the perspective of a morally ambivalent animist relational ontology such encounter-narratives disrupt the sacred-profane dichotomy per se.

Wilby persuasively argues for early modern animism in Britain. While it was the official religion, a veneer of Christian belief overlay enduring pre-industrial folkways, with Catholicism itself having many 'pagan' aspects and Protestantism being the main harbinger of change. Wilby is persistent in reminding us that early modern life was starkly different from our own, not only in terms of hardship and daily toil, but in relationships – between humans, animals and otherworldly creatures, with spirits often living nearby, in a stone, tree, crystal or bottle (p77). She offers evocative descriptions of intimate engagements with animals, hinting at why it is that frogs, snails, rabbits, cats and hares might be perceived as 'visionary familiars' (p228-31). Previous literature has neglected these familiars and Wilby's attention to detail leads to a more nuanced consideration of how these familiars were constituted as 'envisional spirit-guides' (p242). Scholars have also focussed on elite conjurations of spirits to the neglect of examples of conjuring among cunning folk and witches (p81), and concentrated on the witch's journey to the Sabbath (as did the persecutors of witches) because these accounts are so bizarre and titillating, at the expense of the rich resource of encounter-narratives (p174). Rather than highlight hysterical elite narratives (balancing Davies' [2003] focus on elite discourse and neglect of encounter-narratives [p51]), Wilby's attention to encounter-narratives situates everyday magic in community relations. Those that are able to intercede in the 'supernatural' may be able to help but they also have the resources to cause harm, and cunning folk and their spirit familiars were demonised as witches and demons by neighbours. This situating of everyday magic vis-à-vis witchcraft accusations is reminiscent of indigenous contexts (e.g. Evans-Pritchard [1937] on Azande witchcraft and in Amazonian shamanism/sorcery [e.g. Fausto 2004]).

Scholars have also supported a 'downward filtration' (p112) of witchcraft belief, originating with elite theologians. Wilby revises this trend, arguing that the reality was more complex, involving an upward process (p164):

while the learned discourse on witchcraft and demonology indeed filtered down, the already extant, enduring and widespread beliefs in fairies and other folklore likely also influenced the elite. The established assumption that the cunning person/witch did not believe what they were saying/confessing is, Wilby argues, overstated (chapter 6, especially p96), indicating how fairy and other indigenous beliefs fed into elite narratives. Many witches who initially denied involvement in witchcraft and subsequently confessed under torture, explained their denial as a silence/secrecy pact made with the devil. It is compelling that relationships with fairies often involved similar silence/secrecy taboos (and tellingly, this reluctance to talk may be one reason why we know so little [p90-1]). The witch's pact with the devil may derive as much from encounter-narratives including specific demands from fairies in return for help, as from elite Christian sources (p163). In some cases, cunning folk saw no incongruity over their Christian beliefs and engagements with elves and fairies: 'Joan Tyrry (1555) claimed "the power of God taught to her by the ... fairies be both godly and good" ' (p97). Yet, 'the devil told Suffolk witch Mary Skipper (1645) to go to church "and make a great show, but if she attended diligently he would nip her" ' (p98). While demons might demand that the Christian faith be renounced, so too did fairies. And both witches and cunning folk might be required to bargain with their soul, engage in marriage and/or sexual relations, and make sacrifices/offerings of blood and milk, to their spirits/demons. Again, Wilby argues this is evidence that such negotiations were as much a part of indigenous belief as of elite narratives of witch-pacts (e.g. p101).

Wilby offers sustained discussion of witches/cunning folk as early modern shamans. In her reading of the sources, spirits were used for healing, finding lost goods, identifying criminals, divining the future and talking to / mediating the dead – indeed many familiars were 'ghosts' themselves (p68-9). When healing, cunning folk used blowing and sucking techniques and these are strongly reminiscent of shamanic practices (p137). They also endured dismemberment, had their souls stolen and undertook hazardous journeys and magical flight to the otherworld (p151). When entering the fairy realm (for the cunning person) or travelling to the Sabbath (for the witch), the spirit/soul left the body, perhaps constituting evidence for trance practices (p102). She identifies trance as a defining feature of shamanism and instead of assuming encounter-narratives are fictional, she addresses these experiences, sensitively, as a 'reality' (p164, 168).

Less convincing is the focus on the visual nature of the trance-encounter-narrative which might tell us more about ourselves as specularist moderns than about early modern (or indigenous) ontologies. Scholars of shamanism have tended to over-emphasise the visuality of altered consciousness and the discrete nature of 'trance'. Rather, altered consciousness is fluid, aural and somatic experiences may be as crucial as vision, and the senses may be entirely disrupted (synaesthesia). With the notable exception of Rasmussen's ethnography of arctic shamanism, Wilby's sources on shamans are consistently secondary (which seems out of character for a historian), and framed by transpersonal psychology (e.g. Kalweit) and neo-shamanic discourse (e.g. Drury, Harner). The onus is on cunning folk and witches as mystics and monists, revealing a bias to her reading of the sources in the latter part of the book (p219-20). Wilby sees shamanic marriage / sexual relations as 'a metaphor for mystical union' reflecting 'a universal symbol of mankind' (p238) and suggests that 'to some degree the visionary capacities of medieval saints and mystics can be seen as expressions of the perennial "shamanistic tendencies" of the psyche' (p223). This interpretation is at the expense of shamans as agentic animists pragmatically negotiating with other-than-human people, as the new animism approach to shamanism suggests. The way in which the book covers such a range of sources might give the misleading impression that the disparate sources across Britain and through two centuries are coherent and related. And while Wilby briefly mentions contemporary witchcraft and neo-shamanism, I think it is incumbent on scholars to engage with these contemporary manifestations more rigorously, particularly given the influence academic works have on contemporary practice.

I have argued elsewhere (e.g. Wallis 2002, 2003, 2004; also Blain & Wallis 2006) that altered consciousness (if not trance) is useful when approaching many shamanisms; yet for purists, 'shamanism' in the *locus classicus* of Siberia is incongruous with 'trance' (e.g. Hamayon 1993). Certainly, application of the terms 'shaman' and 'trance' both within and outside Siberia requires caution. Hamayon (1996) proposes that the 'spirit marriage' is more relevant than 'trance' when approaching Siberian shamanisms – and Wilby herself offers numerous examples of this practice among cunning people and witches. So, not only does the term 'shaman' work consistently in what might appear to be an incongruous setting, but it also re-configures our understanding of witches and cunning folk. They were not practicing an enduring shamanic old religion, nor were they an elite-formulated fabrication. Approaching them as animist shamans embedded in local community relations constitutes a considerably nuanced analysis.

References:

Blain, Jenny and Robert J. Wallis. 2006, Ritual reflections, practitioner meanings: disputing the terminology of neo-shamanic performance, *Journal of Ritual Studies* 20, (1), 21-36.

Evans-Pritchard, Edward E., 1937, *Witchcraft, Oracles and Magic Among the Azande*, Oxford University Press, Oxford.

Fausto, Carlos, 2004, 'A Blend of Blood and Tobacco: Shamans and Jaguars among the Parakanã of Eastern Amazonia', in: Neil L. Whitehead and Robin Wright (eds) *In Darkness and Secrecy*, Duke University Press, Durham, NC.

Hamayon, Roberte N., 1993. Are 'Trance', 'Ecstasy' and Similar Concepts Appropriate in the Study of Shamanism?, *Shaman* 1, (2), 3-25.

___. 1996. 'Shamanism in Siberia: From Partnership in Supernature to Counter-power in Society' in Nicholas Thomas and Caroline Humphrey (eds) *Shamanism, History and the State*, University of Michigan Press, Ann Arbor

Harvey, Graham and Robert J. Wallis, 2006, *Historical Dictionary of Shamanism*, Scarecrow Press, Lanham, MD.

Wallis, Robert J., 2002, 'The *Bwili* or 'Flying Tricksters' of Malakula: a critical discussion of recent debates on rock art, ethnography and shamanisms', *Journal of The Royal Anthropological Institute*, 8, (4), 735-60.

___. 2003, *Shamans / neo-Shamans: Ecstasy, Alternative Archaeology and Contemporary Pagans*, Routledge, London.

___. 2004, 'Shamanism and Art', in Mariko N. Walter and Eva N. Fridman (eds), *Shamanism: An Encyclopedia of World Beliefs, Practices, and Culture, Volume I*, ABC-CLIO, Santa Barbara, CA.

Robert J. Wallis

Andy Letcher, 2006, *Shroom: a cultural history of the Magic Mushroom*, Faber, London. 360pp, index, bibliography, illustrated, photographs, ISBN 0-571-22770-8, Paperback, £12.99.

There seems to have been a recent upsurge in the publication of intelligent and 'crossover' books on the cultural aspects of entheogenic substances in the last few years. These include Daniel Pinchbeck's *Breaking Open The Head*, which was a fascinating part-travelogue/part-participant observer adventure in the use of worldwide shamanic substances, as a sceptical journalist started to unwittingly become a shaman, and the somewhat earlier *One River* by the ethnobotanist Wade Davis, in part a laudatory overview of the work of the great botanist Richard Schultes, and this book.

Shroom consists of numerous interwoven threads, dealing with (among others) mycology, biochemistry, psychology, neurology, law, medicine, international politics, history, economics, sociology and anthropology, all of which is explained in terms which the intelligent layman would have no difficulty in comprehending. Indeed the book is not intended as a purely academic project, despite Letcher being a double PhD working freelance, but more a wider-appeal study.

This impressive work examines the oft-repeated notion that 'magic mushrooms' have been in use by human societies since time immemorial. Further, that the Witches Sabbath had them as an essential part of the flying ointment, that the Greeks at Eleusis ate them by the handful, that Siberian Shamans munched them in profusion, that the ancient Druids and Celtic pagan priests were hardened 'trippers' and that in the 21st century scientific world we are again seeking aid from these remarkable natural neo-sacramental products as a means of re-enchanting the dull materialist life, and using them as a gateway to entheogenic experiences and linking with our ancestors. This seems especially so as the 'natural, organic' mushroom, unlike many lab-produced synthetic entheogens, seems to specifically heighten the perceptual experience and appreciation of 'the natural'- animals, trees, plants, stones and the very earth itself, and Letcher rightly points out the very 'Tolkienesque' and neo-pagan nature of this experience.

An overall conclusion of this book is that volitional Western magic mushroom use (other than very occasional accidental 'trips' by naive culinary users, who usually experienced terror, thinking they had been poisoned and were imminently going to die) can only so far be dated to the 1950s, and the more widespread use to even later. The mythologising of a cultural heritage stretching back to the distant past in part derives from the poetic assumptions, wish-fulfilments and personal experiences of many influential figures. These include Aldous Huxley, Robert Graves, the powerful banker Gordon Wasson- upon whose amateur but erroneously-influential scholarship Letcher is rather harsh, but justifiably so, Timothy Leary- of who Letcher gives a well-reasoned and balanced summation, the multi-faceted Carlos Castaneda, Terrence McKenna (who similarly to Leary receives a reasoned discussion), Marion Zimmer Bradley and others. These mythologies are usually based on, and extrapolated from an extant and real mushroom-entheogenic culture in small parts of Central America and tiny areas of Siberia only. Letcher believes that to a large extent the mythos is now used in an attempt to legitimise the global practice in the face of increasingly punitive legal machinations as to their use, and (for example) that many of the claims relating to mushrooms being an ingredient of Witches' flying ointments are literary devices, not factual. This is especially interesting given the historical overview that Letcher provides of an extant continuous drug use culture (and often a literary one) in the West, including Coleridge and De Quincey's work while on opium, which gave a visionary frame of reference under which mushroom use would, and perhaps should, have been given a set of psychic co-ordinates, from which would-be shamans and trippers could attempt to re-enchant their world. However to a huge extent mushrooms as a whole (not just the entheogenic kind) were always a culinary taboo and considered poisonous, and the psychedelic effects were not appreciated in the 'civilised' West until the 1950s, and later researched by the CIA in search of drugs for military and intelligence uses.

Letcher argues convincingly that a more coherent and believable history and understanding of the mushroom in global cultural use would actually be a powerful tool in the legitimisation and credibility of their spiritual uses, rather than woolly-headed wishful-thinking and far-fetched invoking of 'tradition' being the only legal defence for the very recent industrial increase in the practice of cultivating and using the mushroom. This book is a robust contender for establishing that coherence.

In rather a similar way that Ronald Hutton's Triumph of the Moon meticulously examined and massively re-modelled the mythologising of 'the survival of an aeons-old witch-cult to the present day', this book performs a similar task on the notion of a presumed 'worldwide mushroom cult, which has existed for millennia, and directed human evolution'. That this longevity and global spread seems spurious should not be a disappointment, rather we should celebrate the more likely truths that Letcher has uncovered (that to a large extent the highly flawed postulations of Wasson and others about a universal, eternal succession of mushroom use actually *created* a new mushroom culture, in much the same way that Margaret Murray's equally flawed theories on age-old witch cults laid the foundations for the creation of modern Wicca), and we should be reassured that despite the invented history the 'global mushroom cult' is a real phenomena, justifying further study. If anything the reality uncovered herein is even stranger than the baser fictions espoused by many adherents, and we should rejoice that there is still room for such delightful and intricate independent scholarship, written in an engaging fashion, and with such stimulating findings.

A stunning debut book, which I cannot recommend highly enough to anyone studying cultural history, mycology, the study or practice of shamanism and neoshamanism or the urge to religious experience. Copious endnotes and a detailed bibliography also provide a wealth of leads for anyone wishing to follow their own lines of research, More simply this work is an exemplar of how to chase down a host of disparate and potentially confusing leads and blend them into a coherent, compelling, humorous and hugely intelligent narrative that crosses and transcends many academic boundaries. It is perhaps one measure of book quality is that one reaches the end and is either glad, unmoved or saddened to have finished it. Turning the last page of this left me almost bereft; it had been so educational and entertaining.

Having completed a (sadly still unpublished) excellent PhD thesis on the Role of the Bard in Modern Druidry, Dr Letcher is now working on a new book on Modern Paganism, which I await eagerly. Quite Excellent.

Dave Evans

Helen A Berger (ed.), 2006, *Witchcraft and Magic: Contemporary North America*, University of Pennsylvania Press, Philadelphia. 216pp, ISBN-10: 0812219716, Hardback £26, Paperback £12.99.

This is the latest addition –the 7th instalment – of the deservedly popular Athlone/University of Pennsylvania Press series on the history of magic. Although it is an edited collection, like previous instalments, unlike those previous texts it does not invite 3 authorities to write long chapters on aspects of esotericism taking a more conventional approach this time around.

The collection is introduced by the Sociologist of Religion Helen Berger. She, in a short introduction, tries to contextualise the magic of North America by linking it to its spiritual contours in Paganisms and the New Age interestingly avoiding mention of the sorts of Occultism linked to American Christian Fundamentalism discussed in *The Occult Tradition* by David S. Katz (reviewed in this journal). She pulls no punches by mentioning esotericism in the context of Satanism and Neo-Nazism, even if it is to play down their significance to more mainstream forms of magical practice.

The first chapter proper is devoted to a discussion of the relationship between the New Age and magic by Michael York. York delivers an economical piece which functions as a development of his doctoral work on the sociology of the New Age. York uses the latest scholarship to highlight the importance of the New Age to Western culture linking it, in a North American context, both to Transcendentalism and Eastern spirituality, but, following Pearson's work on Wicca, for example, making important connections to the Renaissance high magic tradition as a form of Gnosticism. York spends comparatively large tracts of his chapter to discussions of well-rehearsed criticisms of The New Age and the development of New Age theologies. Given the volume's overall aim of mapping magic in North America it is perhaps surprising that York's discussion of New Age magic is so brief, occupying less than 3 pages. Maybe this is a function of the fact that not only is the New Age diverse in terms of belief and practice but the movement's perspective on magic is likewise varied and fragmented. York struggles to argue that the New Age and Neo-Pagan movements are linked by hermetic affinities, but ultimately there are as many perspectives on magic as there are branches of the New Age.

In the next chapter Helen Berger discusses magic and Neo-Paganisms. She begins by a brief sociological analysis which shadows and summarises her own work on the sociology of Paganisms, most notably contained within her 1999 book *A Community of Witches*. She then goes on in very general terms to give a broad outline of some mainstream Pagan practices via their Gardnerian roots. Therefore it has to be said that Berger has a tendency to reduce the plurality of Paganisms to a narrow Wiccan focus. Like York, given the plurality of Pagan paths, Berger finds it difficult with any sense of unity to talk about a specifically Pagan view of magic. Instead she is forced to describe various ends of magic, particularly healing, whilst offering only a superficial analysis of magical theory rooted in energetic models of magical efficacy. The remainder of the chapter offers something of a retread through North American Paganisms which will be extremely familiar to any scholar of Paganisms, though offers an accessible introduction to the field for others. She firstly discusses American articulations of Gardnerianism, though makes a huge leap between the influence of Buckland to that of

Starhawk and beyond to teen witchcraft leaving huge historical stones left unturned in between. She then goes on to discuss differences between various Pagan paths interestingly leaving out many forms of spirituality which have strong magical focuses, particularly Left Hand Paths. She concludes by looking at various Pagan organisations and the importance of festivals. Again, the chapter is dominated by a scholarly description of Paganisms with magic as something of an afterthought.

Chapter 3, by Wendy Griffin, focuses on Pagan feminism. It takes the form of an engagingly and intelligently crafted history of Pagan feminist spirituality in North America. Anyone having read such analyses in Adler's *Drawing Down the Moon* or Salomonsen's *Enchanted Feminism* will be familiar with these histories already. Again magic is largely implicit in this article though it does end with a skilfully created account of the fluidity and immanence of spiritual feminisms which, without making an analysis of feminist magic, goes in some way to explaining the role of magic in feminist praxis.

York returns in Chapter 4 for a discussion of shamanisms and magic. He first differentiates between the dynamics of Indigenous Shamanisms – largely rooted in a discussion of Siberian Shamanisms, North American indigenous Shamanism, New Ages Shamanism and Pagan Shamanisms. Whilst this is valuable, especially to an audience not already versed in these distinctions, a similar discussion in Robert Wallis' excellent Shamans and Neo-Shamans makes similar points in more innovative ways. Again it is significant that York's discussion of magic and Shamanisms is brief and, as such, tends to reduce the influence of Shamanisms on the larger magical community to that of trance states and psychonautic activities. Whilst important this is just the tip of the iceberg in terms of influence and I would have liked to have seen York really engage with other spheres of influence outside of core shamanic activity.

Chapter 5 is a fascinating exploration of Lucumí, a form of Afro-Caribbean diaspora religion, by Ysamur M. Flores-Peña. Flores-Peña begins by giving an outline of the development of Lucumí in Cuba, discusses its major beliefs and then its diaspora to North America, including Canada. It has to be noted that the author, whilst highlighting its spiritual contours, does not emphasise its unique magical qualities rather than to outline its healing practices. What makes this of especial interest to scholars of esotericism and religion, however, is the way in which the author charts the spread of Lucumí and its interactions with other diaspora religions, particularly the *Palo* sorcery of the Bantu and the *Curanderismo* of Central America to create new and syncretic forms of spirituality and esotericism. This is an important living case study of what results from the mix of indigenous magics and Western Capitalism.

Stuart Wright's chapter focuses on Satanic Ritual Abuse (SRA) and its construction as a modern form of witch hunt. Wright gives an excellent and economical account of the major sociological factors present in the creation of the SRA and the construction of "Satanists" as Cohenesque *Folk Devils*, primarily by Christian Fundamentalists. Having said this, his analysis rarely breaks much new ground, his evidence being firmly rooted in the tradition of Jean La Fontaine – indeed her longer chapter in the previous volume of this book series on the magic of The Twentieth Century makes much of this chapter superfluous – and Jeffrey Victor. The advantage of Wright's chapter is that it covers a lot of ground thoughtfully and could be employed usefully as a class reading on the topic.

The final chapter of the collection, by Tanice Foltz, is also arguably its most engaging and innovative piece. Foltz gives a thoughtful sociological overview of the role that witchcraft – here defined broadly – plays in Western cultures, particularly the double edged role that witchcraft plays in commodification processes. She begins with an excellent overview of how witchcraft is construed and constructed in contemporary culture ranging her analysis from TV through film and literature. This is engaging enough but her chapter ends with a critical analysis of such commodification processes develop the ideas of Doug Ezzy that, in contradistinction to forms of esoteric knowledge associated with the New Age, Witchcraft is transmitted as a gift. It is clear that Foltz's analysis is an important article in regard to the commodification of magic and will be a touchstone for future studies in this area.

Overall, this collection is a worthy addition to the book series, if descriptive rather than analytic. The major problem I have with this book is that it sets out to be about the magic of contemporary North America but magic here is more implicit than explicit and often gets included as something of an afterthought rather than the foundation of the articles. This is especially true of the beginning few chapters of the book. Furthermore, the articles on Lucumí and SRA aside, the collection is very much an analysis of Right hand Path spirituality and therefore takes a very narrow view of North American magical spirituality. I would have welcomed something more boundary pushing with perhaps some more radical forms of magical practice on offer here. For example, there is little mention of the legacy of Discordianism. In sum, this is an interesting overview of the dynamics of Pagan spirituality in North America which would be a useful addition to academic libraries but is not an essential purchase.   Dave Green

Kim Farnell, 2005, *Mystical Vampire - The Life and Works of Mabel Collins,* Mandrake, Oxford. 240pp, ISBN 1869928-857, Paperback £12.99.

Since the launch of the quarterly journal "Theosophical History" in 1985, there has been a significant increase in work of academic quality about the organisations and personalities of the Theosophical Society and its offshoots. (www.theohistory.org) Although the main attention has been on leaders such as Madame Blavatsky, there has also been some useful work on secondary characters. Among these scholars, London-based Kim Farnell has gained a place, heralding her work with papers at the International Conferences on Theosophical History held at the Theosophical Society, London. (The next such conference in July 2007 marks the death centenary of founder T.S. president Henry Olcott.)

Farnell first offered a pioneering study of Walter Old ("Sepharial") who had been one of Blavatsky's inner circle in her last days (Farnell 1998) and who eventually lead a double life as astrologer and British Israelite. She has now written the first biography of one of the leading women Theosophists, who became an opponent of Blavatsky, but is now a revered figure in the devotional side of Theosophy.

Mabel Collins (1851-1927), daughter of writer Mortimer Collins, was a private Spiritualist medium in the 1870s, also known as Mrs Keningale Cook. She began to receive inspired material of an Egyptian nature, later published as "Idyll of the White Lotus" and interpreted as a spiritual allegory by Theosophists. Her most famous work however was "Light on the Path, a treatise written for the personal use of those who are ignorant of the eastern wisdom, and who desire to enter within its influence"(1885).

This is constantly reprinted and is widely used as aid to occult development by Theosophists. Her numerous later works and her work for animal welfare are just a footnote to this achievement in her early thirties, though not the least merit of Farnell's biography is that she fully answers the question- what happened after M.C. became esoterically famous? In fact, she was already known in the USA as well as Britain, but as a romantic novelist (Mystical, p.60).

Mabel Collins provided a first home for Madame Blavatsky when she came to live in England in 1887. But after some turbulent months, Mabel was expelled from the recently formed Esoteric Section of the T.S. This may have been because of sexual involvements; at any rate, Theosophy in England soon became dominated by a new convert, Annie Besant. The main centre of magical activity moved to the Golden Dawn, which Mabel did not join, though in her numerous later books she used some of its terms (Mystical, p.102.).

Kim Farnell has pursued Mabel's involvement with feminist, anti-vivisectionist and literary circles with great vigour. The woman who emerges had a difficult life and faced many reverses in a hostile world. If there is anything to add, it is in the exploration of the continuing influence of "Light on the Path" on which C.W. Leadbeater, for example, gave many talks, and to which Rudolf Steiner often referred., The book remains one of the most influential magical texts of the Victorian era, and we are greatly indebted to Kim Farnell for a moving and most entertaining biography of its author.   Leslie Price

Kennet Granholm, 2005, *Embracing The Dark: The Magic Order of Dragon Rouge - Its Practice in Dark Magic and Meaning Making*, Åbo Akademi University Press, Åbo, Sweden. 364pp.

Granholm begins his monograph by noting that the study of Western esotericism is an emerging field and that while 'magic' has received some attention (citing e.g. Susan Greenwood's work), the 'left hand path' specifically has only recently been explored (citing Justin Woodman's 2004 thesis on Chaos Magick in Britain), with very little published work to date. *Embracing the Dark*, Granholm's PhD thesis, attempts to rectify this imbalance with a detailed and theoretically engaged analysis of 'Dragon Rouge', a Magical Order founded in Sweden in 1989 by Thomas Karlsson. Karlsson (b.1972) relates how a variety of supernatural experiences throughout his childhood lead to a sustained study of the occult from the age of 12 (p.161). As a young man standing in Jamaâ El-Fna square in Marrakech, Karlsson encountered a Sufi dervish who pronounced 'The old shall be destroyed and a temple shall be built for the Red Dragon' (p163). Dragon Rouge was then founded 'as an unprejudiced search for a darker spiritual ideology or path' (p164). Dragon Rouge members define their esoteric interests as 'left-hand path': the left side stands for 'chaos, darkness and freedom', while the right side represents 'order, light and restriction', and those on the left tend to prefer 'an individual situational morality' over traditional, systematic ethical systems (p28). The 'true will' (of Aleister Crowley) is crucial to this ontology, since the Dragon Rouge magician uses 'dark magic' to refine 'will' and thereby 'become a god' (p.27). Dark magic is exemplified in the Order's use of the qabbalistic tree of life, *Otz Chiim*, in traversing the qlippothic 'tunnels' (and their demons) on the reverse side rather than the traditional 'paths' of the sephiroth – a system clearly derived from the Typhonion Trilogies of the British mage Kenneth Grant. Drawing on Grant as well as other magicians such as Crowley, the Order professes an eclectic synthesis of esoteric themes from diverse cultures, focusing on 'dark' goddesses such as Kali and Hecate, and such 'left hand' practices as Tantra, additionally infused with more mainstream practices including neo-shamanism and heathenry.

Granholm completed fieldwork as an initiated member of the Order, and his comments on the methodology and reflexivity of participant-observation and interviewing, as well as his sensitive approach to fieldwork ethics, are noteworthy. While there has been a specialized body of 'insider' scholarship on paganism, it is refreshing to read an analysis by an 'outsider' who 'goes native' (with the permission of the informants) for the purpose of research. Much of the volume outlines Granholm's theoretical approach which engages with discourse analysis and 'meaning-making', as well as the Order's practices, locating the latter within the wider context of the New Age, esotericism and contemporary paganism (although his presentation of the New Age and 'neopaganism' is rather generalist [pp.90-101]). Granholm situates Dragon Rouge's emphasis on individualism, personal responsibility for spiritual growth and engagement with such issues as gender inequality, as a 'late modern' phenomenon. He cites key sources on research into paganisms for context, such as work by George Chryssides, Graham Harvey and Michael York, as well as a range of studies by Scandinavian scholars which, unfortunately, are unavailable in English and unpublished. I was surprised not to find citation of Jenny Blain's important work on Northern shamanism and contemporary paganism (or indeed my own work *Shamans/neo-Shamans*), however, given Granholm's attention to neo-shamanism and Northern mythology in the Order.

Granholm identifies six discursively constructed aspects of Dragon Rouge for detailed scrutiny: 1) magic-is-all-encompassing, 2) self-evolvement, 3) individuality, 4) magic-is-demanding, 5) nature and 6) women's rights discourses. He notes that while they are not comprehensive, these aspects do provide a useful framework for discussing the work of the Order. Further, while they might work in unison as part of a Dragon Rouge 'complex', there are contradictions – and this is something we should expect in instances of contemporary spiritual meaning making (p.257). While aspects of femininity and perhaps even feminism are privileged in Dragon Rouge's magical practice, for instance, with an emphasis on 'dark goddesses' and in addition the existence of a 'women's circle', it is ironic that there is a gender imbalance in the structure of the Order with many senior roles being held by the men. And, while the Order foregrounds the interconnectedness of all things, challenging what it sees as the privileging of humans over nature in Christianity, it is somewhat contradictory that the aim of magical practice is self-evolutionary and transcendent, towards 'being a god'.

While Granholm unpacks some of the contradictions of Dragon Rouge's magical practice, this could go further. The book consists mainly of description with only 60 pages of 317 (pp. 257-317) involving analysis. Such analysis might unpack the pressing issue of why it is that Dragon Rouge operates with the (perceived) 'dark' in the first instance. Dragon

Rouge's use of the runes is 'dark' in that it uses the 'Uthark' over the better-known *Futhark*: the name repeats the order of the first six runes and Dragon Rouge situate the first 'F' rune of the *Futhark* at the end of the rune row to form an idiosyncratic 'Uthark' (following Sigurd Agrell [1881-1937]). According to Agrell, the 'F' rune was a form of misdirection planted by rune-magicians in order to preserve the 'true secrets' of the 'Uthark'. It transpires that these 'true secrets' are only available to 'dark' magicians: one informant opines that not only is there a significant difference between 'dark' and 'light' magic, but only the dark magician 'dives deeper' (p296) into the mysteries to see things are they really are.

Yet, for all their rhetoric on 'dark magic', the integrity of the system and substance of the practice (such that it is) is not effectively conveyed in Granholm's ethnography, and nor do the comments of informants substantiate the hyperbole. Agrell's 'Uthark' is based on only one piece of evidence, contradicted by numerous others – yet this facilitates a conveniently 'dark' approach to runecraft for Dragon Rouge. Another informant 'told me that he can be a devoted worshipper of Christ in one ritual and a devoted worshipper of Satan in another', according to the aim of the ritual (p.259). It might be argued that such eclecticism reveals a form of spiritual creativity suited to postmodernity (although Granholm does not explicitly state this), but engaging with an eclectic range of gods and goddesses, angels and demons, from a range of cultures, might also raise issues of eurocentric appropriation, homogenisation and neocolonialism.

Granholm's discussion of eclecticism and the 'why' of dark magic is more generally conceived, with these sections of the book disengaged from the ethnographic description and comments of interviewees. I would like to have seen these better integrated, with more sustained critical engagement; instead, I was left with the impression that Dragon Rouge discourse is self-fulfilling to the point of indulgence and self-obsessed erring on arrogance, shunning rather than contributing to contemporary society or even debates in magic. Perhaps, though, this inconsistency in practice and gothic magniloquence is the mark of a new organization, finding its feet, maturing in its worldview, and gaining coherency in practice. In summary, the book serves principally as ethnographic description of a little-known Magical Order, one significant to the history of European esotericism and the 'left-hand-path' in particular, and so is essential reading for scholars of magic and esotericism – even if it does not deliver satisfactorily in terms of discourse analysis.   Robert J. Wallis

Adam Possamai, 2005, *Religion and Popular Culture: A Hyper-Real Testament,* European Interuniversity Press, Belgium. 176pp, ISBN-10: 9052012725, Paperback £21.99.

In this book the Australian scholar of religion Adam Possamai seeks to illuminate the relationship between religion and popular culture under conditions of postmodernism, a relationship that is of increasing concern both to spiritual leaders and scholars of religion and cultural studies. The paperback version of this book appears bound like a journal or monograph rather than a conventional book and this might alienate a more mainstream audience. This would be a shame as Possamai has a lot of interesting things to say about religion and popular culture which can be extrapolated to esotericism and magic.

Possamai begins by elucidate his project firstly by skilfully giving the exemplar of the shifting boundaries between art and religion and art and popular culture; and then by outlining his Weberian methodology through which he explicates how 'new phenomena create new forms of religiosity adapted to our postmodern view' (p. 23). Indeed he tends to takes this potmodernization of society for granted whilst rooting his own methods in the classical sociological concept of *Verstehen*.

Chapter One of the books seeks to understand the cultural and religious shifts implicated in the postmodernization of Western society. As Possamai argues this involved 'a profound metamorphosis ... at the individual level which gives legitimacy to individuals to seek religious and spiritual content by themselves and for themselves' (pp 23-4). To his credit Possamai does not merely rehash old versions of the modern-postmodern debate in sociology but demonstrates the increasingly oppressive and repressive nature of modernity – another concern of Weber – by examining the works of psycho-social theorist Cornelius Castoridis, born-again postmodernist Zygmunt Bauman, and that architect of the postmodern condition Jean-François Lyotard. Whilst Possamai convinces in his argument that the *metanarratives* of modernity are in crisis and meltdown I am not sure that is different from saying that the transition to a postmodern society has been effected. He appears to infer this. Indeed, the shift from institutionalised forms of religiosity to individual forms of spirituality which he charts seem to point to a radicalisation of modern individualism rather than a shift to a new kind of society, but this is a moot point.

Chapter Two examines new relationships between religion and consumption and argues that this postmodernization process has meant that we now consume religion much like we consume other aspects of culture. Some forms of spirituality, particularly the New Age, and even more particularly those elements of New Age spirituality which have borrowed heavily from indigenous forms of spirituality such as Aboriginal religions, have become particularly suited to such consumption – they have become *hyper consumerist*. Possamai uses the work of Bauman, Baudrillard and Ritzer to make sense of such hyper consumerism. Whilst this is sound again the same theorists can be used to argue for a radicalization of modernity rather than its postmodernization. Despite this the author makes many interesting points on the role of spiritual consumption which will become important springboards for future research in the area.

Chapter Three looks at the *subjectivization* of society and mythology. That is we, following Baudrillard, inhabit a *hyperreal* world of signs and symbols – including spiritual signs and symbols – fragments of which we are invited to consume in order to create our own subjective spiritual mythologies. In many ways Possamai is intellectualizing about the obvious here but he skilfully illuminates these processes by using examples culled from Science Fiction and fantasy literature in particular; for example, the works of H.P. Lovecraft, the Star Wars sextet, and the works of Robert Heinlein.

The next chapter continues these arguments demonstrating the processes by which these subjective spiritualities are formed from popular cultural fragments and mythologies. He does with specific and fascinating reference to the creation of the Jedi Religion. The author grounds these processes in the works of the arch *postmodernist* Baudrillard and the arch *late modernist* Ulrich Beck. Although reasonable Possamai fails to acknowledge the contradiction of such a theoretical position, and this undermines the seamlessness of his personal methodology to some extent.

In Chapter Five continues these themes by demonstrating how postmodern spiritualities – here construed as The Human Potential Movement – can have their effects and aims galvanised and amplified through the use of cultural borrowings. So, for example, Possamai shows how superheroes are often used as motifs for liberating human potential in postmodern spiritualities. Such commodification of the higher self again reinforces both notions that we spiritually buy in postmodern mythologies and that religions are comprehensively commodified.

Chapter Six demonstrates how the commodification of spirituality can have significant effects not just upon its doctrines but also upon the way that spiritual knowledge is disseminated. In particular he uses the case study of Western forms of esotericism to demonstrate how once secret wisdom is now transmitted to all comers through the internet, and the effects that this might have upon its doctrines. Following Peter Koenig, with heavy theoretical borrowings from George Ritzer, Possamai argues that we now have a *McDonaldization* of occult culture (occulture) whereby complex occult ideas are often dumbed down for a mass audience of global consumers. Such knowledge is now sold *en masse* rather than being transmitted as a gift to a few chosen acolytes.

The next chapter continues the theme of this capitalization of esoteric and spiritual knowledge by looking to the work of Frederic Jameson concerning Capitalism and The Postmodern. Through this, Possamai provides further evidence for new forms of postmodern religion which, ironically, are forced into cultural borrowings and syncretism through the very fact that these are the only ways in which they can innovate in the current cultural climate.

The penultimate chapter looks at the ways in which religious actors are able to shape the cultural landscape sometimes making it an exclusive landscape where only certain individuals, or followers, are allowed access to certain religious and cultural activities. Here Possamai is thinking of fundamentalist forms of religion and the ways in which the media, for example Tele-Evangelism, can be manipulated to produce certain exclusive meanings of religious "truth". In particular the author shows how fundamentalists seek to ban certain cultural artefacts – for example certain Christian stances on the Harry Potter books – in attempt to re-assert foundational truths (often, ironically, accomplished through the use of the media).

The book concludes with very brief restatement of Possamai's overall position – that these *hyperreal* forms of religion are the ones best suited to postmodern society.

What makes this book stand out from others is the fact that Possamai has sought to make it accessible to a more general readership through the use of numerous engaging examples of the ways in which religions use popular cultural works and icons in order to thrive in a postmodern world. The author himself is an extremely skilled and intelligent cultural commentator and something of a polymath. The major problem is, however, the book is just not as accessible as it might have been. It is far too complex a work and too replete with sociological jargon to gain the wider audience it definitely deserves. The general tone and presentation is that of a published PhD monograph rather than a polished book suited to a more general readership. This is a real pity as Possamai skilfully blends cultural theory with cultural practices and it is no means a dry text, just one laden with theory. Indeed, with theory in mind, I think that Possamai all too often presents the postmodernization of society as a *fait accompli*. This is misleading and does not represent a balanced view of the current state of sociological debate on the matter. Indeed, there are a number of ambiguities in Possamai's theorising, for example the use of the late modernism of Ulrich Beck, which actively contradict his main thesis. I am nit-picking. Possamai's book is innovative, inventive and thoughtful, but I fear that his intelligent comments will remain the preserve of sociologists of religion rather than being the popular – but certainly not dumbed down - text it could have been. Recommended for readers with an interest in religion and esotericism with some background in the social scientists, and students of Sociology, Cultural Studies, and Religious Studies.

Dave Green

The Journal for the Academic Study of Magic (JSM)

Back numbers

JSM 1: ISBN 978-1869928 674, £13.99, Airmail $25, 200pp
Beyond Attribution: The Importance of Barrett's Magus/
Alison Butler * Shadow over Philistia: A review of the Cult of Dagon/John C. Day *
A History of Otherness:Tarot and Playing Cards from Early Modern Europe/Joyce Goggin * Opposites Attract: Magical Identity and Social Uncertainty/Dave Green * 'Memories of a Sorcerer': notes on Gilles Deleuze-Felix Guattari, Austin Osman Spare and Anomalous Sorceries./Matt Lee * Le Streghe Son Tornate: The Reappearance of Streghe in Italian American Queer Writings/Ilaria Serra * Controlling Chance, Creating Chance: Magical Thinking in Religious Pilgrimage/Deana Weibel

JSM 2, ISBN 978-1869928 728, £19.99, 420pp
Alien Selves: Modernity and the Social Diagnostics of the Demonic in 'Lovecraftian Magick': Woodman/Wishful Thinking Notes towards a Psychoanalytic Sociology of Pagan Magick: Green/A Shell with my Name on it: The Reliance on the Supernatural During the First World War. Chambers/The Metaphysical Relationship between Magick and Miracles: Morgan Luck/Demonic Possession, and Spiritual Healing in Nineteenth-Century Devon: Semmens/ Human Body in Southern Slavic Folk Sorcery: Filipovic & Rader/Four Glasses Of Water: Snell/The Land Near the Dark Cornish Sea:. Hale/Kenneth Grant and the Magickal revival: Evans/Magic through the Linguistic Lenses of Greek mágos, Indo-European *mag(h)-, Sanskrit màyà and Pharaonic Egyptian ¡eka: Cheak/The symbolism of the pierced heart: Froome/ Nicholas Roerich: McCannon/Book Review, etc.

JSM 3, ISBN 798-1869928-964, 300pp, £19.99 (post free)
Buffy and Beyond: Language and Resistance in Contemporary Teenage Witchcraft: Sanders/Witchery as a New Language of Female Identity: Lee/Creative Revolution: Bergsonisms and Modern Magic: Green/Discovering the Witch's Teat: Magical Practices, Medical Superstitions in The Witch of Edmonton: Hayes/The Re-Enchantment of the Medical: An examination of magical elements in healing: Lowery/ Apparitions, Ghosts, Fairies, Demons and Wild Events: Virtuality in Early Modern Britain: Marshall/Living the Mystery: Sacred Drama Today: Laity/ Is there esoteric symbolism in H.P.Lovecraft's The Dream-Quest of Unknown Kadath?: Geall / Becoming a Sorcerer: Jean-Pierre Bekolo's Quartier Mozart and the Magic of Deleuzian and Guattarian Becoming: Gorman / Book Reviews

Mandrake

Fire Child; The Life And Magic Of Maxine Sanders 'Witch Queen'
978-1-869928-97-1 - 300pp - illustrated £19.99/ US$40

FIRE CHILD is the long awaited autobiography of Maxine Sanders, one of England's most celebrated Witch Queens. In this book, Maxine talks about her early life and her partnership with husband Alex Sanders, with whom she co-founded the Alexandrian Witchcraft tradition. She will reflect on her vocation as Priestess of the Goddess and teacher, as well as a respected spiritual catalyst.

Ithell Colquhoun : pioneer surrealist artist, occultist, writer, and poet by Eric Ratcliffe

978-1869928-98-8 - 314pp - 90 ills (25 in colour)
The skills of Ithell Colquhoun in her main practice, that of artist and pioneer in this country of surrealistic art, have been long recognised. Additionally, other interests - alchemy, Earth-magic, active occultism, poetry, druidism, the pre-Christian Pagan calendar, the history and membership of the Golden Dawn - and writing of and involvement in these interests by book publication and in a widely scattered field of correspondence, have created a miscellany of truly gargantuan proportion. Eric Ratcliffe considered it was time to get together some of these pieces, to add something of what is known of Colquhoun's early life and family history and to take the opportunity of listing a comprehensive calendar of her work and exhibitions. The result is neither strictly biographical nor a treatise on any one subject, but it is a first gathering of the roots, passions and multi-directions of this artist. It is a patchwork containing many launch-pads for exploration of the magical and mythical atmosphere which this artist existed in and created. Here therefore is a contribution towards solving a jigsaw and a wind-catch of the minor cyclones of Ithell's dedicatory interests, also serving as a record of her accomplishments in the art field.

Jesus the sorcerer: Exorcist, Prophet of the Apocalypse By Robert Conner
978-1869928-957 320pp £12.99/$25

The most complete summation to date of the New Testament evidence for magical practice by Jesus and the early Christians.

Documentary Evidence / Infancy Narratives / Confrontation / Resurrection as Ghost Story / Apocalyptic Prophet / Apocalypse Postponed, / Magic and Mystery, / Jesus the Magician / Spirit Versus Spirit, / Ecstatic Inner Circle, / Christian Mysteries, / Secret Gospel of Mark, / Beloved Disciple, / On the Use of youth in Magic, / Apocalypse, Magic, and Christianity, / "Son of David." / Mary Magdalene

111 Magdalen Rd
Oxford OX4 1RQ
Tel 01865 245301
Fax 01865 245521

mail@innerbookshop.com
Open 10-5.45 - **Mon-Sat**
Books for mind, body and spirit

*From Alchemy & Chaos Magick
to Wicca & Zoroastrianism*

Thousands of titles
(new, secondhand & bargains)
search & orderable on our website

www.innerbookshop.com

Visit us (and the Magic Café next door) and see our **Noticeboards** for Oxford and National events or use our **Mail-Order Service** via telephone or fax as well

Journal of Alternative Spiritualities and New Age Studies
www.ASANAS.org.uk and www.open.ac.uk/Arts/jasanas/
ISSN (print) 1750-3191, ISSN (online) 1750-3205
A multi-disciplinary, peer-reviewed journal,
co-edited by Marion Bowman and Daren Kemp

JASANAS Volume 3, ISBN 978-0-9557007-0-5
The Epistemological Foundations of Esoteric Thought and Practice, *Julia Iwersen*; The Epistemology of Esoteric Culture: Spiritual Claim-Making within the American Neopagan Community, *Marty Laubach*; Towards a Sacramental Understanding of Dextromethorphan, *Joseph Gelfer*; Complicating Spiritual Appropriation: North American Indian Agency in Western Alternative Spiritual Practice, *Christina Welch*; Modern Paganism in the United Kingdom, *Ieuan Jones*; Spiral Bound: Spaces, Selves and Cosmologies of Contemporary Magick, *William Redwood*; Spiritual Direction, Life Coaching and Culture; *Andii Bowsher*; Conference Reports; Book Reviews

JASANAS Volume 2, ISBN 1-4196-2696-5
New Age thinking in the light of CG Jung's theory of synchronicity, *Roderick Main*; The Marsden Imbolc festival: A case of civic paganism? *Ieuan Jones*; Globalisation, charisma, innovation, and tradition: An exploration of the transformations in the organisational vehicles for the transmission of the teachings of Prem Rawat (Maharaji), *Ron Geaves*; Does the counter-cultural character of New Age persist? Investigating social and political attitudes of New Age followers, *Franz Höllinger*; New data on who joins NRMs and why: A case study of the Order of Christ/Sophia, *James R Lewis*; A psychological study of New Age practices and beliefs, *Miguel Farias*; Weber and the witches: Sociological theory and modern Witchcraft, *Leo Ruickbie*; Positions; Book Reviews

JASANAS Volume 1, ISBN 1-4196-0359-0
Wanting to Have Your New Age Cake and Eat It Too, *Michael York*; Spectral Evidence of New Age Religion: On the substance of ghosts and the use of concepts, *Wouter J Hanegraaff*; The Invisible Inside the Visible – The Visible Inside the Invisible: Theoretical and methodological aspects of research on New Age and contemporary Esotericism, *Christoph Bochinger*; Gurdjieff, 'Old' or 'New Age': Aristotle or Astrology? *Sophia Wellbeloved*; Heaven's Gate: End-Time Prophets in a Post-Modern Era, *George D Chryssides*; New Age and the Discursive Construction of Community, *Olav Hammer*; The Rise of Mind-Body-Spirit Publishing: Reflecting or Creating Spiritual Trends? *Elizabeth Puttick*; Conference Report; Book Reviews

Printed in the United States
200991BV00004B/109-111/A